Quine and Analytic Philosophy

⊒⊑ Bradford Books

Edward C. T. Walker, Editor. EXPLORATIONS IN THE BIOLOGY OF LANGUAGE. 1979. The MIT Work Group in the Biology of Language: Noam Chomsky, Salvador Luria, et alia.

Daniel C. Dennett. BRAINSTORMS. 1979.

Charles Marks. COMMISSUROTOMY, CONSCIOUSNESS AND UNITY OF MIND. 1980.

John Haugeland, Editor. MIND DESIGN. 1981.

Fred I. Dretske. KNOWLEDGE AND THE FLOW OF INFORMATION. 1981.

Jerry A. Fodor. REPRESENTATIONS. 1981.

Ned Block, Editor. IMAGERY. 1981.

Roger N. Shepard and Lynn A. Cooper. MENTAL IMAGES AND THEIR TRANSFORMATIONS. 1982.

Hubert L. Dreyfus, Editor, in collaboration with Harrison Hall. HUSSERL, INTENTIONALITY AND COGNITIVE SCIENCE. 1982.

John Macnamara. NAMES FOR THINGS. 1982.

Natalie Abrams and Michael D. Buckner, Editors. MEDICAL ETHICS. 1983.

Morris Halle and G. N. Clements. PROBLEM BOOK IN PHONOLOGY. 1983.

Irvin Rock. THE LOGIC OF PERCEPTION. 1983.

Jon Barwise and John Perry. SITUATIONS AND ATTITUDES. 1983.

Elliott Sober, Editor. ISSUES IN EVOLUTION: A Book of Readings. 1983.

Robert Cummins. THE NATURE OF PSYCHOLOGICAL EXPLANATION. 1983.

Stephen Stich. FOLK PSYCHOLOGY AND COGNITIVE SCIENCE. 1983.

Jerry A. Fodor. MODULARITY OF MIND. 1983.

George D. Romanos. QUINE AND ANALYTIC PHILOSOPHY. 1983.

Quine and Analytic Philosophy

George D. Romanos

————————————

A Bradford Book
The MIT Press
Cambridge, Massachusetts
London, England

Second printing, August 1984

Book design by Mary Mendell.
Jacket design by Irene Elios.
Set in Palatino by The MIT Press Computergraphics Department.
Printed and bound by The Murray Printing Co. in the United States of America.

Library of Congress Cataloging in Publication Data

Romanos, George D.
  Quine and analytic philosophy.

  "A Bradford book."

  Includes bibliography and index.
  1. Analysis (Philosophy) 2. Semantics (Philosophy)
3. Quine, W. V. (Willard Van Orman) I. Title.
B808.5.R65 1983   149'.94   82-24984
ISBN 0-262-18110-X (hardcover)
ISBN 0-262-68038-6 (paperback)

To Brenda

Contents

Foreword

George D. W. Berry was my student at Harvard forty years ago, and took over my teaching when I went off to war. He is now a professor of long standing at Boston University, and has been honoring me there with a seminar year after year on my philosophy. It is now my custom to meet with his students at the end of term and belabor with them a string of questions and comments of their compiling. A star pupil of Berry's, in turn, has brought light and liveliness to these discussions each year, namely George Romanos.

When Romanos received his doctorate, he sent me his dissertation. Much of it, as I told him, bore the promise of an admirable book; now, after two more years of scholarly inquiry and critical and creative thinking, the manuscript of such a book is before me.

The book is rich in historical background, perceptively interpreted and interrelated. There are three interlocking themes whose philosophical significance Romanos explores: the flight from intension, the priority of sentence and truth over word and object, and ontological relativity. His insights are deep and his arguments convincing. In the end one comes away satisfied that philosophy will never be the same.

W. V. Quine

Acknowledgments

This book grew out of my Ph.D thesis at Boston University and was written over the course of a half-dozen years. I am particularly grateful to Paul T. Sagal, my early mentor, for providing me the intellectual stimulus and personal encouragement to undertake this project, and to George D. W. Berry, whose keen philosophical instincts and judgment helped guide the manuscript through numerous revisions and whose determination to see it finally into print was matched only by my own. To Judson C. Webb go my sincere thanks for making invaluable critical suggestions at several stages and for putting his formidable knowledge and rich philosophical insight at my disposal. Of course, I have profited immeasurably from Professor Quine's own patient and enlightening responses, during George Berry's annual student-faculty seminars at Boston University, to questions posed on virtually every facet of his philosophy, as well as from his painstaking and extensive critical commentary on two separate versions of the manuscript. I would also like to thank Tyler Burge for a number of helpful comments and suggestions which improved the final manuscript in many respects.

In addition, I owe a special debt of gratitude to my friend and colleague Ilona Lappo, who through her exceptional intelligence, generosity, and innumerable technical skills has been instrumental from the start in bringing this book into being.

Introduction

For fifty years W. V. Quine's books and articles have stimulated intense discussion and debate in the fields of logic and the philosophy of language. During the latter half of this period, perhaps no other figure has had a greater impact on the focus and direction of philosophical research and argumentation.

In spite of the keen interest and attention which Quine's published views have invariably aroused, however, some of the most important and far-reaching implications of his work seem to have escaped the notice of most contemporary analytic philosophers. These implications have to do with the familiar and fundamental question of the relevance of linguistic inquiry and analysis to traditional philosophical issues. The purpose of this book is to explore the philosophical significance of Quine's work within the context of twentieth-century analytic philosophy. I argue that the simple but elusive philosophical perspective which underlies and supports most of Quine's writings—and, particularly, his essay "Ontological Relativity"—represents, in its own way, as radical a departure from prevailing modes of philosophical thinking as did the celebrated rejection of traditional metaphysics by the logical positivists of the Vienna Circle.

"Ontological Relativity" represents, by Quine's own admission, the most complete formulation of his mature thought. The essay contains his most comprehensive treatment of the role and scope of human convention in language construction and interpretation.

Quine brings together here several themes from his earlier work (including, most notably, his collateral theses of the indeterminacy of translation and the inscrutability of linguistic reference) and relates them carefully in order to develop his relativistic thesis, according to which our ultimate understanding of a language's subject matter—that is, its ontology—is held to be thoroughly relative to our at least partially arbitrary choice of how to interpret or translate that language in terms of another.

Quine's thesis of ontological relativity has been subject to frequent misinterpretation as expressing, or implying, a relativism akin to Kuhn's incommensurability thesis, or Whorf's hypothesis. In light of the extralinguistic philosophical significance such claims about language are almost automatically accorded by philosophers today, such misconstruals are not surprising. What I shall attempt to show here, however, is that what the relativistic thesis really undercuts is not so much a belief in the objectivity of our knowledge of the world as, simply, the prevalent preconception of most analytic philosophers that the analysis of language is, in one form or another, essential to the solution, resolution, or dissolution of outstanding philosophical problems.

In doing philosophy one may eschew questions of language altogether and devote one's attention directly to the task of discovering the first principles or truths concerning the ultimate nature of reality or the basic categories of existence. This is classical metaphysics. On the other hand, one may become impressed with the seriousness of epistemological limitations on our ability to directly "grasp" or apprehend such metaphysical truth and so adopt an indirect way of approaching these questions by looking closely at the way we do, or ought to, speak about the world. Here the basic structure or meaning of language is viewed as presenting a picture of the metaphysical facts, or at least providing suggestive hints or clues to the ultimate truth. This is the perspective of Russell's early "logical atomism," and of Gustav Bergmann's approach to the construction and study of the "ideal" language. Among latter-day adherents of so-called ordinary language philosophy, essentially the same metaphilosophical outlook is discernible in the writings of Austin, Ryle, and Hare. These philosophers may be referred to as analytic metaphysicians. Like traditional metaphysicians, they are ultimately interested in the fundamental nature of extralinguistic facts and our knowledge of those facts. Their concern with language does not reflect a distaste for traditional philosophical problems, but only a belief that the most fruitful approach to solutions for such problems is through an investigation of language, because of the special role language is imagined to play in mediating between us and the world around us.

There is another, somewhat more radical, linguistic response to traditional metaphysics. Here the traditional philosophical questions are rejected out of hand, or perhaps reinterpreted as merely linguistic, as questions concerning the grammar of a language, the reference of terms, the usefulness of a linguistic framework, and so forth. Talk about the world as it really is, apart from considerations of language and theoretical science, is viewed as unintelligible, incoherent, and meaningless. Historical philosophical controversies are held to arise either from confusion caused by the vagueness and ambiguity of ordinary language or, conversely, from philosophical misuse and abuse of ordinary language. This staunchly antimetaphysical approach took shape dramatically with the early Wittgenstein and the Vienna Circle positivists and endures in the attitude of the later Wittgenstein and the ordinary language philosophers most heavily influenced by him, such as Strawson, Hampshire, and Toulmin. These linguistic Kantians, as I shall call them, may be primarily interested in doing "therapeutic" analysis, conceptual history or description, or epistemology in the form of philosophy of science, but in each case their ultimate concern is just linguistic or conceptual systems themselves rather than some supposed realm of being beyond. All meaningful inquiry into the extralinguistic world is generally conceded to lie in the domain of the natural or empirical sciences which employ given linguistic or conceptual schemes as the tools of their trade.

Underlying the philosophical outlooks of both groups is the analytic conception of language—the idea that the structure or meaning of language (individual expressions or linguistic systems as wholes) can be objectively examined and analyzed in some fundamental way in which extralinguistic reality, as such, cannot. A language may thus be held to embody a general way of "seeing," representing, or conceptualizing the world or our experience of it. The analytic metaphysician studies the linguistic data only for the light it may shed on traditional philosophical questions concerning what there is or what the world is really like. He also worries a bit about whether the language he is studying is the right or correct one, in the sense of providing a true or accurate picture of reality. The linguistic Kantian rejects any idea of one true or ideal language; he studies language for its own sake, to discover our basic patterns of conceptualization and perhaps to find some more fruitful ones.

The central concern of this book is to examine the validity of this single shared conception of language, which is basic to both metaphilosophical traditions within twentieth-century philosophical analysis. Special emphasis will be put on the crucial role the analytic conception of language plays in linguistic Kantianism, where language is held to constitute virtually the entire legitimate subject matter of philosophy. It is, indeed, the utter rejection of metaphysics itself that finally presents the most serious obstacles to any effort to render an intelligible, coherent, and meaningful account of this conception of language. What I wish to accomplish here is to present and focus Quine's critical arguments and observations about language in such a way as to reveal clearly the implausibility and meaninglessness of the analytic conception of language itself, apart from any independent metaphysical assumptions. One may thus view this project as either an attempted refutation of the analytic conception of language or an indirect proof of the sound footing of metaphysics.

Considered independently of metaphysics-ridden theories of an ideal language, essentially two basic versions of the analytic conception of language remain, corresponding roughly to the split between ordinary language philosophers and linguistic reformers. According to one version, usually identified with the proponents of linguistic reform and the construction of artificial languages, the basic meaning, structure, or conceptual content of a language is capable of full and explicit codification by means of a complete set of syntactical and semantical rules. These rules are viewed as entirely the product of human artifice and convention, and they define just what basic features or conceptual categories the language in question applies to the world. According to the second version of the analytic conception of language, explicit codification of the meaning or content of a language is out of the question. The analyst must instead pay close attention to the actual use or functioning of linguistic expressions in everyday life, noting carefully the variety of different circumstances in which their use is appropriate and keeping track of the systematic relationships they exhibit with other expressions in the language. Both versions of the analytic conception of language are to some extent distillations or idealizations of views actually held with greater or lesser admixtures of conscious or unconscious metaphysics. They are not altogether mutually exclusive, but may simply represent different areas of emphasis.

Chapter 1 deals with the rise to prominence of linguistic analysis as a response to the difficulties of traditional philosophy, and with the explicit emergence of the analytic conception of language which supported the linguistic movement. Chapters 2 and 3 treat directly the impact of Quine's views on the two versions of the analytic conception of language just outlined. Chapters 4 and 5 relate these consequences more specifically to issues in contemporary semantics, particularly with respect to Tarski's semantic analysis of truth, and sketch an integrated picture of the relationship between language, science, and philosophy that requires neither traditional metaphysical assumptions nor the analytic conception of language to hold it together. The ultimate aim is to show the broad and devastating implications of Quine's philosophical writings for the essentially linguistic or analytic approach to philosophical problems, and the analytic conception of language underlying it. It is my contention that Quine's work, despite his own seeming preoccupation and obvious fascination with questions of language, marks the beginning of the end for this fundamental and all-pervasive view of language, which has dominated analytic philosophy in one form or another from Moore and Russell to the present day. What is finally revealed, most dramatically perhaps in Quine's doctrine of ontological relativity, is that the philosophical method of analysis is at root no less speculative—and with that, no more plausible or coherent—than the more traditional brand of metaphysical inquiry it was originally intended to supplement or replace.

Quine and Analytic Philosophy

1 The Rejection of Metaphysics and the "Linguistic Turn"

1 The Positivist Creed

If substantial philosophical agreement was ever achieved on a number of important and interrelated philosophical problems, it surely was by those philosophers and scientists who made up the famed Vienna Circle. These early positivists prized philosophical agreement above almost all else, and this led to a remarkable convergence and conformity of opinion on several key issues. Although a great diversity of views certainly prevailed concerning myriad details of formulation, there remained a standard overall point of view and a generally recognized orthodoxy with regard to a central core of theses which have come to define the movement of logical positivism.

First on the positivist list of priorities was unquestionably the overthrow or elimination of traditional metaphysics, particularly the post-Kantian variety. The means for accomplishing this objective was to be the logical analysis of language. Statements purporting to deal with some transcendental reality, or being in itself, were to be regarded not simply as false, but as cognitively, or theoretically, meaningless, through failing to admit, even in principle, of verification—or at least confirmation.

Verification—the key to cognitive significance—was believed to be of two basic, mutually exclusive and mutually exhaustive varieties: logical and factual. That is, truly meaningful assertions must either be analytic (true under any empirical circumstances in virtue of considerations of language alone) or synthetic (factual assertions to be verified or falsified according to specific empirical procedures).

Logic and mathematics were guaranteed significance, and their a priori epistemological status was preserved, by counting their truths among those of the analytic category. The statements and laws of empirical science were taken to comprise all those of the synthetic category. Social sciences like psychology or sociology were placed here on an equal footing with natural sciences like physics or biology.

The proclamations of metaphysics, however, seemed to fit neatly into neither the analytic nor the synthetic category and thus were taken to violate the very logic or rules of significant discourse. Whatever significance might be granted metaphysics was to be assessed only in literary or poetic terms. Theology was treated in identical fashion. The normative disciplines of ethics and aesthetics—for which various versions of "expressive" or "emotive" theories soon emerged—were similarly excluded from the realm of legitimate theoretical inquiry. Though any of these disputed fields might serve as the sociological subject matter for an appropriate empirical investigation, their various individual claims were seen as based neither on language nor empirical fact, and were thus not simply to be refuted but to be rejected outright as meaningless, or devoid of "cognitive content." Positivists, therefore, viewed themselves as undermining metaphysics and related fields not on the basis of their admitted empiricist epistemology but rather through a logical critique or analysis of language itself.

The linguistic conception of analytic truth was of crucial importance for positivism, for it provided an account of the nonempirical and certain character of logico-mathematical knowledge without an essential appeal to metaphysical first principles or abstract entities like concepts or ideas. Among positivists there was a healthy respect for modern logic and mathematics and a deep appreciation of their fundamental role in physical science. They shrank from an extreme empiricism such as that of Mill, which saw the propositions of logic and mathematics simply as empirical generalizations or hypotheses, like those of the empirical sciences (though more general in scope) and, in principle, just as susceptible to refutation by empirical evidence. By treating the truth of these propositions as grounded in the very nature of language (its structure or meaning, rules or conventions) as revealed through logical analysis, the positivists seemed to have found a way of rendering the a priori status of logic and mathematics compatible with a thoroughgoing empiricism. They could still hold that, although our understanding of language might derive from experience, logical or mathematical truths based only on the nature of this understanding itself were not themselves empirical propositions. Thus, Wittgenstein called analytic truths tautologies—empty statements that "say nothing" about the world.[1] Ayer, stressing the conventional origins of language, wrote that the propositions of logic and mathematics "simply record our determination to use symbols in a certain fashion."[2]

With logic and mathematics secured within their revised empiricism, and with metaphysics banished once and for all from the domain of significant inquiry, all that remained was to find a place for philosophy itself, and this was immediately suggested by the very method of logical analysis which had proved so useful in achieving the first two objectives. This mode of critical inquiry and analysis seemed to offer a way of doing epistemology without indulging in the metaphysics of rationalism or the psychologizing of traditional empiricism. Various characterizations of "analysis" emerged. At one extreme were the early views of Schlick and Wittgenstein, who saw it as a sort of mental activity ("search for meaning"[3]) whose results were, in principle, incapable of explicit formulation. At the other extreme were the writings of Carnap, in which "analysis" came more and more closely to resemble a particular branch of theoretical science itself, closely related to empirical linguistics.[4]

The fundamental difference, however, between philosophy as logical or linguistic analysis and science proper was still to be found in the former's purported concern with language or meaning as opposed to fact or truth. Whatever might be conceded or denied in the way of methodological likeness, this distinction in subject matter was surely supreme. Empirical science exhausted the legitimate questions of truth about the extralinguistic world; there was no higher or transcendent realm for philosophers to investigate, there was only language—the tool employed by scientists engaged in their several different theoretical investigations. The aim of analysis was first and foremost to clarify language and make it more precise, thereby simultaneously exposing the traditional "pseudo-problems" of philosophy and exhibiting the exact nature and extent of genuine theoretical issues. Whatever difficulties positivists encountered in precisely characterizing this new philosophical method of analysis, the fundamental difference between philosophy and the rest of science was believed to be as basic and irreducible as the difference between language and the world that language describes.

There was difference of opinion also with respect to the particular aspect of language with which logical analysis was taken to be concerned. Early analysts liked to emphasize a distinction between *grammatical* or *syntactical* questions concerning the (logical) structure or form of linguistic expressions and *semantical* questions concerning the meaning or content of these expressions. Some early positivists, impressed by this distinction and suspicious of the metaphysically tainted notion of 'meaning,' sought to speak exclusively of the syntactical features of language; others, following Schlick, settled for talk of linguistic meaning outright. Carnap once attempted to interpret all significant semantical notions in terms of purely syntactical ones, but later, after having become increasingly impressed with the philosophical importance of semantics as an independent discipline, proposed the "semiotic" analysis of language, which would take into serious account both syntax and semantics as well as a third domain called "pragmatics."[5] However, although the distinction between syntactical considerations of form or structure and semantical considerations of meaning or content retained a surface plausibility and intuitive appeal, its precise theoretical nature and importance resisted explicit and unproblematic formulation. Most nonmetaphysical attempts to account for either of these purportedly distinct sorts of linguistic phenomena appealed, in the end, to the same considerations of linguistic behavior or to the rules or conventions believed to govern such behavior.

At present it is not necessary to pursue this question beyond the point of observing that, as in the case of analysis itself, the peculiar features of language at which analysis is to be aimed have come under various alternative descriptions. Whether these terminological discrepancies do in fact signal any significant substantive distinctions of far-reaching philosophical importance it is our purpose here to examine.

2 Background of the Positivist Manifesto

The most important circumstance leading to the positivists' philosophical revolt was the hopeless disarray of philosophy around 1900. Ironically, the work of Kant, the great antimetaphysician, sparked some of the most chaotic and unprecedented extremes of metaphysical system building in the history of philosophy. In anchoring science to the perceptual and conceptual features of human experience, Kant had hoped to save human knowledge from the skeptical doubts of empiricists while simultaneously avoiding the excessive metaphysics of rationalists. In so definitively limiting scientific understanding to the realm of what was admittedly mere "appearance," however, Kant excited fresh philosophical interest in that transcendent realm of reality, or being in itself, which, it seemed reasonable to think, must lie beyond such appearance. That knowledge of some transcendent reality was in fact possible was argued just from Kant's having been able to draw the boundaries he did.[6] Instead of undermining metaphysics altogether, then, Kant's *Critique* had the effect rather of breathing new life into it by severing once and for all its increasingly tenuous union with science and setting it up as a distinct and autonomous mode of inquiry, with its own separate domain of concern.

Science, secured by the added support which Kant's comprehensive and authoritative scholarship lent to common sense, pursued its course with renewed confidence in the legitimacy of its claims to knowledge. Metaphysically minded philosophers, on the other hand, freed from the conceptual strictures within which scientists were now believed destined to toil, looked to a higher level of understanding or cognition by which they might grasp the ultimate nature of reality itself. Metaphysics thus became a self-consciously speculative enterprise. Once their bonds with the everyday world of science and scientific understanding were decisively cut, metaphysical systems proliferated on a grander and more vigorous scale than ever, limited only by the capacity of each individual philosopher's imagination.

The impossibility of adjudicating competing metaphysical claims soon became the outstanding obstacle to philosophical progress. Empirical scientists had standards for assessing the merits of alternative systems; but metaphysicians, except for the requirement that each system be internally consistent (which was itself interpreted in novel ways by Hegelians) had no such generally recognized standards. Denied, in effect, the very possibility of adducing evidence objectively, debate became deadlocked, and advance was hopelessly stalemated. Opposing schools quarreled incessantly with one another and within their own ranks, without making significant headway toward the resolution of their differences. Manley Thompson describes the situation: "Each metaphysical system defines for itself the circumstances within which all metaphysical systems are to be tested, so that proponents of rival systems can hardly expect to find circumstances within which they can seek agreement."[7]

Without shared standards to serve as a basis for arbitrating metaphysical disputes, matters took a predictably subjective turn. Attempts at justifying a metaphysical system invariably culminated in special appeals to some sort of inexplicable insight, romantic intuition, or religious faith. A system was as likely to be embraced for its creative originality, its speculative boldness, or its grandeur and elegance as for any element of truth it purported to contain. Metaphysics had become a question of taste, and *de gustibus non disputandum est*. This moral, however, could not be observed, for the philosophers' claims were still ultimately to truth and not merely to likes and dislikes, and *de veritate multum disputandum est*.

This stultifying situation, which found philosophers isolated from one another within the confines of their idiosyncratic metaphysical systems, arguing futilely and always at cross purposes, repelled the scientifically trained and scientifically minded positivists. The spectacle of philosophers caught in a tangle of imaginative fantasies, with rational debate all but forsaken in favor of tactics of persuasion, contrasted sharply with the received view of the sciences, where cooperative efforts, rational discussion, objective decision procedures, and systematic progress had by now come to be taken for granted. With the virtues once considered so distinctive of philosophy itself now best exemplified elsewhere, the conviction grew that there was something fundamentally awry. Positivists came to see these so-called debaucheries of post-Kantian metaphysics as the outgrowth of a deep-rooted misconception of the true nature of philosophy, and thus turned their attention to the task of reconsidering the philosophical enterprise itself.

The optimistic nature of Moritz Schlick rebelled against the suggestion that philosophical progress was impossible and the accompanying "historicist" doctrine that philosophy consists primarily in its own history.[8] Positivists had no sympathy for a reformulation of philosophy as an essentially irrational or nonrational activity where fruitless controversy was inevitable. They were intent, rather, on reinvesting philosophy with a semblance of its traditional status. Thus, Ayer began his famous English exposition of positivism as follows: "The traditional disputes of philosophers are, for the most part, as unwarranted as they are unfruitful. The surest way to end them is to establish beyond question what should be the purpose and method of philosophical inquiry."[9]

It is not surprising that in revising their conception of philosophy the positivists came to focus on questions of language. There was, first of all, the fact that philosophers have historically been obsessed with questions of the form "What is x?" or "What is the nature of x?"—which have always looked suspiciously like requests for definitions or accounts of words.[10] Schlick viewed philosophy as the "search for meaning," most clearly exemplified by Socrates himself as portrayed in Plato's *Dialogues*.[11] Ayer likewise found it plausible to assert that "the majority of those who are commonly supposed to have been great philosophers were primarily not metaphysicians but analysts,"[12] which is to say, according to Ayer, that they were "not concerned with the physical properties of things . . . but . . . only with the way in which we speak about them."[13] These "great philosophers" were taken to include, among others, Plato, Aristotle, Kant, and all the British Empiricists, from Hobbes through Mill.[14] However, the mere fact that the historical interpretation of philosophy as definitional or simply linguistic in character has always had a certain appeal can hardly explain the fervor and unanimity with which positivists embraced it or the distinctive form this interpretation took in their hands.

A second key factor can be traced to the very features of the situation that sparked the demand for a new conception of philosophy—namely, the futile debates and controversies of post-Kantian metaphysics, against which positivists were directly reacting. These disputes were so severe and seemingly so remote from possible resolution that not only was agreement hard to come by but communication itself seemed wanting in most cases. Besides

simply disagreeing over what they held true, opposing metaphysicians seemed frequently to differ with respect to what they
meant. As Thompson has urged, a system typically sets not only
the standards for deciding its own claims, but also the meanings
of the words used in making them; this itself suggests that disputes
between systems may often be only verbal.[15].

However, as conducive as the above circumstances must have
been to the ultimate choice of logical or linguistic analysis as the
sole task of philosophy, the most overwhelming factor was undoubtedly the startling successes of the new method of analysis,
brought to bear (chiefly by Russell) on a number of outstanding
philosophical problems. The most remarkable and widely celebrated
of these "successes" was the reduction of mathematics to logic
believed to have been achieved by Russell and Whitehead in *Principia Mathematica*. Here the construction of basic mathematical
concepts out of purely logical ones held promise of an ultimate
derivation of all truths of mathematics from just logical principles.
This culmination of work begun earlier by Frege gained immediate
and widespread recognition and served as dramatic testimony to
the power and utility of analysis as a philosophical tool. The doctrine
of mathematics as essentially a matter of pure logic soon figured
as a rallying point for positivistically inclined philosophers.

A related area of major importance in which the use of analysis
seemed to hold similar promise was indicated by Russell's envisioned scheme for exhibiting the three-dimensional physical world
as a "logical construction" of more primitive sensory elements. The
idea was, in short, to do for physics what *Principia* was thought
to have done for mathematics. For positivists such a program appeared to open a pathway between the Scylla and Charybdis of
metaphysics and psychology by casting their empiricist epistemology into the form of a purely logical issue. Though Russell
never attempted to carry this enterprise forward on any large scale,
he succeeded ingeniously with a limited but suggestive treatment
of the concepts of space and time,[16] and the ideal of a complete
reduction of the physical world to that of immediate experience
quickly became a powerful driving force among early positivists,
who regarded it as the central objective in the effort to clarify the
foundations of empirical science. The closest this ideal ever came
to realization, however, was in the brilliant but ill-starred constructions of Carnap's famous *Logische Aufbau der Welt*.

The method of analysis was also to prove remarkably fruitful when directed against metaphysics. One well-known example which had a tremendous impact upon the development of positivism and linguistic philosophy in general is Russell's theory of definite descriptions.[17] This purported account of the correct logical form of a particular grammatical construction of ordinary English made essential use of the logical symbolism of *Principia* and was deployed in devastating fashion against the perversely swollen ontologies of Meinongian semantics. The analysis of definite descriptions thus came to serve as the prototype for efforts to tie the origins of various metaphysical claims to confusion over the proper logical form or structure of statements in ordinary language. Such an approach was the basis for Wittgenstein's view of philosophy as a "critique of language," which aimed thereby to show that "the deepest problems are in fact *not* problems at all."[18] Taking the cue from Wittgenstein, positivists followed this same course by launching a wholesale assault on a wide range of traditional philosophical issues, from the problem of universals and the ontological argument to Heidegger's conception of "nothing." Here linguistic analysis proved a powerful critical weapon whose importance, in one way or another, was readily conceded by many philosophers.

Another even more decisive way of utilizing analysis in a critique of traditional metaphysics can be traced to Russell's theory of types, set forth in the *Principles of Mathematics* to preclude formation of a certain troublesome class of propositions of set theory. Set-theoretic statements heretofore regarded as grammatically correct and significant were deemed now to violate proper logical form through failing to observe certain so-called type distinctions between individual component expressions, and were thus put aside as meaningless strings of symbols. This idea of trying to demonstrate not the falsity but the meaninglessness of undesirable assertions, which Russell employed in trying to resolve the paradoxes of set theory, was adopted by positivists as a general strategy for directly undermining all of metaphysics. The theory of types was itself generalized to apply to all theoretical discourse, with the result that a multitude of metaphysical assertions were now claimed to have been revealed as cognitively meaningless "pseudo-statements" in which "predicates which should be applied to objects of a certain sort are instead applied to predicates of these objects or to 'being' or to 'existence' or to a relation between these objects."[19] Meta-physicians were thus alleged to be doubly misled by ordinary grammar, first in taking the apparent logical form of ordinary state-ments to be the real form and second in failing to notice that their own philosophical assertions violated canons of correct logical form and were thus insignificant.

Whereas analysis according to the theory of definite descriptions could do no more than explain the psychological genesis of meta-physical issues as a result of confusions over ordinary language, analysis along the general lines suggested by the theory of types appeared to provide a logical critique of the very philosophical discourse constituting these disputations as itself involving the mis-use and abuse of language. While the former approach could at best only "cure" some metaphysicians, the latter aimed directly at eliminating metaphysics entirely. The more direct attack on meta-physical "pseudo-doctrine," irrespective of supposed origins, thus proved much more to the positivists' taste, and verifiability soon appeared on the scene to supplement—as well as to provide a more general replacement for—logical form as the criterion of cog-nitive or theoretical significance.

It should be no wonder, then, that positivists, bent on refor-mulating philosophy to preserve it as a significant and integral branch of knowledge, seized upon the method of analysis as an alternative to speculative metaphysics. The brilliant success and promise of the new method contrasted sharply with the futile meta-physical controversies of the preceding century. This versatile new mode of inquiry seemed to have accomplished precisely what spec-ulative metaphysics had for so long failed to do: it had led to significant progress in the resolution of outstanding philosophical problems, and it had provided a basis for substantive philosophical agreement. At the same time, it offered what seemed to be an illuminating explanation of the origins of metaphysics itself as well as the logical grounds for its complete overthrow. Carnap thus described analysis as having both a positive and a negative use:

> The researches of applied logic or the theory of knowledge, which aim at clarifying the cognitive content of scientific state-ments and thereby the meanings of the terms that occur in

the statements, by means of logical analysis, lead to a positive and to a negative result. The positive result is worked out in the domain of empirical science; the various concepts of the various branches of science are clarified; their formal-logical and epistemological connections are made explicit. In the domain of *metaphysics*, including all philosophy of value and normative theory, logical analysis yields the negative result *that the alleged statements in this domain are entirely meaningless.*[20]

However, Russell and many of his followers employed the method of analysis primarily not as an alternative or a means of attacking or eliminating all metaphysics but as a means of conducting metaphysical inquiry itself. The analysis of definite descriptions was utilized, therefore, in conjunction with the principle of parsimony (Occam's Razor—*Entia non sunt multiplicanda praeter necessitatem*) in order to defeat one ontological view in favor of another, more modest one. So, too, the wholesale reduction of mathematics to logic in the *Principia* was regarded as support for an ontological claim of the existence of just classes or properties rather than numbers. Likewise the proposed view of physical things as logical constructions of sense data was aimed eventually at demonstrating the ontological priority of sense data.

Positivists, however, in rejecting outright the transcendental realm of being, which had served as the basis for so much fruitless speculation, were entirely committed to the view that any and all genuine questions of truth or existence fell totally within the domain of science proper. Therefore, as philosophers, their objective in analyzing and clarifying the concepts and propositions of science was to be purely epistemological rather than metaphysical. The analysis of definite descriptions was regarded as simply revealing one example of how metaphysics arises from linguistic confusion. The reduction of mathematics to logic was not viewed as lending support to any claim of the existence or nonexistence of classes, properties, or numbers, but as showing only that mathematical knowledge was as certain and as firmly based as logic itself. In like fashion, Carnap in the *Aufbau* viewed his "logical construction" as demonstrating only the epistemological rather than the ontological priority of phenomenal entities.[21]

3 Linguistic Reinterpretation

The positivist attack on metaphysics was mitigated to some extent by efforts to reconstrue metaphysical claims not simply as meaningless pseudo-statements but as significant assertions concerning language rather than the extralinguistic world. It has been noted that the history of philosophy shows a preponderance of "What is" questions, which have always suggested the possibility that something on the order of mere verbal definitions might, in fact, be required by way of answering them. So long as one's view of definition remains sufficiently Aristotelian, this suggestion hardly need threaten the integrity of the metaphysical enterprise as such. Positivists, however, were willing to accord significance to such philosophical questions only when these were reconstrued as strictly linguistic:

> In other words, the propositions of philosophy are not factual, but linguistic in character—that is, they do not describe the behaviour of physical, or even mental, objects; they express definitions, or the formal consequences of definitions. . . . Thus, to ask what is the nature of a material object is to ask for a definition of "material object," and this . . . is to ask how propositions about material objects are to be translated into propositions about sense-contents. Similarly, to ask what is a number is to ask some such question as whether it is possible to translate propositions about the natural numbers into propositions about classes. And the same thing applies to all the other philosophical questions of the form, "What is an x?" or "What is the nature of x?" They are all requests for definitions . . .[22]

Now, disregarding the dubious accuracy of any historical claim to the effect that the great philosophers of the past actually viewed the questions they posed as primarily linguistic in character, Ayer's suggestion here is clearly that this is how they ought to have viewed them, and how we too ought to view them now if we wish to make any progress toward answering them.

Ayer's remarks stem in large part from Carnap's doctrine of quasi-syntactical sentences set forth in his *Logical Syntax of Language*.[23] Such sentences are said to occupy an intermediate domain between genuine factual (object) statements and linguistic (syntactical) statements, for they "are formulated as though they refer . . . to objects, while in reality they refer to syntactical forms, and, specifically, to the forms of the designations of those objects with which they appear to deal. Thus these sentences are syntactical sentences in virtue of their content, though they are disguised as object sentences."[24] For the sake of clarity and precision, quasi-syntactical sentences may be translated out of the material mode of speech, wherein they appear to treat of objects, into the formal mode of speech, wherein, through the use of such devices as quotation marks, their actual linguistic content can be made explicit. Thus the pseudo-object sentence "Five is a number," which like the genuine object sentence "Five is an odd number" appears to be about the number five, is held to really concern the word "five" and so to be best reformulated as the purely syntactical sentence " 'Five' is a number-word."

An important class of these quasi-syntactical or pseudo-object sentences is said to result from the use of certain so-called universal words or predicates (*Allwörter*), examples of which are "number," "class," "property," "relation," and many others. These words, which appear to designate basic classes or categories of objects, are instead held, in the words of Victor Kraft, to "represent the conceptual or grammatical categories which are discriminated by the logical grammarian."[25] Thus, when a universal word is employed in a sentence as a predicate applicable to a certain kind of object—such as "number" in the above example, "Five is a number"—it is to be treated as a disguised linguistic, or syntactical, predicate, which actually applies to all linguistic expressions of the corresponding type appropriate for designating such objects; in the present example these would be numerical expressions, like "five." The factual content of a sentence like "Five is a number" is therefore seen as null, and the sentence—as well as any others resulting from the substitution for "five" of any other numerical expression—is to be regarded as trivially and analytically true, reflecting only the syntactical type distinctions of a given language.

The occurrence of universal words in the material mode of speech abounds, according to Carnap, in philosophical contexts, where it causes the mistaken impression that what is under investigation is the nature or existence of fundamental categories or features of reality, when it is in fact only a question of the basic types of expressions employed by a language. This confusion and the ir-resoluble conflicts and disputes to which it gives rise can best be dispelled, in Carnap's view, by translation out of the material mode of speech and into the formal mode of speech.

Carnap cites the logicist-formalist debate over the nature of num-ber as one typical philosophical dispute that can be brought to a quick and satisfactory resolution once the apparently conflicting claims are formulated so that the peculiarly linguistic nature of the issue is brought to the surface.[26] Thus, the two opposing theses

[L:] "Numbers are classes of classes of things."

[F:] "Numbers belong to a special primitive kind of objects."

which are according to Carnap misleadingly formulated in the ma-terial mode of speech, may be translated into the formal mode of speech as follows:

[L':] "Numerical expressions are class expressions of the second level."

[F':] "Numerical expressions are expressions of the zero level."

Here L and F are pseudo-object sentences that appear to deal with extralinguistic objects (namely, the natural numbers) but whose transformations, L' and F', reveal them to be actually concerned with language (numerical expressions). The stage is now set for resolution of the dispute, but the opposing parties still have to specify the particular language with reference to which their re-spective assertions, L' and F', are made. Failure to note the need for such a specification is itself reckoned as one other major cause of confusion arising out of the use of the material mode of speech:

> ... the use of the material mode of speech gives rise to obscurity by employing obsolete concepts in place of the syntactical concepts which are relative to language. . . . The use of the *material mode of speech* gives rise . . . to a *disregard of the rel-ativity to language of philosophical sentences*; it is responsible for an *erroneous conception of philosophical sentences as absolute.*[27]

Once the language in question is indicated, however, checking the validity of such claims as those above is presumed to be a routine and unproblematic procedure.

Carnap cites the disagreement between phenomenalists and realists over the nature of material objects as another representative example where reformulation of the opposing theses to bring out their true linguistic "content" leads the way to a speedy settlement of the matter. The pseudo-object sentences

[F:] A thing is a complex of sense data.

[R:] A thing is a complex of atoms.

are then rendered in the following purely syntactical form:

[F':] Every sentence in which a thing designation occurs is equipollent (equivalent)[28] to a class of sentences in which no thing-designation but sense-data designations occur.

[R':] Every sentence in which a thing designation occurs is equipollent (equivalent) to a sentence in which space-time co-ordinates and certain other descriptive functors (of physics) occur.[29]

Again, specification by both parties of the languages in question is necessary in order to allay the ambiguity and underscore the relativity of their respective claims. (This is, by the way, neglected by Ayer in his discussion of these matters.)

Here, then, is Carnap's suggested scheme[30] for treating philosophical questions as merely questions concerning the forms and interrelationships of expressions employed in particular languages (questions of "definition" for Ayer). Therefore, to say from within an explicitly logicist language that numbers are classes of classes of things, or from within a phenomenalist language that material objects are complexes of sense data, is to say something uninteresting, empty, and trivially true. Just as in the case of "Five is a number" taken within the context of arithmetic, these statements simply reflect the verbal conventions or rules governing the expressions of the language in which they are understood to occur. But it is only the nature and import of these conventions themselves that interest the philosopher as analyst, rather than any corresponding absolute claims concerning the nature of reality.

Now, this purported clarification of traditional philosophical is-

sues as entirely linguistic was not sufficient to quiet old-style
controversies, even among positivists. There was, after all, a ten-
dency for familiar metaphysical issues, such as the nominalism
versus realism and phenomenalism versus physicalism debates, to
reassert themselves within this new linguistic setting. Once questions as to the nature of the rules and conventions of various languages had been apparently resolved, or shelved for a time, the
question quickly arose as to what language was to be preferred.
That is, proponents of a nominalist language debated with proponents of a realist language over which language ought to be used
for mathematics. Likewise, proponents of a phenomenalist language
disagreed with proponents of a physicalist language with regard
to what sort of language was required for natural science. To critics
of positivism these supposedly linguistic disagreements seemed
rather poorly disguised versions of the traditional metaphysical
arguments concerning the existence of universals and the reality
of the external world, suggesting that the material mode of speech
was, perhaps, the proper philosophical idiom after all.

Carnap's response to this sort of criticism derives from his principle of tolerance invoked in the *Logical Syntax of Language* to permit
the free and unhampered construction and exploration of various
linguistic alternatives without the establishment of a priori restrictions on what sort of language might ultimately be admissible for
any given purpose—as in the case of the development of non-
Euclidean geometries:

> *It is not our business to set up prohibitions, but to arrive at*
> *conventions. . . . In logic there are no morals.* Everyone is at liberty
> to build up his own logic, i.e. his own form of language, as
> he wishes. All that is required of him is that, if he wishes to
> discuss it, he must state his methods clearly, and give syntactical
> rules instead of philosophical arguments.[31]

This principle leads Carnap to consider the possibility that perhaps
not all philosophical theses are best regarded as actual statements
about language after all:

> It is especially to be noted that the statement of a philosophical
> thesis sometimes . . . represents not an *assertion* but a *suggestion*.
> Any dispute about the truth or falsehood of such a thesis is

quite mistaken, a mere empty battle of words; we can at most discuss the utility of the proposal, or investigate its consequences.[32]

This is the origin of Carnap's suggestion for the reformulation of traditional metaphysical or ontological claims as *linguistic proposals*, which achieves its clearest and most complete expression in his later essay "Empiricism, Semantics, and Ontology," in which he offers an explanation for the appearance of metaphysical disputes within the positivists' own movement, in addition to a somewhat more sophisticated statement of the positivist case against speculative metaphysics. In doing so, Carnap stresses the importance of recognizing "a fundamental distinction between two kinds of questions concerning the existence or reality of entities."[33] These two sorts of questions, which depend on what he calls a linguistic framework, Carnap labels internal and external.

Internal questions concern the existence or reality of entities belonging to a given system of entities. These questions can occur only from within the specified contexts of some linguistic framework designed specifically for the purpose of talking about such entities. Internal questions, and possible answers to them, are formulated according to the rules of the framework, which govern all correct use of its constituent expressions. Answers are then empirically tested in the manner specified also by the rules of the framework— unless it is purely a logical question, in which case the truth or falsity of a proposed answer is supposed to follow from just the rules alone. For example, once we have accepted the thing language (cf. system of thing designations)[34] and its accompanying rules, we may meaningfully ask and answer such factual questions as "Are there any black swans?" In similar fashion, once we have the arithmetical framework (cf. system of numerical expressions) and its rules in hand, answering such questions as "Are there any prime numbers over 100?" should be a routine, logical matter. Internal questions, therefore, which are held to fall completely within the domain of the various special sciences and to exhaust all theoretically significant questions concerning any given sort of entity, are entirely relative to an accepted linguistic framework, with its rules for formulating and testing all statements concerning such entities.

External questions, on the other hand, occur outside the context of any particular framework and concern the existence or reality of a system of entities as a whole, such as the system of physical objects or that of natural numbers. External questions are like the "absolute" philosophical theses mentioned earlier in that they are formulated without reference to any particular language or framework and purport to deal with the basic categories or ultimate constituents of reality itself. Such "philosophical" questions are commonly thought to require answers as a means of justifying the acceptance of a proposed linguistic framework. "In contrast to this view," says Carnap, "we take the position that the introduction of the new ways of speaking does not need any theoretical justification because it does not imply any assertion of reality."[35] According to Carnap, all significant theoretical questions are relative to a specific language or framework in that the formulation of any significant assertion, along with the subsequent determination of its truth or falsity, presuppose the methods and criteria only an already accepted framework can provide. We may, of course, question the existence of a whole system of entities from within the framework that has been designed to speak about them, but the answers to these, now internal questions, are trivially true, reflecting only our decision to accept the framework in the first place.[36]

Thus, absolute ontological, or external, questions remain thoroughly devoid of theoretical significance. Accordingly, Carnap rejects the view that a framework is to be introduced on the basis of its purported correspondence to reality. However, he suggests, there is a way that external questions may be conceded a point, if not a theoretical content, when regarded as practical questions concerning the desirability of employing a framework for certain purposes. Carnap spells out what he means with reference to the external question concerning the reality of physical things:

> Those who raise the question of the reality of the thing world itself have perhaps in mind not a theoretical question as their formulation seems to suggest, but rather a practical question, a matter of a practical decision concerning the structure of our language. We have to make the choice whether or not to accept and use the forms of expressions in the framework in question. . . . If someone decides to accept the thing language, there is no objection against saying that he has accepted the world

of things. But this must not be interpreted as if it meant his acceptance of a *belief* in the reality of the thing world; there is no such belief or assertion or assumption, because it is not a theoretical question. To accept the thing world means nothing more than to accept a certain form of language, in other words, to accept rules for forming statements, and for testing, accepting, or rejecting them. . . . The purpose for which the language is intended to be used . . . will determine which factors are relevant for the decision. The efficiency, fruitfulness, and simplicity of the use of the thing language may be among the decisive factors. And the questions concerning these qualities are indeed of a theoretical nature. But these questions can not be identified with the question of realism. They are not yes-no questions but questions of degree.[37]

Thus, while Carnap strongly affirms that philosophers talk nonsense when they declare the truth of a framework, he is willing to grant their remarks a legitimate practical import when construed simply as linguistic proposals, hinging only upon the comparative utility of given frameworks intended for specific purposes.

When the seemingly metaphysical disputes of positivists are viewed within this suggested overall perspective, the air of paradox is quickly dispelled; they are seen simply as disputes over the practical merits of employing different languages or frameworks for various specific purposes. The issue of a nominalist versus a realist language then appears not as a disagreement about the existence of universals but, rather, as the question of which language is best suited for the foundation of mathematics. Similarly, phenomenalists and realists are debating not which entities, physical or phenomenal, are truly real, but only whether a phenomenalist or a physicalist language best serves the purpose of natural science.

Another view of ontological inquiry that somewhat resembles that of Carnap has been put forward by Gustav Bergmann. Bergmann shares the general positivist interest in mathematical logic and the philosophy of science, as well as the basic conviction that questions of language are of fundamental importance for philosophy. Bergmann suggests the reformulation of ontological claims as proposals for an ideal language. Even the rationalist metaphysics of Spinoza or Leibniz are, according to Bergmann, best interpreted as such linguistic proposals. His view of the issues of nominalism versus realism and phenomenalism versus physicalism has what is, by now, a familiar ring:

> Consider the thesis of classical nominalism that there are no universals. Given the linguistic turn it becomes the assertion that the ideal language contains no undefined descriptive signs except proper names. Again take classical sensationalism. Transformed it asserts the ideal language contains no undefined descriptive predicates, except non-relational ones of the first order, referring to characters exemplified by sense-data. . . .[38]

The crucial difference between Carnap and Bergmann lies in Bergmann's conception of the ideal language. According to Bergmann, "One does not, in any intelligible sense, *choose* the ideal language";[39] one rather "discovers" that it is adequate to represent reality. The ideal language is, then, no mere question of practical expediency, but purports to provide a true representation of the extralinguistic world. Bergmann proposes construction of the ideal language as a means of actually doing "descriptive metaphysics." He explains this by comparing the relation between language and reality to that between a picture and what it represents: "To say that a picture, to be a picture, must have certain features is, clearly, to say something about what it is a picture of."[40] Unlike the positivists, who see philosophy as purely and simply linguistic, Bergmann's view is that "philosophical discourse is not just about the ideal language, but rather, by means of it, about the world."[41] Whereas Carnap and other positivists adopt linguistic reformulations of classical philosophical theses as alternatives to what they believe to be meaningless metaphysical discourse, for Bergmann the move is merely a strategy for sidestepping such charges of meaninglessness while continuing to do metaphysics: "I know of no other way to speak of the world's categorial features without falling into the snares the linguistic turn avoids."[42]

Bergmann's view, however, seems to offer no way of proving the adequacy of, for example, a nominalist language, short of establishing in the first place the metaphysical claim that universals do not exist. So viewed, Bergmann's suggestion that we can discover the ideal language is surely metaphysics in a linguistic guise and is alien to the positivist temper. Carnap's proposal, on the other hand, is far more attractive from a more stringently antimetaphysical outlook. The idea that ultimately only pragmatic considerations lead us initially to speak of physical objects, numbers, and the like also brings Carnap close to the views of American philosophers like C. I. Lewis, while remaining essentially consistent with classical positivism. Carnap offers a more complete and well-rounded account of both science and philosophy and simultaneously sheds further light on the reasons for the alleged failure of speculative metaphysics.

The philosopher's chief task remains, for Carnap, that of asking and answering definitional "What is" questions—that is, the task of exploring and examining the conceptual parameters, or conditions of significance, imposed by the rules (syntactical and semantical) of various linguistic frameworks, and their consequences. This is, in Carnap's words, scientific philosophy. In opening up the domain of choice between alternative forms of language as a practical rather than a theoretical issue, however, Carnap accommodates traditional philosophical questions of the more straightforward "What is real?" or "What exists?" variety without compromising his antimetaphysical principles. Within this broad perspective the "scientific philosopher" is like the scientist himself in that he furnishes tools for the attainment of certain practical objectives. The philosopher provides useful linguistic or conceptual frameworks for the scientist, who employs these in fashioning theories for more direct technological application.

4   Kantian Ingredients in the Positivists' Redefinition of Philosophy

An apparent truism from which positivists inevitably began arguments for their view of philosophy as essentially logical analysis was that before you can decide whether some particular statement is true you must first understand what the statement means. Positivists latched onto this almost universally accepted dichotomy between meaning and truth (of propositions, statements, sentences, or whatever) and took it to reflect the division of labor between philosopher and scientist. As Schlick puts it,

Here then we find a definite contrast between the philosophic method, which has for its object the discovery of *meaning*, and the methods of the sciences, which have for their object the discovery of *truth*. . . . I believe Science should be defined as the *"pursuit of truth"* and Philosophy as the *"pursuit of meaning."*[43]

The philosopher is to seek and clarify the meanings of the statements of science, to construct or reconstruct the language of science; the scientist, language in hand, then proceeds to decide questions of truth or falsity and to build theories with the language at his disposal:

As I have stated the scientist has two tasks. He must find out the truth of a proposition and he must also find out the meaning of it. . . . In so far as the scientist does find out the hidden meaning of the propositions which he uses in his science he is a philosopher.[44]

What that simple distinction between meaning and truth did, besides provide a basis for distinguishing between science and philosophy, was to supply a basis for philosophy's claim to priority over theoretical science proper as a mode of human inquiry. Just as knowing the meaning of a statement was recognized as a logical prerequisite to the ability to verify it, the task of the philosopher was viewed as logically or epistemologically prior to that of the scientist. The philosopher, by setting forth (or at least discovering) the nature and extent of significant discourse, sets the parameters of scientific inquiry itself (that is, determines the limits within which scientific or theoretical truth may be established). In defining the range of legitimate theoretical inquiry—what may and what may not be established as true or false—the philosopher fixes the conceptual limitations of scientific investigations. Thus, by focusing on the rudimentary distinction between meaning and truth, and the apparently intimate relation between them, positivists were able to characterize logical or linguistic analysis as a genuine sort of "first philosophy" or epistemology, a discipline concerned with the conditions of the possibility of all knowledge (science). Again, we turn to Moritz Schlick for exemplary clarity on this point:

We see that meaning and truth are linked together by the process of verification: but the first is found by mere reflection about possible circumstances in the world, while the second is decided by really discovering the existence or non-existence of those circumstances.[45]

Or, in the words of the early Wittgenstein, to whom Schlick was so indebted,

Philosophy sets limits to the much disputed sphere of natural science. It must set limits to what can be thought; and, in doing so, to what cannot be thought. It must set limits to what cannot be thought by working outwards through what can be thought.[46]

There was more than a slight Kantian flavor, then, to the positivist program. Where Kant reacted in part against the excesses of German rationalism, positivists were reacting against the "debaucheries" of post-Kantian idealism. Where Kant sought to secure scientific knowledge itself from the skepticism of a Hume, positivists sought, in a similar spirit, to establish its 'logical foundations.' The cutting edge of Kant's approach was the observation that there could be no pure perception of reality unmediated by human conceptualization; that knowledge of the world requires the application of conceptual categories which shape and mold experience into some cognitively digestible form. Thus any knowledge of the world is necessarily relative to such a conceptual scheme, and the idea of any absolute or direct apprehension of reality is rejected as an impossibility. This is essentially the same outlook positivists came to adopt, except that, whereas Kant had located the organizing conceptual manifold through which all experience is filtered in the structure of the human mind, the positivists saw it now as embodied in the very language of science.

Just as the psychologically entrenched concepts or categories were for Kant a prerequisite to all human knowledge, for positivists language, as the actual embodiment of all human thought, was a precondition of any science. For positivists, then, the 'conditions of the possibility of human knowledge' came to be identified with the 'conditions of the possibility of meaningful discourse.' Positivists clearly perceived the task of the scientist as that of establishing systems of true propositions, statements, or sentences as such; therefore, identifying the conditions of meaningfulness of such propositions with the conditions of theoretical knowledge followed naturally. According to Schlick,

> The content soul and spirit of science is lodged naturally in what in the last analysis its statements actually mean; the philosophical activity of giving meaning is therefore the Alpha and Omega of all scientific knowledge.[47]

Kant's strictures against projecting the features of our conceptualizations onto reality itself were paralleled by similar positivist strictures against projecting the features of linguistic systems onto their subject matter. But now, instead of simply denying the possibility of knowledge of a transcendent realm, the positivists' identification of the conditions of knowledge with the conditions of significant discourse enabled them to deny the very meaningfulness of the conception of such a transcendent realm in the first place. And, as one might have expected, the charge against Kant, that in presuming to set the limits of knowledge one thereby presupposes something beyond those limits, was echoed by analogous objections to positivists' claims (such as that of Wittgenstein quoted above) about the limits of significant thought and discourse.[48] Whereas for Kant all knowledge of the world was relative to human conceptualization and categorization, for positivists all such knowledge, as well as the very significance of any talk whatever about the world, becomes relative in exactly the same way except that language assumes the role initially played by the conceiving mind.

Shifting the conceptualizing burden from human nature to language was also important in establishing the logical independence of the new epistemology from the rest of science. It represented a move away from psychological introspection to purer "logical analysis":

> Psychology is no more closely related to philosophy than any other natural science. . . . Does not my study of sign-language correspond to the study of thought-processes, which philosophers used to consider so essential to the philosophy of logic? Only in most cases they got entangled in unessential psychological investigations . . .[49]

These remarks of Wittgenstein were later echoed by Ayer, who observed that positivists make the impossibility of a transcendental metaphysics a matter of logic, whereas for Kant it was only a matter of fact (which is to say, a question of empirical science itself).[50]

The relativity of all knowledge of the world (and of the very significance of our conceptions of reality) to language, or the conceptual scheme(s) therein embodied, was therefore an essential, if sometimes only implicit, ingredient in the positivist antimetaphysical stance. This Kantian theme was captured in Neurath's widely publicized figure of the "conceptual boat" in which we are presumably cast adrift, unable to disembark in order to reconstruct it anew in accordance with the precise nature of extralinguistic reality but forced instead to rebuild it plank by plank while remaining afloat in it, warping it to fit the world even as the world itself is perceived only by means of it. There was to be no question of fitting language as a whole to the world, of trying to justify the acceptance of a language on the basis of an appeal to what there really is, for such an appeal to the nature of extralinguistic reality as a basis for judging the acceptability of a language would constitute nothing less than sheer metaphysical speculation, as Carnap so clearly recognized.

An essentially similar view of language—as presenting a "veil of symbols" through which all reality is necessarily perceived— led Henri Bergson to his thesis of the ineffability of our knowledge or perceptions of reality. Bergson traced the origins of traditional philosophical disputes between rationalists and empiricists to the preoccupations of these two schools with what he saw as essentially different features of language, rather than of reality or our experience of it. This analysis of rationalist and empiricist metaphysics as rooted in linguistic considerations of one sort or another is outlined at length in Bergson's *Introduction to Metaphysics* and is very suggestive of the positivists' later view that traditional philosophical controversies stem largely from linguistic confusions. But, whereas the positivists tended to view the relativity of our perceptions of reality to language as militating against the significance of any talk of reality apart from the specific conditions of meaningfulness set by a given linguistic system, Bergson looked to this conceptualizing role of language as a hindrance—an obstacle to our perceiving the world as it really is. For Bergson, then, language was bound to distort reality; for positivists it presented the only picture we could hope to attain. This mystical outlook of Bergson, which others have seen in the writings of Wittgenstein and even Schlick, is, in the end, the only alternative to simply giving up hope of making any sense of an absolute reality lying behind all our linguistic conceptions, once the conditions of linguistic significance and theoretical knowledge are clearly seen to converge.

To retain an absolutist view with respect to the nature of extra-linguistic reality was, then, to endorse the idea that its true nature could only be grasped by some sort of mystical insight or intuition. Positivists could hardly be expected to tolerate this idea. None-theless, their early efforts to articulate a strict empiricist epistemology left them hard pressed to avoid such an interpretation of their views. As already noted, drawing inferences about the structure or nature of reality from observations about the structure or meaning of language was every bit as illegitimate to positivists as projecting the features of the conceptual manifold onto the world beyond was to Kant. While Russell saw the use of logical analysis as providing a way around the Kantian dilemma ("replace inferred entities with logical constructions"[51]), to positivists it simply left an analogous problem: rendering their epistemological preference for sense data compatible with their strict antimetaphysical posture. Positivists had no desire to establish that the real things of the world were sense data, any more than that they were physical objects. Such concerns were clearly perceived as efforts to treat of what lies beyond the conditions of all possible significant discourse, and could not, therefore, be taken seriously. On the other hand, the positivists' original conception of an ideal language having the logical syntax of *Principia* and referring only to data of immediate experience into which all statements should be translatable if they are actually meaningful (that is, verifiable) made strict adherence to these antimetaphysical scruples a tricky business at best.

In the writings of Russell and the early Wittgenstein the ideality of such a language was linked to its possessing the logical structure necessary for its various propositions to correspond with or picture actual 'facts' or 'states of affairs' in the world. Thus, for Wittgenstein the meaning of a statement was the possible state of affairs it "pictured," and if a statement could not be rendered in terms of the ideal language it could not represent a possible state of affairs and therefore could be only a pseudo-statement to begin with. The possible states of affairs which a meaningful statement pictured thus constituted the circumstances under which it was true (its truth conditions). When an actual state of affairs was found to correspond to the state of affairs pictured by a particular statement, the statement was discovered to be true (that is, it was verified). Thus, to be verifiable, and so meaningful, was to picture a possible state of affairs, or, what comes to the same thing, to be couched in or capable of being couched in the ideal language. On this view, notions of truth and meaning are both tied to a metaphysical conception of the nature and structure of the extralinguistic world. The epistemological priority of atomic propositions in the ideal language is reducible, by and large, to the ontological priority of the atomic facts they reflect, describe, or picture.

For the positivists such a metaphysical account of meaning and truth was a source of considerable discomfort. Russell sought to infer the nature (or structure) of the world from that of language—revealed through analysis (that is, translation into the ideal language)—but to warrant this kind of inference he needed something like the "picture theory" of meaning and the correspondence theory of truth to back him up. Positivists had no desire to draw metaphysical conclusions but still needed a theory of meaning and truth to back up their own epistemological claims for analysis, in terms of a phenomenalist language employing the logic and grammar of *Principia*. This forced them to try to explain the special meaningfulness and verifiability of the ideal phenomenalist language without recourse to talk of the world in an absolute sense not conditioned by language itself. Thus, whereas the early Wittgenstein construed the meaning of a statement in terms of its truth conditions (the states of affairs pictured by the statement, which would make it true if found to exist), the positivists eventually chose to speak rather of a statement's method of verification, thereby giving the impression that the meaning of a statement could be given simply by specifying a procedure to be followed in verifying it without requiring reference to any supposed extralinguistic 'facts' that would make it 'true.'[52] However, such specifications amounted in the end to the same translations into sentences of a phenomenalist language (observation terms, protocol sentences, or the like) whose own meaningfulness and verifiability might still be questioned. One might prefer to speak of immediate experience or the "given" in describing the reference of such sentences, rather than of sense data, phenomenal entities, or atomic 'facts,' but the problem of meaningfully characterizing such primitive experience was no easier than making sense of atomic facts themselves. One could not actually have knowledge of such a pure realm of experience, for this would then be some kind of knowledge apart from that achieved by empirical science itself. One could not even legitimately attempt to describe it, because all meaning was somehow ultimately dependent on it. This dilemma led to some doctrines rather like Bergson's of the ineffable just to explain the meaningfulness or verifiability of language, and the epistemological priority of the phenomenalist language in particular.[53]

The problems deriving from the epistemological ambitions of the positivists have resisted a satisfactory solution to the present day. Early on, Otto Neurath suggested looking to a physicalist language as psychologically rather than logically prior. However, this implied the same situation in which Kant had presumably been ensnared: making epistemology, or logical analysis itself, part of science rather than above it or prior to it. Carnap, taking the hint from Neurath's suggestion, did adopt a much more tolerant view (ergo his principle of tolerance) toward the use of physicalist languages, if this should "suit the purposes" of science better. But in retaining the idea that a phenomenalist language might suit the purposes of epistemology better, the same old question remained, only now it was hidden under Carnap's increasing emphasis on the broad scope for linguistic alternatives and the idea that decisions between them are constrained only by practical considerations. If a phenomenalist (or a physicalist) language is, however, to remain epistemologically preferable, then its privileged status among all other languages despite any conceivable "practical" considerations would seem to be ensured.

Still, it was Carnap's devotion to his principle of tolerance and his development of the idea of linguistic alternatives, most fully articulated in "Empiricism, Semantics, and Ontology," that best represented and most clearly expressed the Kantian insight in its linguistic mode. Here apparent metaphysical assertions come to be recognized either as disguised proposals for new ways of speaking or as questions merely concerning the rules of particular linguistic frameworks. The only assertions that can be granted genuine theoretical significance according to this scheme are those made within some given linguistic framework. There is to be no significant discourse about the world except in relation to some language or framework. Carnap's doctrine of linguistic frameworks thus represents the fullest articulation of the linguistic Kantianism implicit in the positivists' basic critique of metaphysics and their advocacy of linguistic analysis as the primary philosophical task. The view in question here is, very simply, that how one 'sees,' 'conceives,' or talks about the world is always relative to the language employed in doing so. How this principle could consistently apply with respect to what is given in immediate experience without sacrificing the claims of a phenomenalist language to privileged epistemological status is a question Carnap never really confronted.

What happens as a result of relocating conceptual schemes in linguistic systems, once a view like Carnap's has been fully spelled out, is that something like the old freedom and spontaneity of speculative metaphysics reappears. With the structure of the human mind seen as determining our view of the world, as Kant would have had it, we are forced to look at the world in the way we happen to. That is, we see things the way we do because we were born that way. There is no other way we could see them. In Carnap's linguistic version, however, we are at liberty to construe reality in any number of alternative ways. We are as unconstrained by the 'facts' as speculative metaphysics supposed itself to be. However, this freedom does not exist because the nature of the facts depends on how we imagine or intuit them to be, but only because there are no such 'facts' to begin with—except relative to some specified linguistic or conceptual framework, which we may wish to accept. We are free to construct as many alternative frameworks for discourse as our own imagination and ingenuity permit, and to accept them to the extent that our own practical purposes make it desirable. The key point is, simply, that acceptance of a framework cannot be predicated on significant beliefs with respect to what really exists or is the case; all significant questions of what there is are 'internal' (that is, relative to some framework itself).

An even more thoroughgoing version of this same philosophical perspective has recently been voiced by Nelson Goodman. Goodman vigorously attacks the idea that it makes sense to think of an absolute and self-contained reality existing independently of some mode of symbolic representation and/or directly given in experience, which we may then either fail or succeed in adequately capturing—that is, the idea that it makes sense to talk of the world, or our experience of it, as it really is.[54] According to Goodman the world is only as it may be described or represented:

What we must face is the fact that even the truest description comes nowhere near faithfully reproducing the way the world is. . . . There are very many different equally true descriptions of the world, and their truth is the only standard of their faithfulness. . . . For me there is no way that is the way the world is; and so of course no description can capture it. But there are many ways the world is, and every true description captures one of them. . . . Since the mystic is concerned with the way the world is and finds that the way cannot be expressed, his ultimate response to the question of the way the world is must be, as he recognizes, silence. Since I am concerned rather with the ways the world is, my response must be to construct one or many descriptions. The answer to the question "What is the way the world is?" "What are the ways the world is?" is not a shush, but a chatter.[55]

According to Goodman, there is no way the world really is, apart from some way of describing or representing it. The idea that there is a single "right" or "true" way of representing the world, says Goodman, implies that there is an objective standard against which to judge the 'faithfulness' of any mode of description or representation.[56] As Carnap would put it, there is no single right or true framework that uniquely fits or corresponds to reality because any truly meaningful claim about the nature of reality must be itself made from within the specific context of such a linguistic framework.

An interesting feature of Goodman's critique is that it is marshaled simultaneously against the analytic metaphysics of Russell, against the mystical views of Bergson, and against phenomenalist epistemological doctrine as well. According to Goodman, neither reality nor our experience of it will cohere in and of itself, but depends instead for its coherence and organization on the application of some conceptualizing or categorizing system of symbols. For Goodman, then, the idea that knowledge arises through some sort of processing of raw materials received through the senses and discoverable "either through purification rites or by methodical disinterpretation"[57] is on the same kind of shaky footing as the idea that there is some way the world really is that our linguistic frameworks, or modes of symbolic representation, may more or less faithfully capture. Notions of the given or ground elements in immediate experience fare no better than that of Bergson's "ineffable." The classifying and organizing function of a symbol system is, Goodman contends, a necessary prerequisite to even having a determinate experience in the first place. Regarding the innocent eye, which is imagined to somehow perceive things just as they are presented or given in experience, Goodman says

> It functions not as an instrument self-powered and alone. But as a dutiful member of a complex and capricious organism. Not only how it sees but what it sees is regulated by needs and prejudices. It selects, rejects, organizes, discriminates, associates, classifies, analyzes, constructs. It does not so much mirror as take and make.[58]

Thus, while clear and explicit recognition of the relativity of all meaningful talk about the world to overall linguistic considerations, along with a full appreciation of its consequences, has come only gradually, as doctrines of the ideal language, the given, and the verification theory of meaning have crumbled, this Kantian-like view remains implicit in the basic rationale of the positivists' critique of metaphysics and their endorsement of 'logical' analysis as a replacement for it. It is clearly expressed in the idea that thought is embodied in language and that man is inevitably cast adrift in a "conceptual boat."

5   The Analytic Conception of Language

If one recognizes (as positivists generally did) the limiting conditions which considerations of language set for questions of genuine theoretical interest, the substitution of an exclusively linguistic investigation for that of traditional metaphysics is not hard to understand. Once inquiry into some completely external and self-contained reality appeared to be beyond both practical and theoretical bounds, attention naturally came to focus upon the mode of human conceptualization itself—in this case, language. If we cannot get out of the "conceptual boat" represented by one linguistic framework or another and gain a clear view of the world as it really is—indeed, if it does not even make sense to imagine such a thing— then why not turn our attention toward the boat itself and the conceptions about reality it embodies? Just as Kant assumed that we occupy something of a privileged position with respect to an investigation of our own concepts or thoughts about the world (even if the world itself should be so distant as to be completely unattainable), so positivists rather naturally adopted a similar attitude; but now such an investigation would have less the character of subjective introspection than of a purely 'logical' analysis of language, the chief instrument of all genuine theoretical inquiry. However, the central presupposition of this move (and of Kant's) is that what is said or thought or conceived about the world can be examined and understood in some ultimate and absolute way in which the world itself cannot—that is, that although there may be no way in which the world *really is*, there is still a way (or ways) that we *really say* it is, or *conceive* it to be.

The idea that the individual words, statements, or linguistic systems we routinely employ in the pursuit and accumulation of theoretical knowledge possess a determinate meaning or content, or embody certain fixed structural or conceptual features, or treat (or purport to treat) of a determinate and identifiable subject matter is hardly unique or peculiar to positivism. This basic *analytic conception* of language is indeed common to all classical approaches to philosophical analysis, whether this method is to be employed simply in an effort to explain the origins and hopelessly irreconcilable character of traditional philosophical disputes or to demonstrate the theoretical meaninglessness of such disputes.

Similarly, whether the aim is ultimately to adduce evidence in favor of or against specific metaphysical beliefs or only to clarify and elucidate the epistemological or 'logical' basis of science, the assumption remains intact that what language really says or is really about is a genuinely significant issue, open to objective philosophical examination (that is, analysis).

The early Wittgenstein thus proposed a view of philosophy as a critique of language whose business is primarily to uncover the true logical form of statements hidden under the superficial and misleading grammatical structure of ordinary language, and he credited Russell with showing that the apparent form of language need not be its real form.[59] In a similar spirit, Ryle proposed examining what is really meant by an expression in order to discover the real form of the facts recorded by it.[60] Where Russell looked to the logical form of expressions as giving clues to the basic constituents of reality, Ayer protested: ". . . the philosopher, as an analyst, is not directly concerned with the physical properties of things. He is concerned only with the way in which we speak about them."[61]

Various opposing views of the character and feasibility of traditional philosophical inquiry thus overlaid a single shared conception of language as inherently possessed of 'real' form, structure, or content, which was presumed to be accessible to the analyst's searching eye without regard to his ultimate philosophical objectives. However, it was for positivists (such as Schlick, with his talk of the "hidden meaning" of scientific propositions, or Carnap, in his discussions of the "logical structure" or "content" of the language of science) that the analytic conception of language assumed the greatest importance and was cast into the sharpest relief, for it was these philosophers who contended that the investigation of such features of language was not only essential to an adequate understanding of the origin, nature, and extent of all human knowledge, but that such an investigation itself constituted the sole realm of legitimate philosophical inquiry.

And so the real form or meaning of our discourse, as allegedly revealed through analysis, was claimed to show that such things as Being, Nothing, the Absolute, properties or universals, and a host of nonentities from Mr. Pickwick to Pegasus, as well as the apparent designations of such 'unique' or 'definite' descriptions as "the king of France," were not really the subjects of statements that appeared to deal with them. Similarly, analysis purported to show that statements like "God exists" do not really attribute a property of being to anything, and the doctrine of type distinctions was claimed to represent a finely grained conceptual structure in language that prohibited the application, under any circumstances, of some predicates to some things while simultaneously guaranteeing the applicability of other predicates under all circumstances. And of course there was the most impressive achievement of analysis—the set-theoretic interpretation of number theory, which purported to show that our apparent talk of numbers is really about classes of classes—along with the parallel effort to show that the language of physical science is really concerned with elements of immediate experience rather than physical objects themselves. In all such instances analysts claimed to be getting at the real structure, meaning, or conceptual import of the portions of language at which their analyses were directed. With this revealed, true meaning or structure was then appealed to in various ways to solve, re-solve, or dis-solve outstanding philosophical difficulties. The particular uses to which the specific results of analysis have been put (explaining metaphysics, attacking metaphysics, or doing metaphysics or epistemology) are thus irrelevant to the generally accepted assumption that language exhibits fixed and determinate meaning or conceptual content that represents a distinctive way of talking about or describing the world and is susceptible to sustained philosophical analysis in one form or another.

To such absolute metaphysical questions as "What is the structure of reality?" or "What really exists?" there correspond such absolute linguistic questions as "What is the structure of our language?" or "What are we really talking about?" The positive achievements of analysis not only seemed to confirm antecedent intuitions that such linguistic questions might be asked, but excited the idea that answers to them might be novel, interesting, and nontrivial. The positivists, wary of absolute metaphysics altogether, embraced this linguistic absolutism wholeheartedly. This eventually led to systematic reformulations (like those of Carnap) of virtually every conceivable absolute metaphysical or ontological assertion in terms of a corresponding absolute linguistic assertion concerning the syntax, structure, or meaning of the expressions of a particular language. In this way, for every statement about what there really is there could be substituted a statement (or statements) about what a certain language (or certain languages), or a portion of the same, *really says* there is. Inquiry into what we really say (or may say) about the world thus systematically replaced inquiry into the world as it really is.[62]

The linguistic absolutism of the analytic conception of language must not, as already noted, be confused with the doctrine of the ideal language or the Picture Theory of meaning. Russell's and Wittgenstein's notion of the ideal language that pictures the world as it really is is, rather, one version of the analytic conception of language—one version, but an exemplary one. The Picture Theory attempts to account for the purported structure and content of (the ideal) language by appealing to a mysterious picturing relation between language and reality. Language pictures the world through projecting the logical form of the 'facts.'[63] "The picture is a model of reality."[64] According to this view, the job of the analyst is to clarify the confused and distorted picture presented by ordinary language with its superficial grammatical structure and to reveal its true sense and structure by means of reformulations in the ideal language, which presents an accurate or true picture (true in the sense of having the right logical form). Once propositions are cast in the form of the ideal language, grasping their meaning or sense is compared with the way it is imagined one recognizes what a picture represents; "The proposition *shows* its sense."[65] The "sense" of a proposition as a whole is actually held to be a function of the logical form it shares with reality (if it is a significant proposition at all) and the particular things its individual component terms stand for as a matter of convention.

The Picture Theory, therefore, attempts to explain what (the ideal) language really says or means by appealing to the way the world really is. Here linguistic absolutism is totally dependent upon metaphysical absolutism. However, we thereby achieve a powerfully suggestive figure of language meaning as a definite and concrete feature that can somehow be immediately grasped or recognized in the way it is imagined that we apprehend what a picture represents. Understanding language (so long as it is language with the proper logical form) takes on the character of a direct and unmediated seeing rather like that privileged mode of cognitive apprehension we normally expect to find associated with metaphysical insight, intuition, or awareness. One examines language, or the picture it presents, as the metaphysician would examine reality. Language thus presents a specific and determinate picture of reality that can be directly examined even though reality itself may be beyond either practical or theoretical reach. Thus was the picture of reality presented by language to become the surrogate subject matter of philosophical scrutiny. The seemingly manifest character of pictorial representation appeared to offer a plausible account of how we might thus come to "see" what language really says about the world, even if we cannot "see" directly the way the world really is.

The irrepressible metaphysical assumptions of the Picture Theory as put forward by Russell and Wittgenstein, and the concomitant supposition that there is only one right or true or ideal language, were, as I have stressed, unappealing to the positivists. However, the graphic and suggestive characterization of the absolute determinacy and the patent accessibility of the structure and content of language continued to exercise a strong influence over positivists and other analytic philosophers, who have striven manfully ever since to find a less compromising explanation for it. Initial attempts to escape the metaphysics of the Picture Theory led to a new emphasis on the rules or conventions believed to govern linguistic discourse. Attempts to account for or vindicate some imagined ineffable relation between language and the extralinguistic world, as the source of what language really says or is about, were abandoned in favor of accounts in terms of linguistic rules or conventions.

The role of convention had, of course, been acknowledged to some degree by the early Wittgenstein as explaining the sense of individual terms. For Wittgenstein, however, this aspect of linguistic representation was secondary to and dependent upon the nonconventional doctrine of a logical structure which we are imagined unable even to talk about directly in a truly significant fashion. The secondary, conventional aspect of language thus could be explained, but the primary structural features could only be recognized or grasped. The idea that both meaning and structure (the whole linguistic story) arise from rules or conventions that may be spelled out, discussed, and reformulated if need be in a metalanguage gained prominence partly as a response to the acknowledged inadequacies of the Picture Theory, its incipient metaphysics and mystical tendencies, but another strong and positive influence stemmed from the increasing interest in the formalization of mathematics and the metamathematical results of Hilbert, Gödel, and Tarski. According to this new view, language is still regarded as presenting a picture, but the origin of this picture is not tied logically to that which is pictured. The key to the picture lies in the rules—formation and transformation, syntactical and semantical, and so on—of the language in question. These rules are not intended to represent links with the extralinguistic world but simply to identify and set the conditions of meaning for the expressions of a given language. What language really says, then, or how it pictures the world, is now seen as fully determined by the rules or conventions governing the use of language. The job of the rules is to spell out just what can be said about the world by means of the language in question, and how. The rules represent a codification of the language's conceptual content, and are thus (if I may parrot Schlick) the Alpha and Omega of the way a language pictures the world.

The doctrine of linguistic rules and conventions appeared, therefore, to provide a release from dependency upon the ineffable "picturing relation" and its associated metaphysical implications, as well as freeing philosophy from Wittgenstein's mystical strictures against the possibility of meaningful talk about the way language represents the world. With this doctrine of the thorough conventionality of linguistic use and meaning, the central antimetaphysical posture of positivism, as well as its basic rationale for analysis as the new "first philosophy," seemed secure. The conceptual bounds within which any scientific or theoretical investigation must necessarily take place are determined not by the immutable and ultimate traits of reality, as reflected in language or otherwise, nor by the structure of the human mind, but simply by the conscious or unconscious adoption by men over the course of time of rules or conventions concerning how they will speak.

In the end, consistent adherence to the principles that led to this conventionalist doctrine of language led also to an analogous theory of picturing itself. As Goodman explains,

> I began by dropping the picture theory of language and ended by adopting the language theory of pictures. . . . You might say that the picture theory of language is as false and as true as the picture theory of pictures; or in other words, what is false is not the picture theory of language but a certain absolute notion concerning both pictures and language.[66]

According to Goodman, then, how we see or picture or view the world, not just metaphorically but quite literally, is as relative to conventionally derived systems of symbolization as is the way we speak about, talk about, or describe the world by means of language.

The "rules of language" thesis accords well, then, with Carnap's principle of tolerance, as opposed to the view that there is only one right way of talking about the world. Our different alternative ways of seeing or describing the world are, according to Carnap's doctrine of linguistic frameworks, as many and as distinct from one another as are the different and distinct sets of rules we may devise for the construction and use of linguistic expressions. In

Carnap's fully articulated scheme of things each framework possesses and is constituted or defined by its own set of rules. To choose a framework, and thus a general way of conceiving of, describing, or perhaps picturing the world, is simply to adopt an appropriate set of rules. The theoretical scientist is viewed as working within the conceptual scheme defined by some such set of rules, and deciding, relative to it, questions of truth and falsity about the world. The philosopher, however, seen as engaged in the task of discovering, identifying, formulating, and reformulating these rules, is viewed as actively engaged in the analysis of the basic structures of these conceptual systems themselves—in the examination, exploration, and comparison of the different conceptual schemes, world views, or world pictures embodied in such rules for speaking. The philosopher's task is to reveal and describe the general picture of reality, as represented in the rules of language, relative to which the scientist may establish theoretical truth.

The conventionalist version of the analytic conception of language is therefore still, in a sense, a picture theory of language. That is to say, it still holds that language presents a fixed and determinate picture of reality, or a conceptual scheme in terms of which all experience is interpreted. This version eventually just opts for a different theory of picturing altogether. Picturing no longer implies as logically prior the something pictured; rather the general features of that which is pictured are determined simply by the rules of the system of symbolic representation employed. Language still presents a fixed and discoverable picture of things, and the philosopher still is concerned with the features of this basic picture rather than directly with features of the world itself; the point is now that this picture, which represents the conceptual parameters of any acceptable science, is constituted only by a set of conventionally adopted and specifiable rules and not by some inexpressible relation with the world in itself. Characterization of the task of philosophical analysis is thus freed from any suggestion of metaphysical concern. In investigating the picture of the world embodied in this or that language rather than the world itself, the philosopher is concerned only with simple rules for the creation and manipulation of symbols. His linguistic absolutism appears now quite free of any metaphysical absolutism and quite compatible with any doctrine concerning the actual *relativity* of metaphysical inquiry (or any corresponding doctrine of the meaninglessness of metaphysics) he may wish to endorse.

Still, the linguistic absolutism of the analytic conception of language, no matter how it is explicated, when joined to the view that talk of the world is meaningful only relative to some applied system of linguistic representation, seems to imply that language itself is not of this world—that the concepts, meanings, ideas, thoughts, form, structure, content, and subject matter of linguistic expressions, or the conceptual schemes, world pictures, and *Weltanschauungen* embodied in whole linguistic systems, may somehow be 'grasped' or 'discovered' in a way that is not dependent upon or relative to language in just the same way as are our ordinary determinations of truth about the world. This is implicit in the view that the analysis of language is (epistemologically) prior to all empirical science, that it explores and determines the conceptual basis of all genuine empirical or theoretical investigations. The view is that the world is not determinate apart from language, but that our conceptions or understanding of the world, as constituted in language, are. We may not inquire significantly into the ultimate traits of reality, but we may seek corresponding absolute answers about the fixed structural or conceptual features of a language. Basic ontology and logico-mathematical truth do not rest on a priori metaphysical principles, but reflect only the limiting features of applied conceptual or linguistic systems.

Thus the antimetaphysical stance of the positivists, and of many analytic philosophers of the succeeding generation, puts the greatest burden on this sort of linguistic absolutism. Conceding that there is no way the world really is, they continue to adhere to the view that there is a way we really say it is or conceive it to be, and that this absolute or determinate conceptual content or meaning of language may properly be subjected to something of the piercing philosophical vision usually associated with the efforts of metaphysicians. Though perception of reality is impossible except relative to conception, our perception of these conceptions is imagined to be clear and distinct. Whether analytic philosophers turn to language in the belief that talk of the world as it really is constitutes outright nonsense or simply in the belief that direct knowledge of such a world is obstructed by more practical sorts of considerations, their common acceptance of the analytic conception of language involves assumptions about the nature of linguistic inquiry that parallel the pretensions of speculative metaphysics regarding our access to extralinguistic reality.

2 What Language Says as Determined by Rules

1 Quine's "Ontological Relativity"

For positivists, then, the analytic conception of language played a crucial epistemological role beyond that of simply supporting analysis as a critical adjunct to metaphysics or "first philosophy." It supported a view of analysis as constituting "first philosophy" itself. Only such a priori claims as could be reconstrued as hinging entirely upon the basic meaning, structure, or content of linguistic expression, rather than the nature of extralinguistic reality (or of extralinguistic thought), were conceded genuine significance or validity. Carnap, we have seen, spelled out this doctrine to the point where considerations of language came to account not only for the difference between logical and factual truth but for that between ontological and scientific questions of existence as well. The existence of basic categories of entities was, as for the truths of logic and mathematics generally, held to result solely from the peculiar characteristics of the particular language or framework adopted—that is, to be a consequence of what the language we choose to speak *really says there is*, rather than what we may suppose there *really is*, apart from all language. And as we noted, the theory that the form and content of any language is totally determined by conventionally adopted rules gradually evolved to replace the picture theory of meaning as the mortar holding the whole positivist and neopositivist edifice together.

Quine has long been known for his strenuous opposition to all efforts to base the logical/factual distinction on linguistic considerations alone and to Carnap's analogous approach to the distinction between scientific and ontological (or 'philosophical') questions of what exists or is real. This opposition has taken the form of a sustained critical examination of the notions of linguistic meaning, rules or conventions, and a variety of related issues, beginning with his early essay "Truth by Convention" and continuing through such well-known efforts as "On Carnap's Views on Ontology," "Carnap and Logical Truth," and "Two Dogmas of Empiricism," and into several important sections of his book *Word and Object*. His more recent essay "Ontological Relativity" pulls together several different strands of his own position which are scattered throughout these and other works and represents, perhaps, the single most compact and comprehensive statement of Quine's views on language construction, the role of convention or "rules," and the theoretical status of questions about language in general. Though in some respects the essay clearly echoes strains of Quine's earlier attacks on the conventionalist view of language and the philosophical doctrines that view is used to support, its unprecedented scope and precision disclose an unexpectedly fresh and unified philosophical perspective that penetrates much deeper than his earlier work—at some points even seeming to contradict some of his own former pronouncements on language.

The exceedingly far-ranging and frequently technical nature of the discussion in "Ontological Relativity" does not suit it to simple and concise summarization. Though individual localized portions may appear lucid and cogent in themselves, their interconnections with one another and their overall philosophical import are apt to seem clouded and somewhat enigmatic. For this reason the following extended outline is included to serve as the basis for further discussion of the essay. The present chapter will focus primarily on the arguments, insights, and observations that militate specifically against the classic linguistic orientation to philosophy best represented by Carnap. Much of this will be reminiscent of familiar criticisms of Carnap and his followers and will suggest certain already well-recognized aspects of Quine's views on language and theoretical science. Succeeding chapters, however, will be devoted to detailing more novel and far-reaching critical consequences for the underlying analytic conception of language, of which Carnap's formulations represent simply one important and influential version.

The central thesis of "Ontological Relativity" is what Quine calls the double relativity involved in all talk about what ontology a theory is committed to or what entities the terms in a theory refer to. According to Quine, the ontological import of a theory can be determined only relative to some further theory or language (itself taken at face value) and relative to some choice of how to translate or interpret the former in terms of the latter. Besides being thus unable to say absolutely what the objects of a theory are, Quine also explains that in some cases we are similarly unable to decide absolutely whether or not a theory imports a universe of discourse to begin with.

Quine begins by covering some familiar ground in connection with his well-known thesis of the indeterminacy of translation and the problem of empirically determining linguistic reference.[1] The reference of general terms, or terms of divided reference, in a remote language is objectively inscrutable, Quine claims, because what such terms are taken to apply to, or how they are determined to individuate or slice up scattered portions of the world, may vary widely depending on how far one is willing to make compensating adjustments in the translation of other words in the language. Specifically, it will depend on how one finally decides to translate a certain "cluster of interrelated grammatical particles and constructions: plural endings, pronouns, numerals, the 'is' of identity, and its adaptations 'same' and 'other'."[2] This group of interrelated devices Quine calls the English apparatus of individuation.

For example, in Quine's hypothetical native language, "gavagai" may be assented to whenever queried in the presence of a rabbit. But a rabbit is present when, and only when, an undetached rabbit part or a rabbit stage is also present:

> The only difference between rabbits, undetached rabbit parts, and rabbit stages is in their individuation. If you take the total scattered portion of the spatio-temporal world that is made up of rabbits, and that which is made up of undetached rabbit parts, and that which is made up of rabbit stages, you come out with the same scattered portion of the world each of the three times. The only difference is in how you slice it. And how to slice it is what ostension or simple conditioning, however persistently repeated, cannot teach.[3]

In order to determine just which things "gavagai" applies to we must be able to ask in the native language such questions as "Is this gavagai the same as that?" and we must therefore rely on some prior translation of the English individuative apparatus. The problem here, however, is that there is no right or wrong way to translate this apparatus, and different translations of it can accommodate correspondingly different interpretations of "gavagai" equally well:

> Then when in the native language we try to ask "Is this gavagai the same as that?" we could as well be asking "Does this gavagai belong with that?" Insofar, the native's assent is no objective evidence for translating "gavagai" as "rabbit" rather than "undetached rabbit part" or "rabbit stage."[4]

Quine finds this situation plausible because of the "broadly structural and contextual character of any considerations that could guide us to native translations of the English cluster of interrelated devices of individuation": "There seem bound to be systematically very different choices all of which do justice to all dispositions to verbal behavior on the part of all concerned."[5] The consequence is, at any rate, that we are left no objective reason for deciding that "gavagai" refers to rabbits instead of undetached rabbit parts or rabbit stages.

Quine treats a further sort of inscrutability of reference in connection with the systematic ambiguity of such terms as "green" and "alpha." These terms may be used as general terms true of individual concrete things such as houses or inscriptions, or as singular terms naming abstract entities like the color green or the first letter of the Greek alphabet. Here the difference in use amounts to a difference in the objects referred to, but again, as in deciding on a translation of "gavagai," we lack any objective criteria for discriminating between the two uses:

> The pointing that would be done in teaching the concrete general term "green" or "alpha" differs none from the pointing that would be done in teaching the abstract singular term "green" or "alpha."[6]

The only way we can determine which use is involved is by paying attention to just how the word occurs in sentences: Does it take an indefinite article, or plural ending? Does it stand as singular subject, as modifier, or as predicate complement? And so on. In order to answer these questions we must again rely on the English apparatus of individuation, but, as we have seen, the translation of this apparatus is itself theoretically indeterminate.

Referential inscrutability is thus bidimensional. First, there is no theoretical basis for deciding among various possible concrete extensions of a foreign general term; second, there is similarly no way of saying with certainty whether the foreign term is being used as a concrete general term to begin with, rather than as a singular term naming some corresponding abstract entity.

Quine mentions, in addition, a certain "dimness of reference" that can be found lingering even in our own "home" language, with its individuative apparatus considered fixed. For example, if we clarify discourse of expressions (to take Quine's example of the protosyntactician) by recourse to sets of atomic inscriptions to serve as single signs and then finite sets of sign/number pairs to represent sequences of signs or compound expressions, are we still talking of linguistic expressions rather than just some corresponding subset of sets? Or, if we choose instead to construe expressions outright as their Gödel numbers, for the sake of simplicity and clarity, in what sense could we argue that we are still talking only of expressions rather than of numbers and their arithmetical properties? Similarly, when we find a set-theoretic model for arithmetic, should we then be construed as talking actually of numbers or of sets?

There appears to be no clear and definite way of answering questions as to which among the several isomorphic universes that may serve as the model of a given theory we actually have in mind at any particular time. We have a real difficulty in saying just what objects any of these theories are really about. Empirical considerations are no help, and our attempt to clarify with words just what we mean seems only to complicate matters further. Quine assesses the implications as follows:

> We are finding no clear difference between *specifying* a universe of discourse . . . and *reducing* that universe to some other. We saw no significant difference between clarifying the notion of expression and supplanting it by that of number. And now to say more particularly what numbers themselves are is in no

evident way different from just dropping numbers and assigning to arithmetic one or another new model, say in set theory.[7]

Quine advances a more provocative claim. He charges that the very sort of extreme referential inscrutability that is inherent in radical translation can be introduced into the home language. Quine points out that we ordinarily translate (more or less unconsciously) our neighbor's words homophonically into our own, and that practically this is well warranted. However, the theoretical justification is not always so clear cut, for as long as we are willing to make compensating adjustments in the way we interpret our neighbor's use of the individuative apparatus we may vary at will what we take to be the referential import of his discourse:

> We can systematically reconstrue our neighbor's apparent references to rabbits as really references to rabbit stages, and his apparent references to formulas as really references to Gödel numbers and vice versa. We can reconcile all this with our neighbor's verbal behavior by cunningly readjusting our translations of his various connecting predicates so as to compensate for the switch of ontology.[8]

We may even, then, ultimately question the reference of our own words, wondering, for example, if our use of "rabbits" refers really to rabbits or to some other just as likely entities.

It is at this point, declares Quine, that we begin to make nonsense out of reference. It is indeed meaningless, he says, to question the ultimate or absolute reference of even our own home language. At home in our own language, with its vocabulary taken for granted, we fix reference simply by saying

> that this is a formula and that a number, this a rabbit and that a rabbit part, this and that the same rabbit, and this and that different parts. *In just those words.* This network of terms and predicates and auxiliary devices . . . is our frame of reference, or coordinate system. Relative to *it* we can and do talk meaningfully and distinctively of rabbits and parts, numbers and formulas . . . reference *is* nonsense except relative to a coordinate system.[9]

We can then meaningfully question the reference of terms in a language only by recourse to some "background" language that "gives the query sense, if only relative sense; sense relative in turn to it, the background language."[10] Absolute questions of reference are as meaningless, argues Quine, as questions of absolute position or velocity. Just as repeated questioning of the positions of spatial coordinate systems can be answered only relative to some further coordinate system, until the regress at length halts, in practice, with something like pointing, so too in ontological inquiry an indefinite regress of appeals to one background language after another can in practice be stopped only by our "acquiescing in our mother tongue and taking its words at face value."[11] Thus, Quine concludes, "What makes sense is to say not what the objects of a theory are, absolutely speaking, but how one theory of objects is interpretable or reinterpretable in another."[12] This, essentially, is the relativistic thesis.

Thus, although a theory is commonly understood to be "a set of fully interpreted sentences," there is no question of fully interpreting a theory except relative to some further background theory:

> In specifying a theory we must indeed fully specify, in our own words, what sentences are to comprise the theory, and what things are to be taken as values of the variables, and what things are to be taken as satisfying the predicate letters; insofar we do fully interpret the theory, *relative* to our own words and relative to our overall home theory which lies behind them. But this fixes the objects of the described theory only relative to those of the home theory; and these can, at will, be questioned in turn.[13]

What makes absolute ontological questions meaningless, says Quine, is *circularity*. A sentence "F is a G" will be satisfactory relative only to our uncritical acceptance of "G." "To question the reference of all the terms of our all-inclusive theory becomes meaningless, simply for want of further terms relative to which to ask or answer the question."[14]

Given only a theory form, there is no sense in speaking of its real or intended model, for any interpretation of it which makes it come out true may be called a model. Which model is meant in the case of a given theory cannot be guessed from its form alone. The intended reference of the theory's terms can be fully learned only through some selected paraphrase of them into antecedently familiar terms. Empirical criteria, or ostension, we have seen to be theoretically inadequate for determining such paraphrase even where empirical relevance seems greatest. "Ontology is indeed doubly relative. Specifying the universe of a theory makes sense only relative to some background theory, and only relative to some choice of a manual of translation of the one theory into the other."[15]

Quine also discusses a further kind of ontological relativity that presents itself when quantification is absent from a theory or is eliminable through truth-functional definition or through specification of the truth conditions of quantified sentences in terms of the truth of their substitution instances. Once it is agreed that a theory's commitment to entities takes place only through the bound variables of quantification[16] (that is, that a theory is only committed to those entities that must be assumed as values of its bound variables in order for the theory to be true), then, when there is no quantification and thus no variables, or when quantification is "substitutionally" construed and variables are thus explained away, the question of the values of the theory's variables also lapses, and talk of its ontology will make sense only relative to a broader containing theory that does employ genuinely "referential" quantification.

According to Quine, the only way a theory can prove that its quantification must be referentially construed is by showing that some open sentence of the theory is true under all substitution instances yet false under universal quantification:

> Ontology is . . . meaningless for a theory whose only quantification is substitutionally construed; meaningless, that is, insofar as the theory is considered in and of itself. The question of its ontology makes sense only relative to some translation of the theory into a background theory in which we use referential quantification. The answer depends on both theories and, again, on the chosen way of translating the one into the other.[17]

In bringing the essay "Ontological Relativity" toward its conclusion Quine summarizes his discussion of the nature of the ontological issues as follows:

> . . . ontology can be multiply relative, multiply meaningless

apart from a background theory. Besides being unable to say in absolute terms just what the objects are, we are sometimes unable even to distinguish objectively between referential quantification and a substitutional counterfeit. When we do relativize these matters to a background theory, moreover, the relativization itself has two components: relativity to the choice of background theory and relativity to the choice of how to translate the object theory into the background theory. As for the ontology in turn of the background theory, and even the referentiality of its quantification—these matters can call for a background theory in turn.[18]

2 Rules and Ontology

The preceding chapter discussed Carnap's doctrine of *internal* and *external* questions, which he set forth in "Empiricism, Semantics, and Ontology." According to this doctrine, traditional philosophical questions about what exists, or is real, occur outside the defined limits of any specific "linguistic framework" and are therefore thoroughly devoid of theoretical significance. These are external questions, to be distinguished sharply from internal questions, which occur and can be answered totally from within the context of some specified framework. Internal questions comprise all those of the formal and empirical sciences and, in Carnap's view, are the only ones that enjoy genuine theoretical significance. External questions, though not straightforwardly meaningful, may be reconstrued as practical questions concerning the desirability of choosing one framework over another.

Thus stated, Carnap's doctrine seems to bear, at least superficially, much resemblance to Quine's relativistic thesis as set forth in "Ontological Relativity." Both philosophers seem concerned to show that ontological questions may be conceded significance only relative to specific frameworks for theoretical discourse. In each case, questions that cannot be thus clearly related are deemed meaningless, and in each case these meaningless questions include questions that many philosophers have heretofore tended to view as both meaningful and important. It seems natural to wonder, therefore, just how closely Quine's division between relative and absolute questions of ontology really comes to Carnap's distinction between internal and external questions of existence, and thus how much, if any, additional light has been shed on the situation by Quine's exacting formulations.

The prima facie similarity between the two doctrines disappears rapidly, however, on closer examination. Carnap's internal/external distinction relates to questions about the world; Quine's relative/ absolute distinction relates to questions about language. Carnap wants to separate such allegedly meaningless questions as "Are physical objects real?" or "Are there really abstract entities?" from such ostensibly meaningful questions as "Do unicorns exist?" or "Are there any prime numbers over 100?" Quine, on the other hand, attempts to demonstrate the meaninglessness of such questions as "What are the real objects of arithmetical discourse?" or "Does such-and-such an alien language really refer to the same kinds of things to which our familiar, ordinary language refers?" as opposed to questions like "Can talk of numbers be reduced to talk of sets?" or "How might we try to simplify our talk of a theory's syntactical structure?" Carnap wants to show that questions about what really exists—absolute metaphysical questions—are meaningless from a theoretical point of view. Quine wants to show, however, that questions about what a language is really about— absolute linguistic questions—are just as insignificant. Carnap's external questions, therefore, are those of traditional metaphysics, which he and other positivists have come to deplore. Quine's absolute ontological questions are instead the very kinds of linguistic queries so many philosophers like Carnap have sought to substitute, in one way or another, for the metaphysical questions. Quine's relativistic thesis, therefore, represents a direct attack on the linguistic absolutism of the analytic conception of language, which is so fundamental to the various forms of philosophical analysis. Our present concern is more specifically with the brand employed and advertised by Carnap.

For Carnap, as we have seen, what a language is really about is determined absolutely by its rules. "It is important to notice," Carnap says in connection with the framework for discourse about propositions, "that the system of rules for the linguistic expressions . . . is sufficient for the introduction of the framework. Any further explanations . . . are theoretically unnecessary."[19] Thus it is imagined that it is possible, at least in principle, to spell out a complete and explicit set of rules for any framework whatsoever. Indeed, even the "implicit" rules of the "thing language," which we have all accepted more or less uncritically and un-self-consciously as children, may, Carnap assures us, be made explicit by means of a "rational reconstruction."[20] Its rules constitute and define each framework, so that the conscious choice between different frameworks comes down, in the end, to the decision to speak in accordance with one or another set of rules. To accept a certain form of language and thus a general way of conceiving or describing the world is for Carnap simply "to accept certain rules for forming statements, and for testing, accepting, or rejecting them."[21]

Basic ontology, according to this view, is determined by the rules of the framework. The rules specify into what basic categories the framework classifies, organizes, or slices up experience. The scientist's search for theoretical truth is carried on entirely from within the basic conceptual scheme defined by some framework's rules, while the existence of these kinds or systems of entities is not itself considered a theoretical matter, but rather a practical question whether to adopt some such set of rules or not. The introduction of new entities into an ontology is therefore considered not a matter of discovering or revealing the basic categories of existence, but simply a matter of choosing or deciding to adopt a new linguistic framework in the form of a set of linguistic rules: "If someone wishes to speak in his language about a new kind of entities he has to introduce a system of new ways of speaking, subject to new rules."[22] We are thus free to introduce new ontologies or systems of entities into existence at will, whenever it suits our practical purposes and in thorough disregard of questions of fact, truth, or the like. Carnap's external questions are ultimately concerned with nothing more than the acceptance or rejection of such linguistic rules.

Few philosophers, if any, have matched the philosophical importance Carnap attached to linguistic rules or the sheer quantity of time he spent and ink he spilled considering the nature and variety of such rules and the role they are imagined to play in regulating and guiding theoretical discourse. The point of view Carnap outlines in "Empiricism, Semantics, and Ontology" can, as has been urged, be viewed as the culmination and fullest expres-

sion of the basic positivist philosophical perspective, and though
what he says there about rules of language is disarmingly simple
and brief in comparison with the mass of technical illustrations
and detailed accounts presented in his earlier work, it will suffice
for our purposes here.

The basic idea is fairly simple: Besides a *syntactical* specification
of all atomic and compound expressions in a language, we shall
need also a *semantic* interpretation—instructions as to the use or
meaning of all these expressions. "The acceptance of a new kind
of entities," Carnap declares, "is represented in the language by
the introduction of a framework of new forms of expressions to
be used according to a new set of rules."[23] The syntactic rules tell
us what counts as the form of a new expression, while the semantic
rules tell us how to use these new forms. Whatever else the rules
of a framework might conceivably encompass, it is clear that they
must include at least a complete list of syntactic and semantic rules.

The semantic rules, in particular, are meant to specify what basic
kinds of entities expressions in a language are applicable to, and
thus the ontology to which anyone adopting the framework is
committed. Carnap sees the introduction of a new framework as
comprising two essential steps: "First the introduction of a general
term, a predicate of higher level, for the new kind of entities. . . .
Second the introduction of variables of the new type. The new
entities are values of these variables; the constants . . . are substitutable for the variables."[24] Defining what kind of entities our new
general term is to be understood as applying to, and what entities
are thus to be assumed as values of our new types of variables, is
how the use of our new linguistic forms is explained; this is, in
effect, the job of our semantic rules. This is also, of course, precisely
the sort of question with which Quine's "relativistic thesis" is primarily concerned.

The central assumption of Carnap's entire doctrine of linguistic
frameworks and his associated distinction between internal and
external questions is that the semantic interpretation of a language
can be carried out in a fully determinate and independent manner.
While Carnap supposes that we are free to select any interpretation
we wish for a given system of expressions, he considers the question
as to what the possible alternative interpretations may be a straightforward matter, amenable to objective investigation and theoretical

determination. It is apparent from Quine's discussion in "Onto-logical Relativity," however, that whenever we undertake the full interpretation of a theory by specifying the values of its variables and extensions of its predicates we do so only from the vantage point of some background theory or language. This is so because the complete sort of interpretation wanted can be achieved only by means of a paraphrase, or translation, of the original framework in terms of the antecedently familiar terms of the background theory. Thus, Quine has urged that the ontology of such a fully interpreted theory is fixed only relative to the background theory and the manner chosen for translating into it, while the ontology of the background theory itself—no matter how familiar its various terms may be —is determinate only relative, again, to some further trans-lation of it into another theory.

Once Carnap's "linguistic frameworks" are clearly recognized as systems of expressions that become interpreted only through trans-lation into the ultimately unexplicated terms of some selected back-ground theory, the adoption of such a framework cannot properly be viewed as a means of introducing new entities into a preexisting ontology, for the rules that specify the ontology of such a framework do not initiate any reference to previously undesignated entities but necessarily rely on the terms of the background theory to des-ignate those objects assigned by the rules as values of the frame-work's variables and extensions of its predicates. These rules, then, serve only to identify the ontology of the interpreted framework as (part of) that of the background theory. The question whether to adopt the entities boils down to the question whether to accept the background theory without benefit of any formal explication at all. Rather than representing the formal introduction of a new ontological system or conceptual scheme, as Carnap supposes, the acceptance of a new framework, subject to explicit rules of inter-pretation, corresponds only to the introduction of a new system of notation for discoursing upon objects already treated of within the unexplicated terms of some background theory.

These difficulties with Carnap's proposal for construing traditional 'ontological' questions as practical questions concerning the choice of linguistic frameworks can be clearly illustrated by reference to the examples Carnap provides of how new systems of entities are supposedly to be introduced through the adoption of corresponding frameworks. Given the framework of natural numbers, Carnap tells us, the statement "There are numbers" is trivially and analytically true, because of the semantic rules governing the use of expressions of this framework.[25] Thus the question of the existence of numbers is held to be reduced to the purely practical question whether to adopt the framework of natural numbers. However, if this framework has been fully interpreted by explicit semantic rules in the manner Carnap proposes, the existence of no new entities of any kind could possibly follow, trivially or otherwise, from adopting it. Such rules would simply provide a translation of the framework into a background theory antecedently recognized as dealing with natural numbers, and thus, in the process, some formula of the interpreted framework would be identified as the translational equivalent of a statement in the background theory already understood to assert the existence of numbers. Adoption of such a framework would thus count as nothing more than adoption of new notation for expressing the background theory and would shed no light on either the nature of numbers or the considerations which might lead us to accept or reject their existence.

Carnap then proceeds to explain that once we have accepted the framework of natural numbers we may add positive and negative integers to our ontology by introducing them as relations between natural numbers. Rational numbers are then to be introduced as relations between integers, and real numbers as "classes of a special kind."[26] We may even add space-time points to our seemingly burgeoning ontology, Carnap further advises, by taking them as "ordered quadruples of real numbers."[27] At each stage of this envisioned process, new types of variables and predicates are to be formally introduced and their values and denotations set accordingly, but always in terms of a background theory in which we must make unhesitating and uncritical reference to natural numbers, relations, and classes of one kind or another. Nowhere is any genuinely new category of entities introduced. All ostensibly new sorts of entities are simply defined outright in terms of antecedently accepted ones. There is merely the introduction of new types of variables and predicates, which are then assigned their own peculiar ranges of values and extensions from within the preexisting domains of natural numbers, relations, and classes.

What amounts simply to rules for translating one language into another will never serve to fix the basic ontological assumptions of either language. If these rules are complete, they will simply provide a way of getting from the sentences of the object language to corresponding ones of the background language via various pairings of the basis expressions and grammatical constructions of the two languages. If there is a basic distinction to be made between objects whose existence is presupposed by the very acceptance and use of the object language and those whose existence must be established as a 'matter of fact' once the language is adopted, we shall somehow have to grasp this distinction without the aid and assistance of any explicit rules or conventions of meaning, for such rules merely transfer the problem of distinguishing between these two classes of entities back to the unexplicated, explicating background language, from which reference to the entire domain originates in the first place. The problem of separating out all those existence questions whose answers depend purely upon language and not on matters of fact is not moved one whit closer to solution by just systematically changing the notational forms of all existence questions or possible answers to them. The problem relates not to the forms of the expressions but to what they purport to say or mean or refer to. And explicit semantic rules can add nothing essential to what individual theories tell us, in their own words, about the nature of their subject matter.

R. M. Martin, in his paper "Category-Words and Linguistic Frameworks,"[28] endorses Carnap's view that brand-new systems of entities can be fully defined and admitted wholesale, full-blown and intact, by means of systematically constructed and interpreted linguistic frameworks. Martin does, however, take pains to point out that the introduction of a new framework does not necessitate both the specification of a new general term and the specification of a new variable type, as Carnap supposed. "Strictly speaking," he observes, "not both of these steps are needed. Either one alone may be made to suffice."[29]

Martin supposes that we are working from within a language L which is formulated "by means of exact syntactical and semantical rules" and whose variables range over "some well-defined domain D of objects." We may introduce new entities, he says, just by specifying some new general term or predicate as applying to all objects of some new domain D'. The range of the old variables of

L is then to be understood as comprising the objects of both domains D and D'. "No new variables are needed, the old variables are merely given a more extensive range."[30] Alternatively we may, according to Martin, simply specify new variables altogether as ranging just over the objects of D' without having to specify at the same time some new predicate applying to these objects. "Such a predicate is in fact definable," says Martin, "as merely a suitable expression for D' itself."[31]

Martin's adjustment to Carnap's procedure does not touch the objection that has been raised against Carnap here, however. Whether one supposes it to be via the specification of new variables or of a new predicate, or both, there is no question of introducing talk of genuinely new entities, for in indicating either the range of our new variables or the extension of our new predicate as the objects of some supposed new domain D' we must rely on a background language (in the present case L) which must be assumed (contrary to Martin's hypothesis that L's variables range over just the objects of D) to possess already some means of referring to the objects of D'.

The utter impossibility of initiating new ontological assumptions in the manner Martin and Carnap suppose becomes manifest upon further consideration of Martin's specific illustrations of just how this is to be achieved. Martin proposes to take D as the domain of physical objects and D' as the domain of properties. L is then assumed to be a framework whose variables range over just the physical objects of domain D and whose predicates apply to just these same objects. Now Martin proposes to show how we may increase our ontology from one containing only physical objects to one containing both physical objects and properties. This is to be done, he explains, by introducing new linguistic expressions— either a new general term or new variables—governed by explicit semantic rules, in the way Carnap has suggested all external existence questions are ultimately to be settled.

Now, if we opt for new variables over new predicates in order to generate talk of properties, Martin assures us, "The introduction of the new entities consists merely in the introduction of variables to range over them."[32] But if we suppose, as Martin urges us to do, that L itself possesses neither variables which range over the properties, nor predicates applicable to them, what terms are we to employ in order to introduce new variables as ranging over properties? How can we specify the values of our new variables when, by hypothesis, we lack in L any means of referring to the entities of domain D'? Martin does allow that "some names of specific properties, i.e. some one-place predicates, may already be available in L."[33] Now names are not predicates, but even so, if L did contain any names of properties, this too would be contrary to our hypothesis about L, for names of properties would be identifiable as such through being substitutable in statements for bound variables taking properties as values and thus some variables of L would have to range over properties after all.

If we choose the alternative approach of specifying instead a new general term or predicate to apply to properties and then extend the range of L's old variables to include these "new" entities, comparable difficulties ensue. Martin proposes such a new predicate, "Prp" (to be read "is a property"), so that by using the old variables "x," "y," and "z" of L we can write such sentences as "Prp(x)" (to be read "x is a property").[34] But in what language is the explicating phrase "x is a property" written? Surely it cannot be L, because "is a property" is a predicate that applies to properties and L's predicates have been assumed to apply only to the physical objects of domain D.

Neither route provides a way of introducing properties into an ontology initially containing only physical objects, because a language like L that speaks only of physical objects will never be capable of providing the sought-after interpretation of new expressions as applicable to or ranging over properties. Specifying new variables or predicates in the manner Martin suggests requires that we work from within a background language (let us call it $\mathcal{L}$) that is essentially stronger than L in that it must allow reference at least to physical objects and properties both. Therefore, if we adopt $\mathcal{L}$ as a means for introducing the new variables or the predicate Prp in the desired fashion, we must also assume the wider domain of objects (let us call it $\mathcal{D}$) over which $\mathcal{L}$'s variables range, and $\mathcal{D}$ must already include, as we have just seen, both D and D' to start with. Martin thus winds up in something of a dilemma. If he takes L as the background language, he will be unable to introduce the new expressions, variables or predicates, via the explicit semantic interpretation he has in mind; if, however, he takes a language like

$\mathscr{L}$ as the background language, he thereby assumes from the start the very entities he is looking to introduce systematically via his semantic rules.

Martin ends up, then, in precisely the same boat as Carnap. Both are convinced that it is possible to spell out explicitly just what objects a theory or language is committed to or about absolutely, but neither succeeds in showing how this might conceivably be done in any individual case. That would require somehow formulating the semantic rules for a framework—that is, specifying the ranges of its variables and/or the extensions of its predicates—in some way other than simply by recourse to a translation of the framework's vocabulary into that of a selected background language.

Carnap's problematic conception of the objectively determinate nature of a theory's subject matter figures prominently in his attack on the view (which he attributes to Russell) that propositions may be regarded as mental entities. That no reference to mental entities takes place within the framework of propositions can be easily seen, Carnap contends, "from a look at the rules."[35] This fact he cites as proof that propositions are not mental entities. Here Carnap seems to violate his own principle of tolerance, for we might simply question whose rules are being consulted. Apart from this, however, we must now also recognize that, regardless of what rules are selected for translating or interpreting the propositional framework, the question as to what propositions are will still depend upon what the ontology of the background theory is taken to be. And the ontology of this background theory, into which we suppose the propositional framework to be translated, will itself be determinate, Quine has shown us, only relative to some further translation of it into some other theory or framework. What propositions really are, or what the propositional framework is really about, is simply not something that can be objectively settled by indicating a set of complete and explicit semantic rules for the "propositional framework."

If there is any ontological significance to the sort of framework construction Carnap proposes, it is not because it serves as a means of initiating talk of new entities, but rather because it serves as a means for eliminating talk of old entities. For example, in construing space-time points as ordered quadruples of real numbers we eliminate the need to talk of space-time points altogether, and by banishing them we gain economy in an ontology that already contains real numbers. In treating all talk of numbers—natural, rational, and real—as talk of various kinds of classes, we can reduce our ontology from one that admits an extensive variety of numbers as well as classes to one that includes only classes. Quine makes this same point in explaining what happens when we employ set-theoretic resources to clarify the notion of natural number: "What we are doing in any one of these explications of natural number is to devise set-theoretic models to satisfy laws which the natural numbers in an unexplicated sense had been meant to satisfy."[36] Thus, Quine concludes,

> We are finding no clear difference between *specifying* a universe of discourse—the range of the variables of quantification—and *reducing* that universe to some other. We saw no significant difference between clarifying the notion of expression and supplanting it by that of number. And now to say more particularly what numbers themselves are is in no evident way different from just dropping numbers and assigning to arithmetic one or another new model, say in set theory.[37]

If the introduction of a new framework is to count as anything more than the construction of an artificial language or a secondary system of notation, then its significance lies on the side of ontological *reduction* rather than *introduction*. The semantic rules of a framework permit us to reduce its ontology to that of a second framework. Perhaps we may then devise a second set of such rules for reducing the ontology of the second framework to that of a third and so on, but we never reach a point at which we are any better able to say just what the objects we are speaking about really are, for such questions always are meaningless, Quine has shown, except when answered relative to some largely arbitrary choice of a translation of our discourse into some selected background language. "What makes sense," Quine reminds us, "is not what the objects of a theory are, absolutely speaking, but how one theory of objects is interpretable or reinterpretable in another."[38]

Within the accepted terms of our most inclusive background theory, however, we may indeed introduce genuinely new types of entities in order to strengthen and simplify the overall theory itself. Such entities are not reduced to or equated outright with any

other objects, but are added directly to the preexisting ontology of
the background theory. What they are is determined not by explicit
rules or definitions but only by the way the laws governing them
are linked with the rest of the theory. Those objects of a more
theoretical and less observable character are frequently described
further with the help of analogies drawn between their behavior
or special characteristics and those of other more familiar and accessible objects within the ontology of the same background theory.[39] This manner of introduction was followed for various sorts
of elementary particles in physics and (originally) for irrational and
imaginary numbers.

The use of analogy itself represents less a means for introducing
objects than simply a means of characterizing objects already introduced. Nor does this characterization in any way represent an
actual reduction or elimination of such entities in favor of others;
that would require the laws concerning them to be wholly translated
into others concerning perhaps more familiar phenomena (in which
case we would not have analogy but literal explication). Apart from
analogy, and in lieu of formal explication, our knowledge of the
objects posited by our background theory—be they ordinary observable physical objects, elementary particles of theoretical physics,
or abstract entities of classical mathematics—rests primarily not on
rules or definitions but on our understanding of the background
theory itself. Quine explains: ". . . our coming to understand what
the objects are *is* for the most part just our mastery of what the
theory says about them. We do not learn first what to talk about
and then what to say about them."[40]

Carnap's view that traditional ontological questions amount to
practical questions of whether to adopt a certain form of language
within which reference to basic kinds or systems of entities takes
place more or less automatically according to the rules of that
language therefore collides head on with Quine's relativistic thesis.
This occurs largely because implicit in Carnap's position is the
assumption that it makes objective sense to speak of what a theory
or framework is really about or what objects it is really committed
to—that it is simply a matter of discovering the conventions or
rules which supposedly determine this. If this assumption were
correct, it might then seem plausible to reduce the question of the
existence of basic systems of entities to that of the practical utility

of some corresponding linguistic framework. However, Quine has shown that such specification of the subject matter of a theory or framework is a thoroughly relative matter, relative, again, to some translation of the theory into another theory which we ultimately accept "at face value."

Therefore, the question of *what* (ontologically speaking) *there is* cannot be settled simply by consulting some set of linguistic rules or conventions imagined as setting the basic conceptual parameters of our linguistic or theoretical frameworks. On the contrary, these "ontological" questions must ultimately take root in our most familiar and all-inclusive idiom, where it is not easy to see how they can be sharply differentiated from the more conventional "scientific" questions, which Carnap calls "internal." Just as no new entities are introduced by Carnap's procedure of framework construction, so also no new (internal) questions about such entities arise thereby. Instead, the rules of our fully interpreted framework enable us simply to translate all questions formulated in terms of that framework into questions formulated in terms of the background framework. In this sense, all questions about the objects of a framework become external to it once it has been fully interpreted.

For example, if the system of real numbers is intepreted by the rules of its linguistic framework in terms of set theory, then all questions (however trivial or important they may seem) about real numbers and their properties are identified as or reduced to questions about sets. Introducing the framework of real numbers in this fashion does not set the stage for a distinction between two sorts of existence questions, internal and external, about real numbers; it simply signals the reduction of all questions about real numbers to questions about certain kinds of sets.

When the introduction of a linguistic framework amounts to the formal construction of an artificial language, or a second system of notation, the rules employed for that purpose do not, of course, provide a means for introducing any new theoretical issues or ontological assumptions; they serve only to preserve antecedent questions and translate them into novel notational forms, perhaps where important internal distinctions and relationships are somehow enhanced. When an actual ontological reduction is accomplished, however, some old questions are translated into what are for them new terms, such that they become indistinguishable from other old questions.

We must reject, then, the notion of a linguistic framework whose basic conceptual content or ontology can be fully specified by a complete and explicit set of rules which tell us exactly what philosophical, metaphysical, or ontological assumptions we make when we decide to adopt the language. Such rules will only refer us to some other background language, where we shall have to begin our questioning anew. Ultimately we shall have to come to grips with a language possessing no such rules, a language in which we simply "acquiesce," to use Quine's word. Without any means of clearly demarcating the irreducible conceptual or logical structure believed inherent in our language, we are thus unable to separate those purely philosophical or ontological questions of existence from theoretical questions generally, and the line Carnap wants to draw between internal and external questions cannot be drawn.

3   Rules and Logical Truth

Carnap's belief that ontological questions are only practical questions concerning the desirability of linguistic frameworks is closely allied with another well-known doctrine long associated with Carnap and extremely popular among most contemporary analytic or linguistic philosophers. This doctrine is the *linguistic doctrine of logical truth*, sometimes referred to as the doctrine of truth by convention. According to this view the truth of certain statements of a language follows by virtue of the rules or conventions governing the expressions of the language in which they are formulated. According to the classical positivist position, these logical or analytic truths comprise all the true statements of logic and mathematics, as well as others, and their truth is grounded in linguistic meaning or convention rather than in matters of fact. Thus ontological existence and logico-mathematical truth both are seen as grounded in purely linguistic or conceptual considerations, and an investigation into either domain becomes not a metaphysical or a scientific enterprise but rather an investigation into language and the rules or conventions governing its use.

Carnap thus employs the conception of a linguistic framework, with its explicitly formulated rules governing the use and application of all expressions, to divide philosophical from scientific existence questions and to divide logical truths from factual truths. Thus, in deciding (consciously or unconsciously) to adopt one or another framework—that is, to speak in accordance with one or another set of rules—we are imagined to be settling not only issues of ontology but a somewhat more extensive domain of so-called logical truth as well. Linguistic rules or conventions are taken as the ground of both logical truth and ontological existence, and Carnap's doctrine of external existence questions might well be labeled "existence by convention" to point up the common orientation and rationale of his views on logic and ontology. Roughly, "truth by convention" preaches that, given a language, such-and-such statements are true; "existence by convention" preaches that, given a language, such-and-such entities exist.

In a relatively early essay, "Carnap and Logical Truth," Quine attacks the linguistic doctrine of logical truth in several of its forms, and most of what he says there is strikingly relevant to our preceding discussion concerning linguistic rules and ontological questions. In showing how neither the somewhat artificial development of non-Euclidean geometries nor the use of conventional definitions in constructing new systems of notation may legitimately be cited in support of a conventionalist view of logico-mathematical truth, Quine brings to light a confusion underlying the doctrine of truth by convention identical to that upon which Carnap's ontological position rests. In audition, observations Quine makes concerning the way convention really does enter matters of truth point up parallel considerations concerning the scope of convention in determining what kinds of objects exist.

In tracing the development of non-Euclidean geometries, Quine first calls our attention to the fact that the original basis of the truths of traditional Euclidean geometry was certainly not anything like convention, but had to do with what were taken to be the actual characteristics of "form and void."[41] While the choice of some of these truths to serve in the role of postulates from which to derive the others can be seen as little more than a matter of conventional choice, Quine notes, this move can hardly be taken to have affected the truth of any of these statements. Viewing Euclidean geometry, thus, as a body of genuine theoretical truths, what might we reasonably expect to say of its ontology? The existence of such entities as Euclidean geometry was taken to treat (say, physical objects of various shapes and dimensions, or perhaps, abstract entities constructed in some sort of ideal space) could hardly have rested on acceptance of the rules governing the Euclidean framework alone, if for no other reason than that just cited—namely, that the acceptance of this doctrine itself rested on what was taken to be the actual nature of physical or ideal space.

The first non-Euclidean geometries appeared, as Quine observes, not as bona fide theoretical formulations but only as "artificial deviations from Euclid's postulates, without thought . . . of true interpretation."[42] While, initially, non-Euclidean geometries developed in a purely conventional manner, questions of truth (and similarly, then, questions concerning whatever objects these truths might be about) were suspended altogether. "There was no truth by convention," declares Quine, "because there was no truth."[43] In like fashion there was no existence or ontology by convention because there was no ontology. As long as non-Euclidean postulates went uninterpreted, considerations of both truth and ontology failed equally to apply.

Over the course of time, though, non-Euclidean geometries have been seriously interpreted, and although these interpretations do come more or less as a matter of conventional choice or decision they bring us no closer to instituting truth itself by convention. As Quine explains,

> This means that ways have been found of so construing the hitherto unconstrued terms as to identify the at first conventionally chosen set of non-sentences with some genuine truths, and truths presumably not by convention.[44]

Here we can recognize the situation previously encountered in our discussion of ontology: Full interpretation of a linguistic framework brings with it no new candidates for truth, just as it was seen to bring no talk of new entities. Just as full interpretation of a system merely involves the assignment of some objects from the ontology of the background theory to comprise the values of the object system's variables and the extensions of its predicates, so too it merely identifies certain well-formed strings in the object system as expressing statements held true in the background theory. To adopt a system fully interpreted in terms of some already accepted theoretical system brings with it no new truths or new commitments to entities simply because it permits no new affirmations, true or false, to begin with.

Perhaps we may envision some non-Euclidean system as being true of the same variously proportioned physical or abstract magnitudes of which Euclidean geometry was formerly held true. There are two possibilities: First, some Euclidean theorems may have come, for whatever reason, to be regarded as false, and some alternative set of truths assumed in their place. These newly postulated truths might then be employed as the basis of a true interpretation of some conventionally originated non-Euclidean system by means of conventionally devised rules of interpretation or translation. On the other hand, non-Euclidean systems are commonly given actual Euclidean models simply for the purpose of demonstrating the formal consistency of the non-Euclidean system. In this second instance the truth of Euclidean geometry is presupposed and the non-Euclidean theorems are merely translated, via conventionally adopted rules or definitions, into theorems of Euclidean geometry. The role of the rules in either case is to preserve reference and truth but not to originate it.

The theorems of a fully interpreted non-Euclidean system become true through such interpretation only because that system is thereby translated into some background system or theory where each theorem of the non-Euclidean system is equated with an independently held truth about independently assumed entities. Truth, no more than ontology, may arise simply out of the conventional adoption of definitions or rules of translation. Quine expresses this point when explaining how convention figures in the simple adoption of new notations for old ones:

> . . . truths containing the new notation are conventional transcriptions of sentences true apart from the convention in question. They become true through conventional definition . . . *together with* whatever made the corresponding sentences in the old notation true.[45]

Conventional definition merely permits us to voice old truths in novel forms, just as framework construction along Carnap's lines allows us only to use novel expressions to refer to the same old entities. The more specific character of the truths we voice, as of the objects we refer to, is similarly determinate only relative to some background language and the way we explicate our forms of expressions in its terms.

I have already called attention to Quine's observation that clarifying or specifying the objects of our discourse is not easily distinguished from reducing those objects to some others, and it should not be too hard to see now that analogous remarks hold if we wish to speak generally of clarifying or specifying the precise nature of some set of truths—in the sense of explicating what they say or mean as a whole rather than simply what objects they concern. Clarifying our true statements in this sense is therefore not meaningfully different from simply reducing them to others via rules of translation or definition. As our attempts to clarify the notion of number may lead us to drop numbers for sets, so by means of this same set-theoretic interpretation of arithmetic we provide an explication of each arithmetical truth by substituting for it a set-theoretic one. Thus, whether we are concerned only with the ontological import of our discourse or more fully with what we might call its total *doctrinal* content, the significance of explicit rules and definitions lies on the side of reduction rather than introduction. Such full semantic interpretation as Carnap envisions for all linguistic frameworks actually precludes rather than facilitates the introduction or initiation of new truths, just as systematically as it frustrates any attempt to initiate talk of or reference to new entities. The whole enterprise of explicit interpretation totally undermines the doctrines of truth by convention and existence by convention, which at first seemed so dependent upon it. We may fully specify (in conventional fashion, of course) rules for interpreting any system or theoretical framework, but always relative to some background theory or language in which we already recognize truth and speak of objects. Carnap's entire doctrine concerning ontological existence questions is after all only a special case of the linguistic doctrine of logical truth, for it relates simply to that subportion of a system's purportedly conventional truths that is deemed to affirm or deny the existence of objects of some kind.

Quine thinks that beneath the linguistic doctrine of logical truth there may lurk a confused analogy with what goes on in the propounding of artificial languages. He asks us to imagine the case of a positivist who, in an effort to refute a metaphysical opponent, describes a hypothetical Martian language that would be adequate for science yet incapable of expressing any metaphysical issues. In specifying this hypothetical language the positivist must tell us "what the Martians are to be imagined as uttering, and what they are thereby to be understood to mean."[46] This amounts to a formulation of syntactic and semantic rules—or what Quine says Carnap might call formation rules and transformation rules, or meaning postulates—for the language in question. Now these rules are, in fact, only part of the positivist's narrative machinery, and they must not be mistakenly viewed as the explicit conventions of the Martians. Confusion enters, Quine explains, when the thoroughly arbitrary nature of the positivist's entire pretense is projected into the story, so that the Martians are misconstrued as having fashioned their language in the totally conventional and arbitrary manner of the positivist and thus as having somehow instituted at the same time some truths by convention.

The Martians, of course, could not have constructed their language by means of the set of syntactic and semantic rules of the positivist, if only for the reason that they are presumed not to have had access to the positivist's language, which would be required as background language for fashioning this particular set of rules. However, even if they did have access to this background language in order to build their own language step by step from scratch, there still would be no sense in imagining that any of the statements of their own language ultimately identified as true became so because of this process of step-by-step construction. Their truth would simply depend, in the final analysis, upon whatever made their translational correlates in the background language true in the first place.

The predicament here is analogous to the above-mentioned dilemma confronting anyone who might attempt to follow R. M. Martin's method for strengthening a language that speaks only of physical objects to the point where it is ontologically committed to both physical objects and abstract properties. Having at hand only the resources of a language like Martin's physical object language L, we will never be able to explicitly introduce new linguistic expressions as referring to properties, whereas if a stronger language like $\mathscr{L}$ is utilized for introducing the new expressions, reference to properties would thereby be presupposed, and so no really new ontological assumptions could possibly accrue.

Carnap, replying to Quine's critique of his view on the nature of logical truth, confesses that he has come to regard characterizations of logical truth as based on linguistic fiat or linguistic convention as misleading and inaccurate.[47] He explains that, while the assignment of meanings to words may be purely conventional, logical truth as such is not based so much on these conventions as on the meanings themselves: "Once the meanings of the individual words in a sentence of this form (i.e., of the form of a logical truth) is given (which may be regarded as a matter of convention) then it is no longer a matter of convention or of arbitrary choice whether or not to regard the sentence as true."[48] Thus, although Carnap thereby clarifies and qualifies his view on the role of convention so far as the ground of logical truth is concerned, he nonetheless reaffirms his commitment to the central view that has been under examination in this chapter—that what language really says or is about, its meaning or content or subject matter, can be fully and precisely articulated by a complete set of conventionally devised semantic rules. And it is Carnap's chief contention above all else that the truth of some sentences in a language and the existence of some of the objects these truths concern are grounded solely in the meanings and references these rules assign, conventionally or otherwise, to the expressions of that language.

Linguistic rules or conventions as employed in theoretical reduction or language construction therefore shed no light on the supposed peculiarly linguistic character of either ontological existence or logical truth. Just as the range of a theory's variables or the extensions of its predicates can be specified only by means of the accepted terms of some background theory or framework, the same goes for any explicit instruction as to the "meaning" or "use" of any of its vocabulary, including all logical particles and constructions. Carnap makes a useful point in clarifying that it is not the conventions or rules themselves that he regards as constituting the basis or ground of logical truth (and ontological existence, we may presume) but rather the meanings these rules assign. The point, however, is simply that these rules do not succeed in clearly and objectively assigning meaning in the sense required. In theoretical reduction the terms of a framework are not so much understood via full interpretation or explication as abolished in favor of the unexplicated terms of the background framework. In language construction we see just the introduction of new notation to express the statements (true or false) of the background language and to speak of its objects. Such full interpretation merely identifies the ontology of a framework as (part of) that of a background framework and its truths as (some of) those of the background framework. It permits us to rephrase all questions about the truth of sentences in the object framework, or the existence of entities referred to by its expressions, as questions concerning the truth of sentences in the background language, and the existence of the entities referred to by its expressions. Preservation of truth, reference, and their internal distinctions, is the test of translation itself. A translation is accepted as satisfactory so long as it is seen as exhibiting here just what was antecedently perceived, and it provides no basis for substantive clarification.

Saying exactly, in a noncircular way, what it means for a certain sentence to be true—explaining, so to speak, the basis or ground of its truth—will ordinarily presuppose understanding some other sentence of which the former may be seen as a translation. The truth of these two statements will never derive from the fact that they are translations of one another, though it will help explain why they are. Similarly, specifying the intended range of some term's application will ordinarily presuppose understanding the intended referential scope of whatever terms are used in the specification. Again, whether such entities exist is inessential to the validity of the explication. Definition or explication in itself can never explain what statements must be true or what objects must exist, as Carnap holds, though it may well equate some statements with others whose truth appears more obvious and some objects with others whose existence we are more inclined to admit. Once we have suspended systematic efforts to clarify our discourse and are content for a time with our understanding of it, the work of deciding what exists or what statements to adopt as true may begin. And here, in a language devoid of any pretense of full and explicit interpretation, is where the line between logical and factual truth, or between ontological and scientific existence questions, must be drawn if it is to be drawn at all.

4 Adopting New Entities and New Truths, Practically Speaking

There is still a role for linguistic decision making of a sort in answering questions of truth and existence, but this does not come through setting down in advance the 'meaning' or 'content' of linguistic expressions to be adopted by means of conventionally devised rules or definitions. In set theory, for example, we find a situation interesting for the contrast it presents with that of non-Euclidean geometry. "Set theory," observes Quine, "is pursued as interpreted mathematics."[49] Set theory, however, is not fully interpreted in the sense we have been discussing thus far. That is to say, there is no presently accepted set of rules that purports to specify explicitly the ontology of set theory or the meanings of its vocabulary. Any set of rules thus sufficient to introduce the framework of set theory would, we have seen, provide a means only of waiving all genuine questions concerning sets and their existence in favor of questions concerning the truth of whatever background theory was employed for such an interpretation, and the ontology of that theory. What occurs in fact is just the opposite. It is the rest of mathematics, including arithmetic and analysis, that is explained in terms of, or is reduced to, set theory. When considering questions of mathematical truth and existence, we commonly end our attempts to clarify or explicate mathematical discourse by finally acquiescing in, or just accepting, set theory itself at face value. Yet in not requiring complete semantic interpretation by means of explicit linguistic rules or conventions we do not thereby accept set theory as merely an uninterpreted calculus or formalism. The truths of set theory and the objects they purport to deal with must somehow be understood and accepted on their own and not on the basis of some prior translation of set theory into some other language or theory.

How, then, are we to answer questions of truth and existence in set theory once we realize these cannot be simply or profitably postponed as questions relating to some background theory in terms of which we might seek to interpret our talk of sets? Oddly enough, explains Quine, it is with respect to set theory itself, where full and explicit interpretation along the lines suggested by Carnap is most clearly lacking, that a doctrine like that of truth or existence by convention begins to take on a certain degree of plausibility:

In set theory we discourse about certain immaterial entities, real or erroneously alleged, viz., sets, or classes. And it is in the effort to make up our minds about genuine truth and falsity of sentences about these objects that we find ourselves engaged in something very like convention in an ordinary non-metaphorical sense of the word. We find ourselves making deliberate choices and setting them forth unaccompanied by any attempt at justification other than in terms of elegance and convenience. These adoptions, called postulates, and their logical consequences (via elementary logic), are true until further notice.[50]

Quine terms making this kind of almost totally arbitrary decision with respect to what theoretical postulates are true "legislative postulation" in order to set it off from "discursive postulation," as exemplified in the case of Euclidean geometry, where there is simply an arbitrary selection from a preexisting body of truths of some of these truths to serve as a basis for logically deriving the others.

So truth may be said to arise by convention during the course of legislative postulation, in the absence of any rules of interpretation, semantic rules, transformation rules, meaning postulates, or the like. And ontologies are admitted in like fashion as part of the same process. For example, in legislatively postulating set-theoretic truths we make a decision to adopt certain quantified sentence forms containing the primitive ϵ as expressing actual true statements, and thereby decide to take the bound variables occurring in these sentences as ranging over some bona fide entities. Our legislative postulation of the truths of set theory amounts to, or includes, the legislative postulation of sets, as objects satisfying the various conditions of sethood established by these truths. The primitive ϵ is never explicitly defined, but rather its sense is at best only 'implicitly' indicated by its sentential contexts which have been legislated true (or false).

Now analogous qualifications are needed with respect to this conception of truth or existence by convention, as were voiced by Carnap concerning his doctrine of logical truth. It is not correct here to view either the truth of set theory or the existence of sets as actually based on, or grounded in, convention as such. Quine points out that conventionality is just a passing trait of the act of legislative postulation and not an enduring characteristic of the legislatively postulated sentence. Even set theory, Quine notes, which is "currently caught up in legislative postulation," may someday "gain a norm . . . and lose all trace of the convention in its history."[51] The adoption of new truths and entities via legislative postulation may arise out of largely practical considerations, but this does not mean that these laws and the objects they concern shall or should be regarded forever after as mere artificial contrivances.

What is interesting to consider now is whether this conception of the role of human convention in matters of truth and ontology can be employed to mark the distinctions between logical and factual truth, or ontological and scientific existence, which Carnap sought so futilely to define by reference to the imagined rules or conventions governing language. Perhaps 'logical' truths may be seen as simply legislatively postulated truths, and perhaps 'philosophical' or ontological existence questions are just those that reduce to practical questions of whether to legislatively postulate certain kinds or systems of entities. This approach, while admittedly in marked contrast to the one based on fully explicit semantic rules, would at least have the virtue of attempting to achieve the wanted distinctions while preserving their felt connection with matters of linguistic decision.

This course is not open, however. Quine notes that the conventionality of legislative postulation, which can be found operating in the domain of set theory, extends beyond mathematics and formal logic into the realm of the natural sciences:

> . . . surely the justification of any theoretical hypothesis can, at the time of hypothesis, consist in no more than the elegance or convenience the hypothesis brings to the containing body of laws and data.[52]

Likewise, empirical content, or significance, must be recognized in reverse fashion, as extending even into the abstract disciplines of logic and mathematics:

> . . . a self-contained theory which we can check with experience includes, in point of fact, not only its various theoretical hypotheses of so-called natural science but also such portions of logic and mathematics as it makes use of.[53]

Therefore, no hard and fast differences are to be found among any of the broad range of theoretical hypotheses which make up the entire corpus of our scientific knowledge, with respect to either the conventionality of their origins or their ultimate relevance to experience. Consequently, recognizing the nature and function of legislative postulation leads us no closer to an objective distinction between logical and factual truth, or between ontological (external) and scientific (internal) questions of existence.

The addition of new truths to our theoretical systems and the inclusion of new entities in our ontologies is never facilitated, therefore, by explicit interpretation of the postulates in question or their component expressions. Such postulates, or hypotheses, must simply be accepted in their own terms. Carnap's program of full framework construction or interpretation, on the other hand, has been shown to have the ironic consequence of systematically precluding the possibility of uttering original truths or talking of novel objects. For this reason, therefore, the truth of a single theoretical hypothesis cannot be fully evaluated solely upon the basis of what amounts to a scheme for translating the hypothesis into other terms. It can be judged ultimately only in light of the particular contribution it (or its accepted translation) makes to the overall predictive power and simplicity of some containing theory, which, as a whole, must be taken at face value. The adoption of new postulates or hypotheses can still be seen as a largely practical affair, but there are here no grounds for a sharp distinction between those hypotheses of set theory or arithmetic that assert the existence of classes of prime numbers over 100 and those of the 'natural' sciences that assert the existence of neutrinos or black swans.

Legislative postulation viewed as the general mode of all scientific hypothesizing may seem deficient from an epistemological standpoint, for it may well appear that before we can rationally consider a hypothesis for possible inclusion in a given body of theory we must possess some prior understanding of what the hypothesis asserts. This is the seemingly unarguable truism at the core of positivist metaphilosophical doctrine—that you must first know what a sentence means before you can decide whether or not it is true. On this basic principle was founded the fundamental distinction between the philosophic concern for linguistic meaning as logically prior to and independent of the scientific concern for theoretical truth. Independent explication of individual hypotheses, at least in principle, seems a minimal prerequisite of rational consideration. If we cannot possess such independent understanding of our scientific hypotheses, how are we to know, in any particular case, what we would thereby be hypothesizing?

The answer is that we simply do not fully know what our assumptions or hypotheses are until we are ready to make them. In selecting one or more hypotheses for possible inclusion in a preexisting theory, we envision a new, broader theory, which itself provides the context for our understanding of the specific doctrinal import of the hypothesis or hypotheses in question. This understanding is made possible by our appreciation of the various theoretical interconnections our new laws and the predicates contained in them have with each other and with the laws and predicates of the rest of the theory, and likewise by our further appreciation of the relation of this entire theoretical structure as a whole to experience. The precision and clarity of our understanding of any particular portion of the theory will increase with the continued articulation of the theory and our growing familiarity with it.

Thus any thought of assessing the significance and usefulness of laws and concepts in total isolation from the theories in which they might be incorporated is an illusion on which the pragmatist positions of Carnap, Lewis, and others rests. It is imagined by such philosophers that the meanings of individual concepts and statements, as well as of whole languages, can be analyzed, abstracted, and understood independent of their employment in an applied theoretical context. But no intelligible account of how we might grasp the meanings of linguistic expression in abstraction from actual theoretical application or everyday descriptive use presents itself. The processes of interpretation and application cannot be sharply separated; linguistic interpretation is theoretical application, and vice versa. In applying new laws and concepts by locating them thoughtfully within more extensive portions of preexisting, applied theory, we come to interpret and understand them—once again in light of their location in the resulting overall structure of the theory and its contacts with experience. This is not full or explicit interpretation in the previous sense, of course, since our understanding of individual expressions is predicated solely upon the structural or contextual considerations which the theory as a whole, in its relations to experience, provides.

In providing a full semantic interpretation of some theory, in terms of some selected background theory, we are indirectly applying the laws and concepts of the object theory to the extent that we are showing that they may be reduced (via our scheme for translation) to (certain of) those of the background theory, whose applicability is already presupposed. All that is required for such interpretation is that the internal structure of the laws of our object theory be mirrored somewhere in the background theory. This in turn helps to explain why absolute questions concerning what a language or theory is about are meaningless, for if the roles which the predicates play in any two sets of laws can be demonstrated to be systematically analogous, so that the two sets of laws are reducible to one another, there will be no real objective sense in talking about the objects of one set as opposed to those of the other. Quine explains the relativity of this understanding by reference to the variously intertranslatable theories of protosyntax, arithmetic, and set theory:

> Expressions are known only by their laws, the laws of concatenation theory, so that any constructs obeying those laws— Gödel numbers, for instance—are *ipso facto* eligible as explications of expression. Numbers in turn are known only by their laws, the laws of arithmetic, so that any constructs obeying those laws—certain sets, for instance—are eligible in turn as explications of number. Sets in turn are known only by their laws, the laws of set theory.[54]

When theories reduce to or are interpretable in one another in this fashion, there is simply no absolute or objective way of distinguishing the ontology and doctrine of one from the ontology and doctrine of the other. Just which objects and which truths we view as basic will depend, so far as this makes any sense at all, upon which theory or theories we adopt as our background theory—or frame of reference—from which all attempts at verbal explication must proceed.

The ontology of a theory was supposed to represent certain fixed features of a conceptual scheme inherent in the very language in which the theory is expressed. Logical truth was, in a way, supposed to reflect these same fixed linguistic features, and therein its claim for certainty lay. However, the failure of the "rules of language" thesis represents the failure of efforts to make such imagined features of language objectively clear and intelligible, with the result also that the very distinction between language and theory itself loses force and the sought-for demarcation between logical and factual truth, as well as that between ontological and scientific existence questions, remains persistently out of reach.

Legislative postulation, as briefly characterized above, offers itself as the general mode of scientific hypothesizing, not to be restricted to the domains of logic and ontology. That their existence or reality is presupposed by the very way we see or choose to speak about the world can be said as appropriately for all entities as for any. Likewise, that their truth is presupposed by our own conscious or unconscious linguistic decisions may as well be said for all as for any true statements. Questions of linguistic meaning or conceptual content cannot thus be abstracted from and treated independently of ordinary questions of theoretical truth.

3 Ordinary Language and Implicit Definition

1 Parallels between the Metaphysical and Linguistic Doctrines

The "rules of language" thesis examined in the preceding chapter constitutes one basic version of the analytic conception of language—the view that language possesses a fixed and determinate conceptual content, or 'meaning,' that is open to objective scrutiny and investigation. According to this general conception of language, it may make no sense to talk in absolute terms about the way the world *really is*, or what *really exists*. However, it still makes patently good sense to talk about the way we *really say it is*, or what we *really say exists*, and it was just such questions as these concerning what language *really says, means*, or *is about* that Carnap's rules were intended to answer.

Carnap's assumption that we can spell out the linguistic rules or conventions that make the meaning or content of linguistic frameworks explicit amounts, then, to the view that we can precisely describe or characterize the various possible ways we may "see," conceive, or "picture" the world. Carnap saw philosophy's primary task as that of examining and comparing the various possible modes of conception or representation embodied in the rules of different frameworks in order to discover which of these might be best suited to pursue specific practical objectives. For others, discovery and reconstruction of the rules of language have been aimed only more generally at resolving or dissolving outstanding philosophical questions, by citing such rules directly or indirectly in order to refute or add additional support to genuine metaphysical claims or to uncover the supposed origins of verbal confusions held responsible for generating entirely spurious philosophical issues. Still, the central problem of formulating the precise rules assumed to govern the way we speak remains that of providing a determinate and explicit characterization of the way we describe or represent experience.

The failure of the "rules" thesis represents, therefore, the failure of the supposedly self-contained and determinate conceptual schemes believed inherent in language to yield to straightforward analysis and description. Just as our understanding of a fully interpreted framework's ontology is always relative to our presystematic grasp of these objects as the references of unexplicated terms of a background language, so the precise mode of conceptualization believed to be embodied in a system of linguistic expressions goes essentially unexplicated throughout such "interpretation." Conceptualization in the form of linguistic meaning looms as recalcitrant and impenetrable as reality or Being in itself. Conceptual truths resist intelligible articulation every bit as much as did those of metaphysics for a mystic like Bergson. It is no longer clear that saying just what it is that we *really say* about the world is any easier to accomplish than saying just what it is the world is *really like*. There are obstacles in principle to be met with in either case, and the reason for this would appear to have less to do with coincidence than with an underlying, shared, philosophical motivation and orientation.

The idea that the specific conceptual content of a language can be explicitly formulated and set forth in the form of a complete set of linguistic rules or conventions involves a vestigial rationalism—a linguistic counterpart of its metaphysical antecedent. This is a rationalism that may reject the possibility of making truly significant claims about the ultimate nature of extralinguistic reality, but sets for itself instead the task of formulating truths about the way we *really* "see" or describe reality. Systematic inquiry into the basic categories and features of existence may be shunned, ridiculed, and rejected in order that a systematic inquiry into the basic categories of representation or conceptualization may take its place. Language simply replaces the world, reality, or Being in itself as the focal point of what still amounts to traditional rational insight.

Surely the sensational antimetaphysical tirades of positivists and their dramatic redefinition of philosophy as the critique or analysis of language seemed a drastic and somewhat revolutionary move at the time. The very idea of suggesting that "mere words" alone were deserving of serious philosophical attention, let alone that they comprised the entire legitimate domain of philosophical investigation, had to appear either insane or ingenious, but in neither case was it inconsequential. Still, now that the uproar has subsided and the linguistic philosophers have had their day, what is striking is the remarkable similarity in the temperament and approach of both the analysts and their more traditional counterparts.

It would be unfortunate if this ostensible radical shift in subject matter were allowed to obscure a basic symmetry of doctrine between traditional metaphysics and a view like that of Carnap. One no longer sought to plumb the very depths of reality, but instead proposed analogous excursions into language and its modes of conceptualization. In this new linguistic version, philosophy remains sharply set off from science proper; the gap between metaphysics and scientific truth is reconstituted in that between conceptual or linguistic truth and theoretical truth. The linguistic analyst still perceived himself, generally, as doing "first philosophy," except for the fact that now he might refer to it as exclusively epistemological. Fundamental principles of language—its logical structure or rules—rather than fundamental principles of reality became the basis for antecedently accepted distinctions between ontological and theoretical existence, or between a priori and a posteriori knowledge generally. Salvaging this latter distinction thus permitted retention of the old and valued idea of the absolute certainty of logic and mathematics as opposed to only the relative probability, and uncertainty, of the tenets of 'empirical' science. Even such metaphysical notions as that of a "category" were linguistically interpreted in terms of Russell's theory of types and Carnap's *Allwörter*. And, as we have seen in chapter 1, valiant and sustained attempts were made across the board to preserve virtually every traditional philosophical question in the form of a "hidden" linguistic query, or at least as somehow dependent upon one. The entire procedure seems now, in many respects, to have involved little more than affixing quotation marks to the entire history of philosophy. What was supposed to emerge at this point was something decidedly more startling and revealing than anything that has yet appeared, although the anticlimax should begin, by now, to seem less surprising.

The basic view of language so painstakingly refined by Carnap over the course of his lifetime simply reflects old metaphysical (philosophical) prejudices and tendencies in a new linguistic setting. Once the general swing to largely linguistic considerations had occurred, rationalistic and speculative predilections took over and fashioned a linguistic philosophy that was in many ways simply the reverse image of the archetypal philosophical viewpoint it sought so stridently to oppose. Just how language is supposed to come by its special relevance to philosophical issues, and how this relevance is to be meaningfully gauged, is less obvious than it once may have appeared. It should come as no great surprise that this observed symmetry between traditional and (positivist) analytic philosophy should now appear on the verge of being matched by an encroaching symmetry of failure and inadequacy, as the emptiness of absolute linguistic questions begins to echo that of absolute metaphysical questions.

The question that really has to be faced is whether it makes any more sense to think we can abstract from all prior linguistic and conceptual considerations in order to explore the pristine and uncharted reaches of language and human conception itself than it does to think we can directly 'grasp' or apprehend the ultimate nature of reality. Relativity to language has emerged as a double-edged sword, and the reservations of the early Wittgenstein and Schlick concerning the possibility of significant discourse about the logical structure or meaning of language have been strengthened and granted additional significance by Quine's relativistic thesis. If the very language we use casts all our thoughts or our basic "view" of the world into a mold that sets absolute limits on what we may perceive or hold true, then the shape and contour of this mold is not accessible to simple and routine description in the form of sets of explicit rules or linguistic conventions. We must seek some basis other than explicit characterization for making sense of such talk of language and the way it limits and constrains how we come to look at the world. We must find some way to talk meaningfully of the sameness and difference of linguistic meaning or conceptual content that avoids the infinite and futile regress of formal explication.

2 Implicit Understanding, Meaning and Use

We may cancel our efforts, then, to discover or formulate explicit rules that precisely determine the conceptual content or ontology of a theoretical framework. However, to say that our theories and frameworks cannot be fully and explicitly interpreted is not to say that they have no determinate meaning, or that we do not so recognize them. We may, perhaps, allow a framework its own distinctive conceptual content so long as we recognize that whatever understanding we ultimately possess of this 'content' is implicit only. Human conceptualization may be viewed as essentially a function of language and experience, determinate enough in principle but incapable ever of explicit verbal formulation. Our linguistic frameworks take on significance, we have seen, only through direct or indirect application to experience in the form of a working theory. Our inability to specify once and for all our ontological or conceptual assumptions need not be taken, therefore, as proving that we do not have any such assumptions or that we do not know what they are.

After all, is not just such an implicit understanding exemplified in our daily unhesitating use of natural or "ordinary" language, especially that core portion in which primitive physical theory is embedded? It seems silly to demand a full explication of ordinary language, for there is no way of speaking which we understand any better. Perhaps we may still have difficulty marking the hard and fast distinctions between ontological and scientific existence questions, or between logical and factual truth, which seemed to depend on making definite sense out of the formal "rules" of language; but who needs rules in this sense to understand everyday talk and what it purports to be about? We might still talk significantly, then, of possible ontologies or different ways of conceiving or picturing the world, even though we must ultimately rely on our implicit recognition of these as characterized in terms continuous with the most ordinary and familiar expressions we have at hand. Surely a theory phrased as ordinarily as possible at least implicitly defines its subject matter.

Of course, it has been quite the rule, since the beginning of analytic philosophy, to draw a sharp distinction between natural or ordinary languages and artificial or formally constructed languages. Carnap himself, so fond of formally constructed linguistic systems, invariably relied on a background language of something like ordinary language as a basis for these constructions. Carnap believed natural language could be nailed down by an appropriate empirical investigation, and he even attempted to sketch the details of such a procedure.[1] Bergmann, another devotee of artificially constructed languages, sees philosophy as "ordinary talk about an ideal language." His cherished "ideal" language is fully explicated in terms of ordinary language, which in turn goes unexplicated. For Bergmann our understanding of ordinary language is direct, immediate, and intuitive in a way that goes beyond anything either formal or empirical semantics is capable of explaining.[2] Many recent analytic philosophers manifest varying degrees of the Carnapian and Bergmannian brands of faith in ordinary language without sharing either Carnap's or Bergmann's reverence for, and fascination with, formally constructed systems.

During the initial stages of the "linguistic turn" the move to reform ordinary language took the form of efforts to analyze and paraphrase the supposedly confused or misleading idioms of ordinary language in terms of the formally constructed ideal language of the *Principia*. The meaning or logical structure of expressions in the ideal language were regarded as more precise and less ambiguous than those of ordinary or natural language which they were designed to replace. Paraphrase in terms of the ideal language was thus looked to as a clarification or explication of ordinary language itself. As the idea that there was only one true, correct, or ideal language fell into increasing disfavor, there remained an avid interest in the construction of formal linguistic systems. This movement, best exemplified by Carnap, still sought to reform ordinary language in a sense, but not so much by replacing it with a truer or more correct language as by constructing systems that, because of their precision and richness of expression, might be deemed more useful for specific purposes. This philosophical approach, most fully outlined in Carnap's "Empiricism, Semantics, and Ontology," sees ordinary language as a sort of hodgepodge of vague, ambiguous, and antiquated constructions, an all-purpose conglomeration made to serve in a variety of different contexts and fields of application other than those for which it was originally adopted. Consequently, "constructionalism," as this viewpoint has come to be called, saw a great advantage to be gained in the systematic construction of specialized languages, consciously designed and engineered to serve the needs of specific theoretical disciplines, which would not introduce the confusion, obscurity, and ambiguity inherent in more ordinary language. In this way, formal language construction is still imagined as aiding the process of philosophic clarification by sharpening the focus on the various issues and determining the precise nature of the subject matter from one theoretical discipline to another.

However, as the constructionalist perspective took hold, an interesting and somewhat paradoxical switch in the role of ordinary language gradually occurred. The phrases and idioms of ordinary discourse, once the object of analysis and clarification themselves, now began more and more obviously to take on the role of clarifying and interpreting the formal or artificially devised systems of notation they were used to construct. The roles of *analysans* and *analysandum* became reversed; ordinary language became (at least during the actual process of language construction) the language of explication.

At this point it may seem reasonable to ask just how the construction of artificial languages helps to clarify issues entrenched in ordinary speech. P. F. Strawson has vigorously advanced the view that, so far as general philosophical purposes are concerned, the construction of artificial linguistic systems is entirely without merit:

> The point I am making is two-fold. First, in so far as the purpose of a constructed system is philosophic clarification, the extra-systematic remarks, so far from being—apart from the minimum necessary to fix the interpretation—comparatively unimportant trimmings, are just what give life and meaning to the whole enterprise. Second, these extra-systematic remarks must include exercises in just that method to which system construction appeared as a rival. . . . This is not to say that the metavocabulary of description and classification should not itself be made as systematic as possible. (*This* aim it need hardly be said, is entirely independent of formal systematization of the concepts which the metavocabulary is used to discuss.) But (1) an adequate set of metaconcepts for the dissection of a natural language will scarcely be found by attending primarily

to artificial languages; and (2) clarity about the metaconcepts themselves will be achieved only by attending to the use that is made of them and hence, ultimately, by attention to the actual functioning of the concepts they are used to discuss. It is the same with the improvement and refinement of such metaconcepts. Classifications are found to be crude and misleading, to obliterate logical features, to blur distinctions; and these discoveries, too, are made by attention to the actual modes of functioning of actually used linguistic expressions.[3]

Strawson thus voices the sentiments of a fairly large-scale movement in contemporary philosophy given great impetus by the views expressed by the later Wittgenstein, after an extended rethinking and readjustment of the position he originally adopted in the *Tractatus*. Formal system construction is seen as more or less systematically missing or avoiding entirely the very philosophical issues it originally set out to capture and illuminate.

The basic working assumption of "ordinary language" philosophy is that it is well-nigh ludicrous to imagine that we do not adequately understand ordinary or natural language. The very suggestion is usually represented as something of a reductio ad absurdum—to wit, if we do not understand ordinary language, in terms of which we come to understand virtually everything else, then we do not understand anything at all. Thus the later Wittgenstein writes

When I talk about language (words, sentences, etc.) I must speak the language of every day. Is this language somehow too coarse and material for what we want to say? *Then how is another one to be constructed*? And how strange that we should be able to do anything at all with the one we have.[4]

The virtual absurdity of supposing that we do not understand or cannot come to understand ordinary language more clearly and adequately than artificial ones has led some philosophers to speak as though the actual use or meaning of ordinary language is somehow self-evident if one simply pays close enough attention to it and does not become distracted by confusions generated by philosophical speculation. It is in this spirit that Austin proposes "linguistic phenomenology" as an appropriate descriptive phrase for the method of ordinary language philosophers.[5] This view of the analysis of ordinary language is frequently endorsed as an alternative to viewing it as simply a part of empirical semantics and so keeping a sharp line between philosophy and natural science. Ryle in "Use, Usage, and Meaning" takes great pains to make this point and draws a sharp distinction between the correct *use* of an expression, which any competent speaker of the language is supposed somehow to be able to grasp or apprehend if he merely makes deliberate enough effort, and the *usage* a term might have, say, from one geographic locale to another, which is, according to Ryle, the only appropriate subject of an empirical investigation and irrelevant to philosophical concerns. R. M. Hare argues for the inadequacy of anything like empirical criteria to establish the actual use or meaning of expressions, and even suggests something like Plato's theory of anamnesis to account for our understanding of it.[6]

These views regarding what we may call the semantics of ordinary language are really quite comparable to Bergmann's view (already mentioned), and there is indeed in such a position more than a hint of the old Logical Atomists' notion of an ideal or correct way to speak and of the implicit metaphysics such a view has been seen to involve. Ryle admits to having held to something like the "ideal language" theory at the time of his early classic essay "Systematically Misleading Expressions,"[7] and it seems to reemerge in a somewhat different form in his doctrine of use and usage. In addition, both in his early essay just mentioned and in his later book *Concept of Mind* Ryle does not hesitate to draw metaphysical conclusions from what he takes to be the real import of language as determined by its "correct" use. Austin, too, comes close to explictly suggesting that the investigation of ordinary language provides one (our best) means of getting at what the extralinguistic world may really be like.[8] Something on the order of Russell's metaphysics-ridden Picture Theory is required here in order to account for the special nonconventional, nonempirical use or meaning attributed to ordinary language, as well as to justify (and make sense of) the drawing of metaphysical conclusions about the world on the basis of what is perceived in language.

Wittgenstein recognized the lure of such a view of the analysis of ordinary language:

> "It's as if we could grasp the whole use of a word in a flash."—

And that is just what we say we do. That is to say: we sometimes describe what we do in these words. But there is nothing astonishing, nothing queer, about what happens.[9]

In Wittgenstein's view, and that of "ordinary language" philosophers more directly under his influence than Austin, Ryle, and Hare, the grasping of the meaning of a word or even of the mental experience it seems to describe is to be explained by the simple fact that we have gained a mastery or competency in our own language, more or less routinely and un-self-consciously, by continual exposure to instances of its appropriate use and our ongoing attempts to employ it correctly under an endless variety of circumstances. That we have learned or come to understand our own language through a long and sometimes arduous process of using it is, Wittgenstein contends, a simple and mundane if not altogether unimportant fact. The process of coming to understand or master one's own language is not sharply differentiated, then, from the process of induction and hypothesis that is assumed to characterize the empirical sciences, except for the relative lack of self-consciousness with which it occurs from early childhood on. Becoming clearer or more precise about the use of ordinary language is thus simply a matter of paying more conscious attention to what we have already learned or acquired through experience.

Much of Wittgenstein's *Philosophical Investigations* is devoted to an examination of the way the use of an expression is indicated by the way it occurs in combination with other expressions of a language, in the variety of complex situations constituting everyday life. One does not, Wittgenstein stresses, come to understand an expression singly, in isolation from others, as in the formal definitions of constructed systems; rather one learns it from seeing the expression "in use," "in application," or "in action"—in its systematic relationships with the other expressions of the language. "One cannot guess how a word functions. One has to *look at* its use and learn from that."[10] The understanding of an expression is not represented, then, by some simple and irreducible mental act of grasping its meaning, but simply by one's having learned to respond appropriately in the various different situations in which the expression occurs as part of statements, demands, commands, requests, and queries. The sense or meaning of a term derives from the language to which it belongs and the way this language is employed to manage experience. The meaning of a term is determined by the numerous different contexts of its proper use or employment and, emphatically, not by simple verbal definition or explication. The point is echoed by Strawson: "To observe our concepts in action is necessarily the only way of finding out what they can and cannot do."[11]

Even the ostensive definition of a term is not to be viewed, writes Wittgenstein, as simply attaching an idea, a meaning, or a concept to an individual expression independent of considerations of where that expression fits into the rest of the language. "So one might say: the ostensive definition explains the use—the meaning—of the word when the overall role of the word in the language is clear."[12] In ostensively defining a term, our understanding of the term will depend on our interpretation of these circumstances in which we are being told the term is appropriately applied, but this understanding is in turn dependent upon the overall linguistic or theoretical framework in terms of which we are construing our experience. Thus to indicate the use of an expression in the sense urged by Wittgenstein, Strawson, and others is to give it an implicit definition, in the sense already urged as the only alternative to full and explicit definition or interpretation of linguistic expressions. That is, we must indicate the distinctive role of an expression in relation to those of other expressions in the laws of an interpreted, or applied, theoretical framework.

For the later Wittgenstein, one's native language constitutes an entire "form of life" in terms of which one's whole life and experiences are interpreted. It is an inherited conceptualizing and interpretive mechanism, passed down from generation to generation. We do not usually recognize that we are employing such a conceptual scheme only because we learn our mother tongue as small children and it thus becomes "second nature" to us. For the later Wittgenstein, therefore, the task of philosophy remains that of investigating language, only now any hint that this means an ideal language, such as he endorsed in his *Tractatus*, is clearly disavowed; the philosopher simply concerns himself with the origins and development of our ordinary mode of speech. This is to be a purely descriptive enterprise, "therapeutic" in its effect, which has also been termed conceptual history or conceptual anthropology.[13]

This proposed mode of philosophizing is to be no more concerned with questions of what *really exists*, or what the world is *really like*, than was philosophy as described by Carnap in his doctrine of linguistic frameworks. The main difference between Carnap's metaphilosophical view and that of the later Wittgenstein is that, according to the latter, the philosopher should not be concerned with the construction, interpretation, and adoption of brand-new formalized linguistic systems, but rather with the study and understanding of the language we already possess. This investigation is to be conducted, again, not by examining formal rules or definitions, but by attending to the various ways and situations in which language is actually used.

Strawson has adopted the label "descriptive metaphysics" for his comparable philosophical program. This is not to be confused with Bergmann's program of the same name; Bergmann, we have seen, is concerned with describing reality in a more or less traditional sense, whereas Strawson is concerned with describing only the conceptual apparatus of our ordinary language. Strawson distinguishes his enterprise from what he terms revisionary metaphysics, in which he would include the programs of both Bergmann and Carnap. Revisionary metaphysics is, in Strawson's view, concerned with the construction of new systems of description and representation, which we are then urged to adopt to replace our old ones. However, according to Strawson, the analyst's first job nonetheless remains that of describing the existing conceptual apparatus, because "the actual use of linguistic expressions remains his sole and essential point of contact with the reality he wishes to understand; for this is the only point from which the actual mode of operation of concepts can be observed.[14]

Such views clearly exemplify the linguistic Kantianism so fully expressed in Carnap's later articulated view; what the world is like is seen as relative to linguistic or conceptual considerations, and no capital is made of the notion of a correct or true or ideal language in the sense of a language that corresponds, somehow, to the way the world *really is*. Such views also embody the same analytic conception of language presupposed by Carnap and other proponents of philosophical analysis—the idea that language possesses a fixed and determinate meaning or conceptual content; that there is something language *really says*, *means*, or *is about* that is open to objective philosophical scrutiny and examination even if the extralinguistic world is not. Strawson clearly expresses this central assumption in the following remark: ". . . I don't see what else there is for philosophy to do other than to conduct inquiry of the type concerning the underlying conceptual schemes, either of particular disciplines, or of daily speech."[15] The basic difference between the approach of Carnap and that of Strawson and Wittgenstein relates to the way this meaning or conceptual content is understood to originate and just how it is perceived or understood by the philosopher. For Carnap, linguistic meaning is seen in a pretty straightforward fashion, as something that can be directly understood and formulated by means of explicit verbal definitions or semantic rules. For Wittgenstein and Strawson, on the other hand, the significance of expressions cannot be directly expressed or described in this formal fashion, but must be understood only implicitly by attending to the actual use of ordinary concepts or expressions in everyday life and the way these relate, systematically, to each other in the language to which they all belong. One may describe these varying uses and relationships, but this is not to directly verbalize or express the meanings themselves in the form of explicit rules of interpretation or formal explications. In either view, however, language is held to embody a basic conceptual scheme in terms of which the world and all our experience of it are necessarily understood.

An interesting offshoot of the later Wittgensteinian viewpoint of language is T. S. Kuhn's thesis of the incommensurability of scientific theories. According to Kuhn, scientific theories are articulated on the basis of conceptual paradigms that derive their very life and meaning from the developing system of laws and concepts in which they are embedded. Because the meanings of the expressions of a theory are relative to the overall conceptual "paradigm" within which or according to which the theory is formulated, Kuhn claims, there can be no independent, objective basis for evaluating, adjudicating, or even understanding the claims of rival theories. To understand and fully appreciate a theory, we are told that we must use it, apply it in laboratory experiments, see the world in its terms, be committed to it. According to Kuhn, this is why we must teach each student a scientific theory by means of textbook illustrations and laboratory experiments—as a "working" theory—rather than by simply schooling him in verbal definitions of theoretical concepts. With the theories we are committed to determining not only the kinds of experiments we run but even the way we interpret their results; the traditional conception of scientific progress must, Kuhn insists, be rejected as an illusion. Because of the alleged incommensurability of different theoretical paradigms, Kuhn argues, theory change is not a systematic, cumulative growth of knowledge but a sudden and often drastic shift from one theoretical perspective to another. In Kuhn's view, one paradigm gains ascendancy over another less as a result of objective experimentation and rational dialogue than because of the vigor, persistence, and persuasiveness of its adherents.

Here Kuhn employs Wittgenstein's version of the analytic conception of language to argue that, because the meaning of expressions takes shape only within the contexts of applied conceptual or theoretical frameworks, there is no way, in principle, that persons "seeing" the world from different frameworks can either communicate or share essentially similar experiences. This is also reminiscent of the well-known "Whorf hypothesis" in linguistics. The starting point for these views is the basic idea that the way the world is is relative to, or dependent upon, one's linguistic or theoretical framework, in combination with the Wittgensteinian view that the meanings of the expressions of a framework are only contextually determined, and can be understood only from within, by adopting the framework and learning to use or apply it as one's own.

Suppose, then, that we view full interpretation of a theory in Carnap's style as merely setting forth the ontological or conceptual import of the theory in terms of some background theory expressed either in ordinary language (which we understand not on the basis of formal "rules" but through having employed it, daily, from childhood in those various situations for which it was fashioned) or in less ordinary and more technical terms we have learned firsthand in conjunction with more specialized theoretical application. In such a case, may we not view the ontology or conceptual apparatus of our background language as implicitly determined and in need of no separate and independent explication? Translation of one theory into another might then be seen as specifying the ontology or conceptual content of the object theory in the sense of reducing it to that of a background theory implicitly understood in this fashion. New entities or concepts could still be introduced and understood, not by means of formal construction, but rather by means of legislatively postulating the appropriate laws to be incorporated into the preexisting background theory. On this hypothesis, mere inability to formally express our ontological/ conceptual assumptions is no proof that we do not have and make such assumptions, in a perfectly objective and intelligible sense, whenever we actively utilize a suitably developed linguistic or theoretical framework.

3 The Indeterminacy of Our Understanding of Ordinary Talk

Have we not finally succeeded in establishing through all this elaborate and circuitous reasoning that we are entitled to make the modest assumption that we do, in fact, know what we are talking about? Is the full import of Quine's "relativistic thesis" merely that complete translation or interpretation of one theory in terms of another will never fully succeed in objectively fixing the ontological/ conceptual import of the former simply because it leaves that of the latter essentially undetermined? Is Quine pointing out that we must understand the terms out of which we propose to construct our formal explanations and explications if they are to be of any practical use? Has this aura of profound and disquieting revelation all been generated from the simple and banal observation that we must assume a prior understanding of some terms in order to construct explicit definitions of others by means of them, and thus that our understanding of these basic terms cannot itself be ultimately based on simple verbal definition, on pain of infinite regress, or vicious circularity? This observation about the limitations of verbal definition or explication hardly rates as a novel or interesting contribution to the philosophy of language.

If this is the full extent of the import of the relativistic thesis, it would appear that the account of how we learn or come to understand our native language as suggested by ordinary language philosophers in the tradition of the later Wittgenstein would be entirely to the point. This approach to language learning does not seem to presuppose, in any obvious way, any prior and independent access to extralinguistic reality, as does the Picture Theory. It also provides a rather plausible account of how we can come to use language effectively and adequately understand its underlying conceptual import without requiring the supposition that the precise nature of this understanding is itself expressible in independent terms. Full interpretation of a theory may be regarded, therefore, as fully adequate for specifying its conceptual import so long as it is accomplished through translation into terms we already understand through extended firsthand practice in their actual use and application. Philosophers like Carnap got carried away a bit, perhaps, in supposing that entirely new conceptual systems could be formally constructed and considered apart from any actual application to experience. However, this misimpression is rectified once the need for something like legislative postulation is clearly recognized as a means of introducing genuinely new talk or concepts into our preexisting frameworks of discourse.

The fact of the matter is, however, that Quine's "relativistic thesis" cuts much deeper than this. According to this thesis, interpretation of a theory in terms of a background theory never really succeeds in laying our ontological/conceptual cards on the table, simply because there are ultimately no such cards to show. The contention is not just that we lack a means for formally specifying these assumptions, but that there is at root nothing to specify beyond what is directly accomplished by the translation itself. Explicit interpretation or translation is not just an indirect, artificial, or formal approximation to the real flesh-and-blood story; it is, in the very impoverished and relative sense already characterized, the whole story. No matter how earnestly and tirelessly we attempt to tie one theory translationally to another, we never reach a background theory whose ontology or conceptual apparatus is any more fixed and determinate than that of the theory translated into it, simply because any sense we are able to make of the notions of linguistic meaning or conceptual content derives from the possibility of such translation itself rather than constituting the basis upon which such translation proceeds. Quine has argued for nothing less than the position that even in our most familiar and all-inclusive "home" language, into which we may suppose that all of our more formally constructed frameworks are ultimately to be translated, our basic ontology or mode of conceptualization remains as essentially inscrutable and indeterminate as ever.

It is precisely our "implicit" understanding of the individual terms of ordinary discourse that is called into question when Quine brings his thesis of the indeterminacy of translation to bear on the so-called "home" language. Quine thereby calls attention to the fact that understanding the precise extension of a term—be it an ordinary word like "rabbit" or its rough equivalent in an alien language—requires, in addition to simple ostension, that one be able to ask and answer such basic questions as "Is this _____ the same as that one?" and "How many _____s are there?," in which the English apparatus of individuation ("a cluster of interrelated grammatical particles and constructions: plural endings, pronouns, numerals, the 'is' of identity, and its adaptations 'same' and 'other' "[16]) plays a fundamental role. It is essential, Quine explains, that we pay close attention to the use of a term in combination with these logical or "individuative" devices and as a part of sentences joined by the standard truth-functional connectives, in order to gauge its proper range of application, referential scope—how it "slices up the world." Wittgenstein, in *Philosophical Investigations*, also describes the ostensive learning of a term as essentially dependent upon mastery of its use in sentence-length contexts where this same basic auxiliary vocabulary is integrally involved.[17] To examine our concepts "in use" or "in action," therefore, is to examine them as they relate to experience and to other concepts—particularly, those more basic logical or general concepts such as identity, number, and existence which derive from the use of this core group of individuative devices. It is from this same perspective, then, that Strawson characterizes the task of descriptive metaphysics as that of detailing "how the fundamental categories of our thought hang together and how they relate, in turn, to those formal notions (such as existence, identity, and unity) which range through all categories."[18] The point Quine considers, which is more or less overlooked by these philosophers, is the question of our understanding of this group of grammatical particles and constructions themselves. How are we to objectively fix an interpretation of this basic subportion of our vocabulary, upon which the understanding of the conceptual import of our language as a whole is so dependent? The answer, Quine explains, is that we cannot, because of the "broadly structural and contextual character" of any considerations that could conceivably guide us in such interpretation, so that "there

seem bound to be systematically very different choices all of which
do justice to all dispositions to verbal behavior on the part of all
concerned."[19] The result is that even so ordinary and humdrum a
word as "rabbit" cannot be said, with any objective assurance, to
"divide its reference" one way rather than another. That is, by
switching our interpretations of some of the English devices of
individuation, while making compensating reinterpretations of
others so as to preserve overall conformity with all observable
dispositions to verbal behavior, we can as easily take "rabbit" as
applying to such odd things as rabbit stages or undetached rabbit
parts as to just plain old rabbits themselves. And Quine's point is
that there is no empirical basis for interpreting these grammatical
devices so as to assure "rabbit" its conventional extension instead
of one of these bizarre alternatives:

> We can systematically reconstrue our neighbor's apparent ref-
> erences to rabbits as really references to rabbit stages, and his
> apparent references to formulas as really references to Gödel
> numbers and vice versa. We can reconcile all this with our
> neighbor's verbal behavior by cunningly readjusting our trans-
> lations of his various connecting predicates so as to compensate
> for the switch of ontology.[20]

There appears to be no objective constraint against rendering
our ordinary theory of physical objects in terms of some less familiar
alternative (time-slice theory, for example) and thus construing our
ordinary talk of physical objects as talk instead of stages or time
slices. This occurs because those very basic concepts—to which
Wittgenstein and Strawson, in addition to Quine, see all the rest
of the terms of our language moored—turn out themselves to be
free-floating and indeterminate in principle with respect to their
own interpretation.

It is at the point when we start to question the reference of terms
in our own most inclusive background language that we begin to
make nonsense out of reference altogether, Quine contends. It is
thus entirely meaningless to ask in any absolute sense—that is,
according to either version of the analytic conception of language—
what we are *really talking about*, or what our words *really say, mean*,
or *refer to*. This is the real thrust of Quine's relativistic thesis. It is
not just an observation concerning fully interpreted theories or

language as opposed to frameworks "implicitly" understood in their actual application to experience. Rather, it concerns the limited and relative nature of the significance that can be attached to talk of any theory's ontological or conceptual import. It is meaningless, Quine urges, to question the references of terms in a theory except relative to a background language; "The background language gives the query sense, if only relative sense; sense relative in turn to it, the background language."[21]

Thus it is both futile and senseless to argue, for example, that we are *really* talking about physical objects rather than time slices in our ordinary everyday language. The difference between these two ostensibly different "ways of speaking" shrinks, in the final analysis, to a question of mere notational variance rather than one of divergence in subject matter. The network of terms, predicates, and auxiliary devices that makes up our background language constitutes, in this sense, our ultimate "frame of reference" or "co-ordinate system" relative to which we must ask and answer all questions concerning what some specific language is *about*, or what some terms *mean* or *refer to*. And this, then, is the sense in which we have noted that Quine likens absolute ontological questions—questions concerning what a theory or language is *really about*—to questions concerning absolute position or velocity, when it is ultimately only the unquestioning acceptance of some system of spatial coordinates that provides the frame of reference necessary for us to speak meaningfully of the location of any other. Thus it is in this full and rather uncompromising sense that Quine tells us that we have no choice but to accept our home language at face value and to acquiesce humbly in its terms. The force of Quine's relativistic thesis is, once more, probably most succinctly rendered in his formulation that "what makes sense is not to say what the objects of a theory are, absolutely speaking, but how one theory of objects is interpretable or reinterpretable in another."[22] We achieve a *full interpretation* of a theory or framework, then, to the extent that we provide a *complete translation* of the framework into some other. This interpretation is full not in the sense that we fix its ontology or conceptual apparatus once and for all, but in the sense that we achieve a *mapping* of all true sentences of the interpreted theory—consistent with all available empirical considerations—onto true sentences of the background theory. We do this by formulating a "manual of translation," a dictionary and grammar for the object language that explains its vocabulary and grammatical constructions in terms of those of the background language. According to Quine's thesis of the indeterminacy of translation, the lack of objective criteria for deciding among the many alternative mappings or translation manuals that are always possible is, in the final analysis, what delivers the crucial blow to any absolute conception of a theory's ontological or conceptual content, for the conceptual systems are as many and varied as the manuals of translation one may derive, and are equally indeterminate from a purely empirical standpoint.

We may have thought that an explicit specification of our underlying ontological assumptions or conceptual schemes (in the manner proposed by Carnap) was impossible only because of our need for always having some language at hand in which to formulate them, and thus the dilemma of infinite regress or vicious circularity seemed unavoidable. But now the situation has been suddenly and radically reversed, for now it turns out that only relative to some such translation of a theory into a background language or "coordinate system" does talk of the theory's ontological/conceptual import make any sense to begin with. Our uncritical acceptance and unhesitating use of a background language, like that of ordinary English, does not, therefore, either engender or in any way represent an implicit understanding of its 'true' referential scope, its subject matter or content; rather it simply signals the suspension of our concern with such matters altogether. Our confident and effective utilization of our most familiar, all-inclusive ordinary language testifies not to our presystematic ontological (semantic, conceptual, etc.) awareness, but rather to the ultimate meaninglessness of such conceptual inquiry itself.

What has occurred is that a blow has been struck against philosophical analysis every bit as decisive and crippling as the positivists' own earlier assault on traditional metaphysics. What has been shattered by Quine's relativistic thesis is the elementary assumption of most analytic philosophers, including both Carnap and Wittgenstein, that *absolute* (philosophical) talk about the *structure, meaning,* or *content* of linguistic expressions makes any objective sense to begin with, regardless of what one supposes the precise nature and origin of these linguistic features to be.

The result is a far more radical departure from traditional philosophical thinking than even Carnap or Wittgenstein envisioned. Not only is reality indeterminate in and of itself, essentially dependent for its organization and coherence upon our linguistic decisions, but now the conceptual import of these decisions themselves appears similarly incomplete and indeterminate in principle. In choosing between such prima facie disparate systems as that of physical objects and that of time slices, we do not seem to be making a choice that makes any objective difference. Major ontological/conceptual discrepancies appear evanescent and ultimately meaningless. What breaks down completely is the analytic conception of language, the idea of a conceptual scheme as an inherent feature of a linguistic or theoretical system that determines, at least in part, how we "see," comprehend, and describe reality. Not only is there no one way the world *really is*, but it no longer even makes any sense to think there is a way we really *say* it is.

Linguistic rationalism—the idea that linguistic meaning may be explicitly codified in a complete set of semantic rules—thus gave way to *linguistic mysticism*—the idea that the concepts embedded in our mother tongue are ultimately ineffable. But neither position retains any plausibility in the face of the relativity of ontology.

Linguistic mysticism is perhaps best represented by Wittgenstein, both early and later. His early doctrine from the *Tractatus* (and that of Schlick) concerning the virtual impossibility of significant talk about the ideal language is well known. However, in his later writings as well he found it equally difficult to grant full-fledged significance to philosophical talk about natural language. In both his earlier and his later writings one finds a characteristic emphasis upon the need for "showing," "pointing to," and "looking at" language in order to grasp its basic meaning, structure, or use, as opposed to any reliance upon systematic definition or explication.

Ineffability, however, provides no more sanctuary for the analyst than for the metaphysician, simply because effability, in the end, is too much to the point. That is to say, effability in the form of translation from one language to another—as relative and arbitrary as this may ultimately be—provides the only framework within which questions about the meaning and the conceptual structure of language can be meaningfully asked. Determinacy and coherence—be it of reality or of our conceptions of reality—are achieved only relative to a linguistic "coordinate system," itself taken "at face value." Just as meaningful doctrine about the world does not arise from the exercise of rational or mystical insight, neither does meaningful doctrine about such doctrine. Rationalism and mysticism are two recurring philosophical (metaphilosophical?) themes that cut across the much-heralded boundary between traditional metaphysics and logical analysis.

4 Atavistic Semantics

James Cornman is an analytic philosopher who has also been critical of the efforts of other analytic philosophers to deal with traditional philosophical problems by means of linguistic analysis. Cornman's criticism of contemporary analytic philosophy is both interesting and instructive because of how he proceeds from considerations of language not unlike those that led Quine to his relativistic thesis to reach conclusions of a drastically different sort.

Cornman's main contention is that before philosophers can say with any assurance, for example, whether mind expressions and body expressions refer to minds and bodies, respectively, or to something else, such as persons, they must first have a theory of reference:

> The kind of a theory which seems to be needed is one like Wittgenstein's picture theory of meaning, the theory that language pictures reality and that certain essential features that language has in common with pictures are the criteria by which we can establish which expressions refer and what they refer to.[23]

According to Cornman, Carnap's semantics does not represent the sought-after theory of reference because all Carnap gives us are what Cornman calls formal reference rules, "rules which connect linguistic expressions with other linguistic expressions."[24] The result, Cornman notes, is that our understanding of the meaning or reference of a term introduced by such formal rules can be no better than our prior understanding of the meaning or reference of the expression of the metalanguage employed in stating the rule.[25] Cornman contends that efforts to formulate reference rules that reflect actual speech usage, as opposed to arbitrarily selected interpretations of formally constructed systems, result in nothing but disguised formal rules, and thus come no closer to providing the kind of theory of reference he feels is needed.[26]

Cornman's argument suggests Quine's own observation in "Ontological Relativity" that *specifying* a theory's universe of discourse is not substantially different from just *reducing* it to (part of) that of a background theory, via some selected manual of translation. Chapter 2 above raised these same considerations against Carnap's doctrine of internal and external existence questions, to show that genuinely new ontological assumptions can never be introduced merely by adopting a set of semantic rules since such rules amount only to rules for translating one theory into the previously accepted terms of a background theory. What is worth noting here, however, is that whereas Quine sees such considerations as militating, generally, against the significance of absolute questions about what objects linguistic expressions refer to, Cornman views them as evidence of the need for what he calls nonformal reference rules, "rules that connect linguistic expressions with reality."[27] It is the lack of such rules, Cornman argues, that prevents analysts from finding satisfactory answers to outstanding philosophical questions: "In all such problems what seems to be required is something other than formal rules, something that goes outside language. . . ."[28]

In his search for nonformal rules, Cornman also considers the ostensive learning of terms of ordinary language as one possible way of breaking out of the linguistic web spun by formal rules. Although he completely neglects the important role played by a language's basic individuative vocabulary, he does reach a conclusion remarkably like Quine's own theses of the indeterminacy of meaning (translation) and the inscrutability of linguistic reference—namely, that while there is, perhaps, some sense in which we can indicate by pointing the "things" we are talking about, available empirical evidence is insufficient to determine just what kinds of "things" these are: whether, for example, they are really physical objects as opposed to, say, Berkeleyan perceptions or "ideas." However, while Quine views the failure of ostension as more or less clinching the case for the meaninglessness of absolute questions of linguistic reference, Cornman stops far short of the relativistic thesis and simply calls for some further alternative to ostension as a means of providing the nonformal rules of reference he is still determined to pursue:

> If we choose ostensive answers as the sort of answers for which we are looking, then although we can connect symbols with reality, we cannot say what we need to say—what it is that a given symbol is connected with.[29]

What Cornman never does succeed in doing is to provide an intelligible and coherent account of how his nonformal rules could ever transcend verbal paraphrase and ostensive definition both.

Cornman even criticizes Quine himself. In his famous essay "On What There Is,"[30] Quine set forth his well-known criterion of ontological commitment, which states that a theory is committed to whatever objects must be counted among the values of its bound variables of quantification in order for the theory to be true. Cornman alleges that this criterion is inadequate because it lacks a theory of reference and nonformal rules of reference, which he believes are needed before one can answer questions about what objects a theory is committed to. He attempts to illustrate his point with reference to Quine's comparison in "On What There Is" of the logicists' position in mathematics with the view of medieval realists concerning the existence of universals. According to Quine, logicism, which prefers a set-theoretic interpretation of mathematics, "condones the use of bound variables to refer to abstract entities, known and unknown, specifiable and unspecifiable, indiscriminately."[31] Cornman thinks that this assessment of logicists' ontological assumptions needs more than Quine's criterion of ontological commitment to support it:

> By his criterion logicism is ontologically committed to whatever certain abstract terms denote. . . . But he can not get from this premise to the conclusion that logicism is committed to abstract entities unless he provides another premise about what abstract terms denote.[32]

Cornman thus rightly calls attention to the fact that Quine's criterion of ontological commitment still only fixes reference relative to a background theory, while suggesting at the same time that Quine, like himself, is interested in providing answers to absolute questions about a theory's ontology. Quine, however, in the passage quoted above, need be interpreted as saying nothing more than that in mathematics logicists opt for a background language of set theory. The assumption that logicists are talking about or committed to sets is based on the acceptance of a specification of the logicist ontology relative to their own chosen background language, namely set theory. The issue is not how we may variously construe and reconstrue the logicist's words, but, rather, how the logicist chooses to construe or interpret mathematics. Quine's criterion of ontological commitment was never proposed, as he has repeatedly emphasized, as a polemical device to foist extravagant existential claims on unsuspecting theoreticians. Rather, Quine's criterion simply makes it possible—if one chooses to utilize the quantificational apparatus and abide by the criterion in the first place—for one to state one's own ontological assumptions as precisely and unambiguously as possible, in whatever terms one chooses. In tying ontological commitment to the use of bound variables, the criterion in effect removes any justification for holding a person committed to the existence of entities other than those he is willing to say, in his own selected words, *exist*.

Still, Cornman's objection is not that Quine takes absolute ontological questions seriously, for Cornman himself takes such questions very seriously. Cornman's objection is, rather, that something like his own proposed nonformal rules of reference—rules that go "outside language" and "connect linguistic expressions with reality"—are needed, in addition to Quine's criterion, in order to properly answer such questions. The fact that such questions may ultimately lack any genuine significance appears to be a possibility he never seriously considers.

Cornman clearly comes to perceive something of the arbitrary and relative character of our ordinary talk of linguistic reference, but shies away from a conclusion like Quine's that all such talk is indeed meaningless, except relative to a background language. Instead, he proposes to search for nonformal rules of reference through an "external" investigation of language, which seeks to answer questions "about what there is regardless of the linguistic frameworks employed."[33] Cornman invokes the old metaphysical notion of a fully determinate and self-contained reality lying beyond all linguistic description or representation in order to provide for talk of linguistic reference the objective determinacy he has found it lacking on its own.

Thus, on the basis of arguments and insights essentially like those that prompted Quine to adopt his relativistic thesis, together with an unhesitating acceptance of the analytic conception of language (the idea that it makes sense to talk about what language really is about, or refers to), Cornman argues, in effect, for the reinstatement of traditional metaphysics. The irony, however, is that now metaphysics is invoked merely to support the kind of linguistic investigations that were originally proposed to support or replace metaphysical inquiry itself.

5 The Reduction of Semantics to Metaphysics

The effort to salvage the significance of what Quine calls "absolute ontological questions" (questions concerning the objects a theory is *really* about, or committed to, which might better be termed absolute *semantic* questions to distinguish them from more traditional *metaphysical* questions of ontology) leads Cornman back to traditional metaphysics. Implicit here is the recognition that talk of the *real* content or referential scope of language (absolute semantic talk) is on a par with talk about the world as it *really is* (absolute ontological talk, in the full-blooded metaphysical sense). The insight that reality is determinate only relative to language actually entails the corresponding truth with respect to what language says about reality.

To see clearly how the meaninglessness of absolute semantic talk follows from the meaninglessness of absolute ontological talk proper, one need only take seriously the fact that the world will not cohere of itself and apply this to the problem of trying to determine objectively how a given portion of language describes or represents reality, as Quine does in his contrived circumstances of "radical translation." The result is the indeterminacy or incoherence of description itself, for to say that there is no single right way of describing, representing, or conceiving the world is to say that there is no objective standard for choosing among certain possible alternative descriptions of the world. But this is just to say that there is no objective difference between the *ways* these purportedly alternative descriptions describe. And this conclusion militates as strongly against the theoretical feasibility of conventional philosophical analysis as traditional metaphysics.

Consider the peculiar nature of the problem facing Quine's field linguist. His theoretical uncertainty concerning the translation of "gavagai" as "rabbit" results primarily from the impossibility of saying absolutely that it is rabbits, and not, say, rabbit stages or time slices, that uniformly correspond with native assent to queries of "gavagai." Whether we determine there to be a rabbit or a rabbit time slice present depends upon whether we are viewing the world from the vantage point of ordinary physical theory or time-slice theory; this is the relativity of the world to language. Whether we judge the natives to be speaking of rabbits or rabbit time slices will similarly depend on whether the "coordinate system" we ultimately employ for interpreting alien expressions is that of ordinary physical talk or that of time-slice talk; this is the relativity of what language says about the world to language itself. The pointlessness of asserting there is *absolutely* a rabbit there, and nothing else, when and only when a native will assent to "Gavagai?" is the same as that of saying that "gavagai" applies *absolutely* to rabbits and nothing else. The evidence is identical in each case, and similarly insufficient, in principle, to decide the issue.

Cornman's analogous illustration of how ostensive definition fails to establish whether a person's words refer to ordinary physical objects rather than Berkeleyan "perceptions," while less complete or technically scrupulous than Quine's treatment of ostension, points up the same problem in a more familiar philosophical context. It illustrates how the objective test procedures that are inherently inadequate to decide the classical realism/idealism dispute fail in exactly the same way to provide a basis for determining who really is a realist or an idealist in the first place.

This brings to mind the uneasiness one is apt to feel concerning Moore's "proof" of the external world, whether it is regarded straightforwardly as a metaphysical claim or (along the lines suggested by Malcolm's famous interpretation) as involving an appeal to the correct use of ordinary language.[34] We may readily concede, without serious qualms, the truth of statements like "Here is a hand" and "Here is another hand" under the appropriate circumstances, or that of "At least two material things exist" anytime, but the circumstances that elicit these concessions are totally indifferent to the questions whether a hand is *really a hand*, or whether material things, more generally, are *really material things*. Likewise, there is nothing in these circumstances that touches the issue of whether "hand" in the above sentence *really* refers to *hands,* or "material things" to *material things.* The purported linguistic or semantic issue embodies the identical vacuity of the corresponding metaphysical issue.

The observation that there is no significant difference between semantic and metaphysical inquiry has been made before. Husserl devoted the entire first section ("Experience and Meaning") of his *Logical Investigations* to a critique of then-current empiricist theories of meaning, concluding that to understand the meaning of a statement requires nothing less than "direct insight."[35] Herman Weyl has written in a more formal context:

> A science can only determine its domain of investigation up to an isomorphic mapping. In particular it remains quite indifferent as to the 'essence' of its objects. That which distinguishes the real points in space from number triads or other interpretations of geometry one can only know . . . by *immediate intuitive perception.*[36]

The point at issue must not be confused with the question whether semantic theories ought to appeal to abstract entities. The point I have been developing here concerns, rather, the virtually identical methodological character of absolute semantic investigations and traditional metaphysics. Max Black has formulated the same point nicely in a criticism of Russell's approach to metaphysics by means of logical analysis:

> The task of determining logical structure i.e. of language demands the capacity to determine the logical structure of certain physical facts. But if we can ever do this we don't need the detour via language. . . . On the other hand if we face some obstacle of principle in dissecting reality, we shall meet the very same difficulties in trying to dissect language.[37]

Perhaps the modes of human conceptualization or description seem significantly closer to home and more naturally accessible to subjective philosophical introspection than does the external reality with which they deal. One may never know whether one's conceptualizations are really accurate (or indeed whether talk of such accuracy even makes objective sense), but the idea that we can at least become clear on the nature of these descriptions themselves surely has an appealing air of humility and common sense. We may grant that experience—the starting point, as it were, of all knowledge—is subjective, in the sense that it is exhausted by the combined gross sensory inputs of a diverse multitude of unique individuals, past, present, and future; however, knowledge or understanding itself does not take shape in the nervous system in a way that permits direct experience of it, or acquaintance with it. Rather, it is a massive and cumulative social and cultural achievement that manifests itself in language, and our knowledge or understanding of this language itself, then, is no less dependent upon language than our knowledge of the world generally. Language is itself one of the most salient and important features of the complex physical and social environment each of us is born into; to suppose we may exercise extraordinary powers of insight or awareness in coming to understand this portion of the world is unalloyed metaphysical pretense.

Recognition that significant talk of the world takes place only relative to a linguistic or theoretical system naturally leads to the demand for a thorough examination of these systems themselves. The lesson "Ontological Relativity" teaches us, however, is to take Neurath's figure of the "conceptual boat" seriously. Both metaphysicians and linguistic philosophers alike have attempted to climb out of and stand free and clear of the boat—the former in order to get a clearer view of the world, the latter in order to take a long, hard look at the boat. But if independent solid ground is to be denied one, why should it be accorded the other?

Absolute semantic inquiry is, then, no better or worse off than speculative metaphysics. The methodological obstacles to both stem from a single common motivation. This motivation is essentially the desire to explain science—scientific theory and scientific truth—in some fundamental way that is prior to scientific explanation itself. "What *really* exists?" "What does our language *really say* exists?" "What is the *true* nature of the world?" "What is the *true* nature of our *descriptions* of the world?" "What is the way the world *really* is?" "What is the way we *really say* it is?" And so on. The force of such words as "really" and "true" in complementary question pairs like these should by now be clear. They transform otherwise unproblematic questions into questions which ordinary science is, in principle, prevented from answering, either during the normal course of theory building or by pointing routinely to theories already proffered and (somewhat less routinely) to the way some of these theories might be interpreted in terms of others.

For metaphysics the idea is to uncover the essential nature and composition of the three-dimensional physical world which science describes. Philosophy as logical, linguistic, or semantic analysis sets itself, instead, the task of examining the conceptual basis of the three-dimensional physical world description which science provides. Metaphysics prefers the material mode of speech whereas semantic and logical analysis demand the formal, but any significant substantive distinction between these two ways of speaking is illusory. Both tasks are definitional. Metaphysicians seek real definitions, analysts seek nominal ones; but the semantic pursuit of linguistic meanings as providing an account of the fundamental nature of scientific truth is a mere reflection, in the formal mode of speech, of the metaphysical search for essences.

The analytic approach to philosophical issues receives its paradigmatic expression with Tarski's famous attempt to provide a formally rigorous definition of truth itself—in the classical sense of "correspondence with reality"—in terms of the semantic concept of satisfaction.[38] While Tarski thus construed truth as an explicitly semantic rather than metaphysical property or relation, he also sought to formally explicate all semantic terms themselves non-semantically in a way that would make such terms more palatable to early positivists like Carnap. For these reasons Tarski's work is of particular interest to us in our examination of the implications of the relativity of ontology, and his "semantic definition of truth" will therefore be given extensive consideration in the remaining two chapters.

4 The Semantic Conception of Truth

1 Sense and Reference

Throughout this examination of the linguistic presuppositions of analytic philosophers I have slipped rather routinely back and forth between talk of the *meaning, reference, ontological import*, and *conceptual content* of language; what linguistic expressions *say* or *are about*; how such expressions *describe, represent*, or *picture* the world; and so on. In so doing I have played fast and loose with the notion of linguistic meaning and have systematically ignored what is commonly regarded as an important semantic distinction between questions of *reference, denotation*, or *extension*, on the one hand, and questions of *meaning, connotation*, or *intension* on the other. It is time, perhaps, to pay more direct attention to this widely observed distinction and to the various philosophical issues on which it is normally seen to bear.

The difference between the *meaning* (or *sense*) and the *reference* of an expression is frequently illustrated by means of Frege's famous "morning star"/"evening star" example. The singular terms "morning star" and "evening star" are said to name, designate, or refer to one and the same object: the planet Venus. However, the two terms are held to differ with respect to sense, intension, or meaning, since, it is observed, their common reference does not follow from a mere understanding of the two terms themselves but was determined as the result of numerous painstaking astronomical observations. Likewise, such general terms as "featherless biped" and "rational animal" may be alike in extension or range of application, yet this coextensionality is judged to be a matter of contingent fact, whereas that of so-called synonyms, like "bachelor" and "unmarried male," is seen as the necessary result of the *meanings* of the two terms in question. Generally, likeness of reference is regarded as a necessary condition of likeness of meaning, but the converse does not hold.

Quine has stressed the importance of the distinction between questions of meaning and questions of reference:

> When the cleavage between meaning and reference is properly heeded the problems of what is loosely called semantics become separated into two provinces so fundamentally distinct as not to deserve a joint appellation at all. They may be called the *theory of meaning* and the *theory of reference.* . . . The main concepts in the theory of meaning, apart from meaning itself, are *synonymy* (or sameness of meaning), *significance* (or possession of meaning), and *analyticity* (or truth by virtue of meaning). Another is *entailment.* . . . The main concepts of the theory of reference are *naming, truth, denotation* (or truth of), and *extension.* Another is the notion of *values* of variables.[1]

Quine's reasons for endorsing this bipartite division of semantics are far more philosophical than pedantic. In particular, they have to do with his long-standing dissatisfaction with the various concepts of the theory of meaning per se as employed by philosophers in the construction of modal or intensional logics and in efforts to explain such phenomena as translation, ambiguity, the so-called propositional attitudes, and especially the purported distinction between analytic and synthetic truth. Gilbert Harman writes:

> Quine thinks that linguistic philosophers have been almost totally wrong about meaning. He denies that appeal to meaning will do any of the things these philosophers have wanted it to do for them. To a philosopher . . . Quine's position is nearly tantamount to disbelieving in meaning.[2]

The basis for Quine's dissatisfaction with, or disbelief in, the concepts of the theory of meaning is the extreme difficulties he encounters in trying to make clear sense of them, as opposed to those of the theory of reference. These difficulties receive detailed and penetrating critical scrutiny in his landmark essay "Two Dogmas of Empiricism," which swiftly earned a place as a classic in the philosophical literature on meaning.[3]

Quine dismisses outright the "museum theory" of meaning (according to which meanings are conceived as abstract ideas arrayed in a gallery of the mind with individual words attached to them as labels) as largely a by-product of confusion between *naming* and *meaning*—a confusion both Frege and Russell had originally sought to dispel:

> Once the theory of meaning is sharply separated from the theory of reference, it is a short step to recognizing as the prime business of the theory of meaning simply the synonymy of linguistic forms and the analyticity of statements; meanings themselves, as obscure intermediary entities may well be abandoned.[4]

Quine traces the notion of an analytic statement, as one whose truth depends solely on the meanings of the words it contains, back to Kant, with earlier roots in Hume's talk of the relations of ideas and Leibniz's conception of truths of reason, and then separates out *logical* truths, like "No unmarried male is a married male," whose truth turns only on the meanings of specific logical particles, such as "un," "no," "and," "if," and "then," from the broader class of *analytic* truths, like "No bachelor is a married male," whose truth depends, additionally, upon the synonymy of nonlogical expressions (in the present example, "bachelor" and "unmarried male"). "The characteristic of such a statement," notes Quine, "is that it can be turned into a logical truth by putting synonyms for synonyms."[5] Thus, with the case of logical truth as such put aside, the problem of explaining analyticity is reduced to that of explaining synonymy.

Definition winds up a dead end so far as accounting for synonymy is concerned, Quine reasons:

> [If the lexicographer] glosses "bachelor" as "unmarried male" it is only because of his belief that there is a relation of synonymy between those forms, implicit in general or preferred usage prior to his own work. The notion of synonymy presupposed here has still to be clarified, presumably in terms relating to linguistic behavior.[6]

Nor does Quine discern any essential difference in the nature of definition as it occurs either in philosophical explication or in other forms of theoretical discourse:

> In formal and informal work alike, thus, we find that definition—except in the extreme case of the explicitly conventional introduction of new notations—hinges on prior relations of synonymy.[7]

The interchangeability of linguistic expressions within various sentential contexts without causing change in the truth value of any such sentence—what Quine (following Leibniz) calls "interchangeability salva veritate"—might appear to be a sufficient condition for the synonymy of the two linguistic expressions involved; however, this holds true only with an important qualification: In order for interchangeability salva veritate to provide a sufficient condition of the synonymy of two expressions—"bachelor" and "unmarried male," for example—there must be available in the language an adverb like "necessarily" that will permit us to write sentences such as "Necessarily, all and only bachelors are unmarried men." The difficulty now arises in trying to come to terms with "necessarily," which, as Quine points out, must be "so construed as to yield truth when and only when applied to an analytic statement."[8] This leaves us back where we started, seeking an explanation of analyticity. Quine sums up the situation as follows:

> Analyticity at first seemed most naturally definable by appeal to a realm of meanings. On refinement, the appeal to meanings gave way to an appeal to synonymy or definition. But definition turned out to be a will-o'-the-wisp, and synonymy turned out to be best understood only by dint of a prior appeal to analyticity itself.[9]

Recognizing, thus, that if an acceptable account of analyticity could be found without making an appeal to the notion of synonymy one could proceed forthwith to explain synonymy in terms of analyticity, Quine turns his attention to Carnap's efforts to define analyticity directly on the basis of semantical rules or meaning postulates.[10] Carnap's use of the conception of semantical rules in trying to account for the distinction between 'philosophical' and 'scientific' existence questions as well as that between logical and factual truth has already been discussed extensively in chapter 2, and Quine's critique of Carnap in "Two Dogmas" follows the same general lines developed in that earlier chapter from Quine's other writings:

> From the point of view of the problem of analyticity the notion of an artificial language with semantical rules is a *feu follet par excellence*. Semantical rules determining the analytic statements of an artificial language are of interest only in so far as we already understand the notion of analyticity; they are no help in gaining this understanding.[11]

Elsewhere, of course, Quine has given much attention to the problems of meaning from the point of view of an empirical investigation of speech usage or linguistic behavior.[12] Far from pointing a way to an acceptable account of either analyticity or synonymy, however, these considerations led quickly to his formulation of the theses of the indeterminacy of translation and ontological relativity themselves, whence our own inquiry first began.

For all these reasons, Quine has come to regard the various concepts of linguistic meaning as totally lacking in systematic theoretical significance and therefore of no use as explanatory concepts. However, in "Notes on the Theory of Reference," a paper of approximately the same vintage as "Two Dogmas," he adopts a strikingly different attitude toward the theory of reference, to which field he assigns his own extensive writings on ontological commitment as well as Tarski's work in semantics.[13] Here Quine sharply contrasts what he perceives to be the superior clarity and intelligibility of concepts belonging to the theory of reference with the "sorry state" of those of the theory of meaning, just recounted.

Despite the annoying presence of the "semantic paradoxes"— from the ancient Epimenides, or "Liar," down to more modern variants —we are reluctant to banish such terms as "true," "true of" (or "denotes"), and "names," whose use gives rise to the paradoxes, from our vocabulary. Quine explains that this is due to their "peculiar clarity," as illustrated by the following:

"_____" is true if and only if _____.

"_____" is true of every _____ thing and nothing else.

"_____" names _____ and nothing else.

without paradox, as long as the statements or terms which fill the blanks belong not merely to L' but specifically to L.[16]

These "paradigms" (more properly, paradigm schemata) are not definitions, Quine points out, because they explain the terms "true in L," "true in L of," and "names in L" only for individual choices of expressions of L by means of the device of quotation, and resist grammatical generalization into a form utilizing genuinely bound variables. Nevertheless, Quine points out,

> the paradigms resemble definitions in this fundamental respect; they leave no ambiguity as to the extensions, the ranges of applicability, of the verbs in question.[17]

These schemata, he contends,

> though they are not definitions, yet serve to endow "true in L" and "true in L of" and "names in L" with every bit as much clarity, in any particular application, as is enjoyed by the particular expressions of L to which we apply them. Attribution of truth, in particular, to "Snow is white," for example, is every bit as clear to us as attribution of whiteness to snow.[18]

There is another important factor which Quine believes warrants our great confidence in concepts of the theory of reference. Tarski, whom Quine credits as the source for most of his preceding reflections on the theory of reference, has shown that if certain general conditions are met, then the concept of truth, in the sense illustrated by its schema, can actually be defined by an explicit general procedure applicable to languages of a particular formalized kind. What is more, Quine notes, the same sort of procedure can easily be extended to construct analogous definitions for truth of and naming.

Because we have both the schemata (which when applied to the sentences, general terms, and singular terms of a language yield paradigmatic illustrations of the concepts of truth, truth of, and naming, respectively) and Tarski's procedure for explicitly defining these notions in the sense revealed through their schemata, Quine concludes that "it is a striking fact that these notions, despite the paradoxes we associate with them, are so very much less foggy and mysterious than the notions belonging to the theory of meaning."[19] Perhaps even more striking now, in retrospect, is the rather startling contrast in tone between this enthusiastic endorsement by Quine of the theory of reference and his more recent relativistic conclusions in "Ontological Relativity," for it is precisely the nature of this once favored province of semantics that he now wishes to qualify so radically.

Although "Ontological Relativity" does indeed focus directly upon what Quine (at least now) clearly perceives to be the partially relative and arbitrary nature of questions of reference per se, the reason I have not restricted the scope of this essay's implications to this domain but have construed it so broadly as to encompass virtually anything that might conceivably be called semantics should now be clear. By any account, the theory of reference represents the most stable and least disputed portion of semantics as a whole. There has been considerable disagreement over whether reference alone suffices to explain everything that needs explaining.[20] However, there has been, overall, far less controversy over whether reference tells some of the story than over whether it tells the whole story. Indeterminacy and relativity do not affect questions of reference instead of questions of meaning, but in addition to them. The problem of relativity now facing the theory of reference comes not simply as one more localized complication for semantics, but as the most crippling broadside yet delivered:

> Certainly likeness of meaning is a dim notion, repeatedly challenged. Of two predicates which are alike in extension, it has never been clear when to say that they are alike in meaning and when not; it is the old matter of featherless bipeds and rational animals, or of equiangular and equilateral triangles. Reference, extension, has been the firm thing; meaning, intension, the infirm. The indeterminacy of translation now confronting us, however, cuts across extension and intension alike. The terms "rabbit," "undetached rabbit part," and "rabbit stage" differ not only in meaning; they are true of different things. Reference itself proves behaviorally inscrutable.[21]

As likeness of reference of two expressions is a minimal condition of their being alike in meaning, so an adequate account of reference generally is a minimal requirement of an adequate account of meaning, and attacks on the theory of reference are, a fortiori, attacks on the theory of meaning. Indeed, some philosophers have recently concluded that the theory of meaning ought not to be considered distinct from the theory of reference at all, but should be construed as part of it.[22] In any case, it is clear that the very least we can ask of a concept is that it have a distinctive application; lacking even this, what further sense can be made of talk of concepts, or of meanings, at all? When reference itself becomes "inscrutable," so much the worse for meaning.

Quine thus poses the following rhetorical question from within the context, once again, of radical translation:

> Can an empiricist speak seriously of sameness of meaning of two conditions upon an object x, one stated in the heathen language and one in ours, when even the singling out of an object x as object at all for the heathen language is so hopelessly arbitrary?[23]

As talk of what the objects of a theory or language are takes on significance only relative to some chosen way of translating the theory or language into a selected background language, itself taken "at face value," so too for our talk of the meanings of the expressions of a language in the narrower sense—except now for the added proviso that the background language contain, in addition to the normal complement of logical and individuative devices, something on the order of a necessity operator as well.

We need occupy our attention no longer, then, with the precise distinction between meaning and reference. Another question now calls for our immediate consideration: how to reconcile what Quine has said of a supportive nature about reference in "Notes on the Theory of Reference" with the apparently negative implications of his current relativistic views. Clearly, the single most pressing issue in this regard concerns the status of the concept of *truth* itself, which we have observed Quine—following Tarski, Carnap and many other philosophers—to assign unhesitatingly to the now-compromised theory of reference.

2   Truth and the Theory of Reference

Now the relativity of ontology clearly raises serious questions concerning the significance of concepts like naming and denotation (truth of), which belong to that portion of semantics Quine calls the theory of reference. These concepts purport to express relations between the singular and general terms of a language and given objects of the language's ontology, and it is precisely questions as to what objects constitute the ontology of a language that Quine has concluded to be so doubly relative in character. The concept of truth, on the other hand, presents, at least on the surface, a somewhat different case. Questions concerning the truth of whole sentences do not automatically raise, in any explicit fashion, questions concerning the reference of individual terms in a language, as do questions of naming and denotation. Before going on to examine more fully the implications of ontological relativity for concepts of the theory of reference as a whole, it will first be useful to consider to what extent truth properly falls within this domain in the first place.

Given the general concern of semantics as the theory of reference with an investigation of the relations between linguistic expressions and aspects of extralinguistic reality, it is natural to view truth as a semantic concept insofar as truth is conceived as a relation of some kind—correspondence, or agreement, for example—between a statement and an objective state of affairs. Such a semantic conception of truth amounts to nothing more than the traditional correspondence theory, as opposed, for example, to the coherence theory, which holds that truth consists just in consistent or coherent internal logical relations between the various members of an overall encompassing system of beliefs or statements. So long as we make no overt effort to further reduce or analyze correspondence in terms of other more elementary referential notions, such as naming or denotation, we are free to construe *truth as correspondence* as a semantic concept of a simple and irreducible sort that does not explicitly raise issues of ontology.

Historically, however, truth has been subject to semantic characterizations of an essentially stronger kind. The stronger version of the semantic conception of truth views the truth of a statement as a function of the references of its component terms. It goes essentially beyond the simple premise that truth consists in correspondence between statement and fact by seeking to analyze the precise nature of this correspondence in terms of more elementary relations—such as naming and denotation—between the corresponding elements of which statements and facts are believed composed.

The above "paradigm" for "true" holds, Quine tells us, "when any one statement is written in the two blanks"; that for "true of" "when any one general term (in adjective form, or, omitting 'thing,' in substantive form) is written in the two blanks"; and that for "names" "whenever any one name (which really names, that is, whose object exists) is written in the two blanks."[14]

Some minor qualifications are needed here, however. First, the three terms "true," "true of," and "names" must all be relativized to the language under consideration and their respective "paradigms" reformulated accordingly, as follows:

"_____" is true in L if and only if _____.

"_____" is true in L of every _____ thing and nothing else.

"_____" names in L _____ and nothing else.

"This is not a philosophical doctrine of the relativity of all fact to language," Quine explains;

> . . . the point is much more superficial. The point is merely that a given string of letters or sounds could constitute at once a statement say of English and a statement (different in meaning, to borrow a phrase) of Frisian, and it might happen in its English meaning to be true and in its Frisian meaning to be false.[15]

Another qualification required in order to avoid nonsense is that the language L, to whose expressions "true in L," "true in L of," and "names in L" apply, is contained in or at least overlaps with L', the language in which the paradigms themselves are formulated. This must occur at least to the extent that the expressions of L which may fill the schematic blanks are also expressions of L'.

Quine then goes on to point out that it is even possible to avoid the semantic paradoxes after all, if, after relativizing "true," "true of," and "names" in the manner just described, we take the further step of banishing these terms altogether from L and admitting them only as expressions of L', the language employed to talk about the expressions of L:

> These terms, appropriate to the theory of reference of L, may continue to exist in a more inclusive language L' containing L; and the paradigms . . . may then continue to hold in L',

For example, suppose we analyze the sentence "Five is a number" into two grammatical components: a subject, "five," and a predicate, "is a number." We may then say that the sentence "Five is a number" is *true* if and only if "is a number" *denotes* what "five" *names*. Truth for the sentence "Five is a number" is thus reduced to naming and denotation, insofar as (given an understanding of simple *predication* itself) to know what sorts of things "is a number" denotes and what, if anything, "five" names is to know the *truth conditions* of "Five is a number" (that is, what it means to say that the sentence "Five is a number" is true).

Though this strong analytic version of the semantic conception of truth is clearly suggested in the earliest formulations of the classical correspondence theory by Plato[24] and Aristotle,[25] it first appears explicitly, perhaps, in the writings of the Stoic Sextus Empiricus, who held that an "atomic" statement such as "This bat flies" is true when and only when the ascribed predicate ("flies") *belongs to* (cf. *applies to* or *denotes*) the individual thing *coming under* (cf. *named* or *designated by*) the demonstrative term ("this").[26] Jaakko Hintikka, a prominent contemporary analytic philosopher who follows Wittgenstein and the positivist tradition by equating the meaning of a statement with its truth conditions and opposes any appeal to 'meanings' in the intensional sense, offers an analogous account of the relation between truth and reference:

> . . . these truth conditions [of sentences] in an extensional language cannot be divested from the references of singular terms and from the extensions of its predicates. In fact, these references and extensions are precisely what the truth conditions of quantified sentences turn on. The truth value of a sentence is a function of the references (extensions) of the terms it contains . . . the references . . . of our primitive terms are thus what determine the meanings . . . of first-order sentences.[27]

Hintikka's statement amply illustrates the need felt by many philosophers to explain the relationship between a true statement and the objective fact that makes it true in some more fundamental way than talk of simple correspondence permits. As Hartry Field has recently put it,

> *Part* of the explication of the truth of "Schnee ist weiss und

Gras ist grün," presumably, would be that snow is white and grass is green. But this would only be part of the explanation, for still missing is the connection between snow being white and grass being green on the one hand, and the German utterance being true on the other hand.[28]

It is this "connection" that a semantic analysis of the statement in question appears to reveal.[29] In Field's example, for instance, the connection is to be explained by the supposed semantic facts that "Schnee" in German *names* snow and "Gras" grass, while "ist weiss" and "ist grün" *denote*, in that same language, white and green things, respectively—in addition, of course, to the fact that the sentential connective "und" has the same logical sense as the English particle "and."

The strong analytic version of the semantic conception of truth thus views truth as entirely reducible to other semantic or referential notions. It holds, in effect, that the nature of the link between a true statement and the world is revealed by a semantic analysis of the statement in question. This, in turn, presupposes both a logico-grammatical analysis of the language involved and a parallel metaphysical analysis of physical facts, along with a complete mapping of the elements of one domain onto those of the other. On this view the relations between individual terms and given objects of the ontology of a language are primary and irreducible, whereas the *truth* of sentences is seen as a secondary construction upon these elementary term-to-thing relations.

In contrast with the first view (which we may call the simple correspondence theory), a semantic analysis of truth or correspondence is bound to raise the same questions of ontology as are required to make sense of notions like naming and denotation, to which truth is ultimately reduced. If we interpret Hintikka's formulation as holding that we must specify the truth conditions of a given statement in terms of the particular objects that make up the references and extensions of its singular and general terms, then, in light of ontological relativity, it is hard to see how we could escape a totally relativized concept of truth. Our understanding of what it would mean to call any sentence true in a given language would presumably be as relative and arbitrary as our understanding of just what objects we take to make up the ontology of the language in question.

Whereas a semantic analysis of truth or correspondence clearly raises ontological issues of some degree or other, the concept of truth that is exemplified in individual instances of the truth schema displays the ontological neutrality of the simple correspondence theory. According to Quine, the biconditional

"Snow is white" is true in L if and only if snow is white

illustrates that "attribution of truth . . . to "Snow is white" . . . is every bit as clear to us as attribution of whiteness to snow."[30] Now, one might interpret Quine's talk here of the attribution of whiteness to snow as implying a view that the truth of "Snow is white" depends upon what we now clearly perceive to be the relative question whether "snow" and "is white" name and denote snow and white things (whiteness), respectively. If this were so, the notion of truth ascribed here would have the relative and parochial character described above.

This interpretation of Quine's remarks is, however, both unnecessary and unwarranted. The right side of the biconditional, which explains "true in L" as applied to "Snow is white," makes no mention of the terms "snow" and "is white" or of any purported relation between these terms and particular extralinguistic objects. There is instead talk only of snow and of its being white. This paradigm tells us that what it means to call the sentence "Snow is white" true is just as clear as the sentence itself, no matter how the specific references of this sentence's component terms, "snow" and "is white," may be construed and reconstrued upon later reflection. The schema explains truth for the individual sentences to which it is applied by using the sentence itself to describe the objective circumstances that must obtain if and only if the sentence is true. In our present example these circumstances relate to the color of snow, not to the references of terms.

Any acceptable translation of a sentence as a whole will describe equally well the circumstances under which that sentence is true.[31] Examples like ours simply illustrate the standard case in which the description of these circumstances and the sentence in question are related through homophonic translation within the home language. However, truth as ascribed to "Snow is white" in our paradigm is not necessarily thereby relativized to this one translation itself, as would be questions concerning the references of "snow" and "is white." The given translation is simply the means for tying the truth of the sentence to the objective whiteness of snow.

Within the context of radical translation, Quine has clearly supposed that what are, in effect, the meanings or truth conditions of at least some native sentences can be empirically determined by querying these sentences for native assent and dissent under a variety of altered circumstances.[32] Arbitrariness enters on a large scale only with the linguist's efforts to fashion a complete manual of translation that equates specific native vocabulary and grammatical constructions with those of his own language and thus enables him to construct for any given native sentence a corresponding one in his own language that, in effect, describes the conditions under which its native correlate is true. Though equally acceptable manuals may achieve the same sentence-to-sentence correlations by charting radically diverse systems of term-to-term connections, it is, in the end, only the relative accuracy of these final correlations themselves, as judged against available empirical evidence, that warrants any manual's achieving them.

Truth, then, as revealed through the truth schema and circumstances of radical translation, retains a distinctively absolute character that transcends the twofold relativity of ontology.[33] It is interesting to contrast Carnap's formulation of the strong semantic conception, which like Hintikka's owes its inspiration to Tarski's formal definition.

In *Meaning and Necessity*,[34] Carnap describes the introduction of what he calls a "semantic system" in terms of three basic steps. First the "rules of formation" (syntactical rules), whose task is to identify the primitive logical and descriptive terms of a language and the way these may be employed in combination with one another to form sentences, must be specified. Next come the "rules of designation" (semantical rules), which purport to relate the descriptive signs to the various individual things and properties to which they refer. Last, the "rules of truth," which explain the meanings or truth conditions of sentences on the basis of the designations assigned to their descriptive constituents, are given. Carnap provides the following example of a rule of truth for his semantical system S_1:

An atomic sentence in S_1 consisting of a predicate followed

by an individual constant is true if and only if the individual
to which the individual constant refers possesses the property
to which the predicate refers.[35]

Carnap emphasizes that "this rule presupposes the rules of
designation."[36]

In the above-cited passage, although Carnap is clearly addressing
himself to the specialized case of formally constructed languages,
what he says about the fundamental importance and role of the
designations of individual terms in determining the truth conditions
of sentences constructed from those terms is meant to apply across
the board to the interpretation and understanding of languages
generally, be they formally constructed or not. Whereas in the case
of formally constructed systems the designations of individual terms
are set by mere stipulation, in the case of natural languages, Carnap
suggests, such designations can be discovered by means of routine
empirical inquiry. In an account written not long after his conversion
from syntax to semantics, Carnap discusses the prospective results
of such an empirical investigation of a hypothetical foreign language B:

> We now proceed to restrict our attention to a special aspect
> of the facts concerning the language B which we have found
> by observations of the speaking activities within the group
> who speak that language. We study the relations between the
> expressions of B and their designata. On the basis of those
> facts we are going to lay down a system of rules establishing
> those relations. We call them *semantical rules*.[37]

These primitive designation relations, as codified in an explicit set
of semantical rules, represent, according to Carnap's view, the fundamental key to the understanding and interpretation of any
language:

> Since to know the truth conditions of a sentence is to know
> what is asserted by it, the given semantical rules determine
> for every sentence . . . what it asserts—in usual terms its
> 'meaning'—or, in other words, how it is to be translated into
> English. . . .
>   Therefore, we shall say that we *understand* a language system,
> or a sign, or an expression, or a sentence in a language system,

if we know the semantical rules of the system. We shall also say that the semantical rules give an *interpretation* of the language system.[38]

Carnap's semantic account of truth is thus founded upon the basic assumption that individual terms are the primary building blocks of a language and that our understanding (interpretation, translation) of such a language is essentially dependent upon a prior determination—whether through formal stipulation or empirical investigation—of the extralinguistic reference of such terms, in addition to the logicogrammatical rules governing their meaningful use in sentences. The mapping of these term-to-thing relations by a set of semantical rules is viewed as the essential groundwork from which our entire understanding of a language is projected.

From this perspective the field linguist is perceived as first having to establish (on the basis of empirical observations) a set of term-to-term correlations from the native's language to his own, and thence proceeding, with the aid of some basic principles of grammar similarly gleaned, to a statement of the meaning or truth conditions of any given native sentence in terms of his own language. The difference between this point of view and that of Quine's contrived situation of "radical translation" is fundamental: For Carnap's linguist it will be the basic set of term-to-term correlations and grammatical rules that will serve as the final arbiter for what meanings, translations, or truth conditions will finally be assigned to native sentences. So far as Quine's linguist is concerned, however, it will ultimately be just the empirically determined truth conditions (meanings, translations) of some whole native sentences themselves that will set the final parameters within which any acceptable manual of translation must fall.

In short, the analytic version of the semantic conception of truth regards the extralinguistic reference of individual terms in a language as a condition of the very possibility of even uttering truth or falsity in the first place—that is, a condition of the possibility of significant discourse itself. Denial or rejection of 'meanings' in the intensional sense to the individual terms of a language may ultimately preclude a precise demarcation between analytic and synthetic statements, construction of modal logics, or the discovery of appropriate objects for the 'propositional attitudes,' but to deny such terms their own fixed reference to objects in the external world would, on such a view, preclude even the possibility of intelligibly describing what it would mean for any given sentence in the language to be *true*.

We have discovered a significant difference, then, between truth as simple, unanalyzed correspondence and truth as explicated in terms of other concepts of reference, such as naming and denotation. Both conceptions may legitimately be classed among the notions of the theory of reference; however, while the relativity involved in specifying the ontology of a language clearly raises questions about the objective significance of notions like naming and denotation, it threatens truth only when explicitly understood or analyzed in terms of these other notions. Truth as revealed by the truth schema and circumstances of radical translation appears to transcend both the relativity of reference and the unintelligibility of meaning. Conceived as a function of the reference of terms in a sentence, however, truth takes on the more obscure and dubious character of concepts such as naming and denotation.

Despite the apparent impunity of the simple, unanalyzed notion of truth with regard to the consequences of ontological relativity, a strong predisposition has prevailed among analytic philosophers to conceive of truth as a function of more primitive forms of reference. This, indeed, is the conception of truth evoked by Quine's own somewhat enigmatic closing statement of "Ontological Relativity":

> In their elusiveness . . . —in their emptiness now and again except relative to a broader background [language]—both truth and ontology may in a suddenly rather clear and even tolerant sense be said to belong to transcendental metaphysics.[39].

The character of Quine's remarks owes much to the treatment truth receives at the hands of Alfred Tarski. It was Tarski's numerous observations concerning the nature of semantics, along with the explicit procedure he provided for defining semantic concepts, that formed the basis for Quine's vigorous advocacy of the theory of reference over the theory of meaning. It was Tarski's semantic definition of truth, in particular—regarded by many philosophers, including both Quine and Carnap, as something of a philosophical milestone—that first succeeded in carrying out the desired reduction of truth to other semantic terms in a formally precise and rigorous manner. Therefore, in considering the implications of ontological relativity for the concept of truth understood in terms of more primitive forms of reference and the extent to which such a notion may be justly consigned (tolerantly or not) to the realm of transcendental metaphysics, it will be of particular interest to examine in some detail Tarski's efforts to provide what he regarded as formally correct and materially adequate definitions of all semantic concepts. Before proceeding to this task, however, we shall first explore the philosophic roots of the semantic conception of truth Tarski sought to capture in his celebrated formal analysis, as well as some of the other philosophical issues he addressed in attempting to set up the foundations of theoretical semantics.

3 The Semantic Conception of Truth and Analytic Philosophy

The seminal formulation of the semantic conception of truth, so far as twentieth-century analytic philosophy is concerned, was undoubtedly Russell's version of the correspondence theory. Defending correspondence against the coherence theories of late-nineteenth- and early-twentieth-century idealists, Russell sought to shed light on two problems Moore's account of correspondence had failed to come to grips with adequately. One was the problem of accounting for error within the general framework of a correspondence theory. This difficulty, raised first in Plato's *Theaetetus*,[40] can be stated simply as follows: Either the object of a false belief exists, or it does not. If it does exist, then the belief must be regarded as true and not false after all. If it does not exist, then the belief is not a belief in anything to begin with. In either case, false beliefs appear to be ruled out. The second problem, upon which a solution to the first seemed to depend, was that of providing a precise analysis of the notion of correspondence itself, which in Moore's treatment had taken on a somewhat mystical, undefinable character.[41]

The approach Russell adopted in order to resolve these difficulties closely paralleled Plato's response in the *Sophist* to the problem of the *Theaetetus*.[42] The approach was essentially that of analyzing correspondence in terms of simpler semantic relations between words and things. Russell rejected the notion that correspondence was a simple, two-term relation between a belief or proposition and an objective fact. He reasoned that both propositions (or beliefs) and facts are inherently complex sorts of things, logically incapable of serving as the terms of such a simple relation. According to Russell's analysis, a proposition is composed of any number of interrelated simple component terms, each of which stands for some correspondingly simple element of a fact. The grammatical rules governing the way simple symbols might properly be arranged in whole propositions was taken, then, to reflect the various possible logical structures of facts in the world. When the arrangement of elements in a fact correctly matches that of the corresponding symbols in a proposition, the proposition is *true*; when it does not, the proposition is *false*.

Russell, thus, succeeded in explicating the notion of "correspondence" and in accommodating the existence of false beliefs by providing an analysis of the relation between a true statement and the fact which makes it true in terms of simpler, more elementary semantic relations posited between their corresponding constituent elements. So conceived, a falsehood does not imply the nonexistence of the objects with which it purports to deal; it is still about something, namely the various 'things' to which each of its component terms individually *refers*. Its falsity results not from any absolute failure of objective reference but only from an absence of correct alignment between its component elements and those of a corresponding fact.[43]

According to Russell's fully developed doctrine of logical atomism,[44] whose refinement, by Russell's own account, owed so much to Wittgenstein's critical influence, reality consists entirely of "atomic facts," which are themselves composed of simple elements (particulars such as "little patches of color, sounds, momentary things"[45]), qualities of particulars, and relations between particulars. Russell regards these simple constituents of facts as the "logical atoms," the "last residue of analysis," from which all facets of reality and our experience of it can ultimately be constructed. Corresponding to atomic facts are "atomic propositions" that express atomic facts and "mirror" their complexity. Atomic propositions have only the simplest grammatical forms, corresponding to the logical structures of atomic facts, and contain only simple, primitive symbols which refer directly to the various elements from which atomic facts are composed: names for particulars, predicates (or adjectives) for qualities, and verbs for relations. All more complex ("molecular") propositions are ideally reducible, or analyzable, in terms of the primitive constituents of atomic propositions. The simple constituent elements of facts to which the simple symbols in atomic propositions refer are the "meanings" (references) of these symbols and cannot themselves be described, analyzed, or defined by means of any other terms; rather, knowledge of their "meaning" rests entirely upon the "direct acquaintance" of the speaker with the objects referred to.[46]

It is, then, according to Russell's view, just the "meanings" (references) of this finite stock of simple expressions, so firmly rooted in each individual's immediate experience, that form the entire basis for our understanding of all propositions in a language and upon which their truth or falsity ultimately turns. The parallel linguistic and metaphysical analyses presupposed by any semantic analysis of truth is graphically illustrated by Russell's classic description of the relation between language and reality that would obtain in the case of a "logically perfect" language:

> In a logically perfect language the words in a proposition would correspond one by one with the components of the corresponding fact, with the exception of such words as "or," "not," "if," "then," which have a different function. In a logically perfect language there will be one word and no more for each simple object, and everything that is not simple will be expressed by a combination of words, by a combination derived, of course, from the words for the simple things that enter in, one word for each simple component. A language of that sort will be completely analytic, and will show at a glance the logical structure of the facts asserted or denied. The language which is set forth in *Principia Mathematica* is intended to be a language of that sort.[47]

Russell, therefore, totally rejected the idea of any simple relation of correspondence holding between a statement and a fact, such as Moore seemed to suggest, and substituted instead an elaborate network of more finely tuned semantic connections between the individual words of which statements are composed and the various corresponding elements into which reality may be analyzed. The result was an analysis of correspondence itself as a logically complex relation which permitted a coherent account of falsehood while preserving the link between language and reality so essential to the correspondence theory. The important thing to bear in mind for our purposes here, however, is simply that this strategy of semantic analysis, which now appears so clearly to be a doubly relative enterprise, is not itself forced upon us simply by virtue of our adherence to the correspondence view of truth, as demonstrated in our preceding examination of the truth schema.

Wittgenstein, in his famous *Tractatus*, embraced Russell's view that all truth about the world is reducible to that of atomic propositions describing atomic facts. He likewise adopted Russell's analysis of the essentially complex nature of propositions and his explication of their truth and significance as a function of the individual *meanings* (or references) of the terms they contain: "To understand a proposition means to know what is the case, if it is true. . . . It is understood by anyone who understands its constituents."[48] Wittgenstein did, of course, make a notable effort to enhance Russell's account of correspondence by construing propositions as "pictures" of the facts that make them true.[49] However, since he explained picturing itself as a kind of structural correspondence between the correlated elements of the picture and what it represents,[50] Wittgenstein's theory of pictures seems to reduce, in the end, to Russell's own original analysis of correspondence.

Wittgenstein took very seriously the idea that anything meaningful that could be said about the world could be said by means of atomic propositions, and he made a determined effort to exhibit all ("molecular") propositions—including generalizations and statements of propositional attitudes—as truth-functional compounds of atomic propositions, so that truth conditions for any such statement could be stated in terms of a particular distribution of truth values among a given set of atomic propositions.[51] While fundamentally flawed, his efforts in this regard proved enormously suggestive, and the underlying assumption—that any significant statement corresponds to a unique combination of possible 'facts' eventually took shape in the positivists' verification principle.[52] Whatever the *Tractatus*'s substantive contribution might have been, surely its most significant achievement was its remarkable success in selling Russell's conception of language in the first place, along with the associated idea of philosophy as logical analysis, which Wittgenstein developed and refined so that it proved virtually irresistible to members of the Vienna Circle.

Wittgenstein effectively portrayed philosophy as wholly concerned with the "critique of language." This was to be an entirely analytic activity, separate from the natural sciences and charged with the twofold task of dispelling traditional philosophical "pseudo-problems" by revealing their origins in the misleading forms of everyday speech and "logically clarifying" the concepts of science itself.[53] It was the apparent availability of a "completely analytic" or "logically perfect" language (represented by the logical symbolism of Whitehead and Russell's *Principia*) whose simple logico-grammatical structure purported to mirror that of reality itself, together with Russell's underlying semantics (which tied this structure definitively to reality at the level of simple sensation and direct observation) that made such an analytic enterprise seem plausible and likely to bear philosophical fruit. Such a language seemed capable of expressing all knowledge in a systematic, explicit, and unambiguous fashion, and thereby laying bare the basic concepts and truths underlying all theoretical science so that their precise logical interconnections and bearing on experience were sharply defined and clearly exhibited. Within this "logically perfect" language it would be impossible even to formulate the spurious issues of traditional philosophy, whereas the precise factual (empirical) significance of any concept or assertion—to the extent that it was significant at all—would be fixed by simple logical rules and definitions. Equipped with the rich logical resources of the *Principia*, such a language promised would-be analysts nothing less than a full reduction of all meaningful theoretical concepts to those of immediate experience and a formal axiomatization of all truth about the world in a basic set of sentences expressing only fundamental 'logical' principles and simple, unanalyzable, observable 'facts.'

This entire picture of language and of the broad potential for philosophical analysis was essentially Russell's creation. In the *Principia* he not only provided the language and logic that were to serve henceforward as the analyst's basic tools, but he also showed, in spectacular fashion, how to carry out the analytical reduction of the entire discipline of classical mathematics. In *Our*

Knowledge of the External World he provided the first concrete examples of how to utilize the same linguistic and logical devices to carry forward a similar kind of project for our knowledge of physical reality as well. And Russell also showed the way toward exorcism of the philosophical confusions induced through the superficial appearance of ordinary, unrefined discourse. The artfully constructed syntax of his "logically perfect" language exposed the notorious paradoxes of set theory as ungrammatical nonsense and permitted an interpretation of "definite descriptions" in the absence of extravagant ontological assumptions.

The program of logical analysis, to the extent that it was directed toward the "positive" task of elucidating the concepts of science, was, as Russell clearly recognized, essentially the Cartesian quest for certainty.[54] Quine has described such investigations—exemplified most prominently by Russell's own work in the foundations of mathematics—as comprising two distinct parts, the *conceptual* and the *doctrinal*:

> The conceptual studies are concerned with meaning, the doctrinal with truth. The conceptual studies are concerned with clarifying concepts by defining them, some in terms of others. The doctrinal studies are concerned with establishing laws by proving them, some on the basis of others. Ideally the obscurer concepts would be defined in terms of the clearer ones so as to maximize clarity, and the less obvious laws would be proved from the more obvious ones, so as to maximize certainty. Ideally the definitions would generate all the concepts from clear and distinct ideas, and the proofs would generate all the theorems from self-evident truths.[55]

To many, Russell and Whitehead's *Principia* appeared to have come close to realizing both ideals with respect to mathematics: by showing how to define all mathematical notions in terms of what purported to be 'clearer' and more 'distinct' ones of logic (including set theory of course), and, thus, how to deduce mathematical truths from what appeared to be, largely, more 'obvious' logical axioms (notwithstanding the acknowledged unobviousness of the *Principia*'s axioms of infinity and choice). Russell likewise envisioned carrying through an analogous project for natural knowledge. This was to be achieved by enriching the original stock of 'clear and distinct' ideas with those of immediate experience, and by enlarging the original set of more or less 'obvious' truths to include direct reports of such experience. Gödel proved that the doctrinal task could never be fully carried out for mathematics even if the Cartesian ideal of certainty was abandoned. The extent to which the constructions of the *Principia* actually achieved the conceptual ideal of 'clarity' and 'distinctness' is , at best, arguable. With respect to our knowledge of the physical world, progress came only on the conceptual side, and there it stalled quickly with Russell's tentative construction in *Our Knowledge of the External World* and Carnap's ingenious efforts in the *Aufbau*. Efforts on the doctrinal side were stymied from the start by Hume's old problem of universal statements—no one of which is ever entailed by any number of singular statements.[56]

The semantic analysis of truth that Russell and Wittgenstein proposed—an analysis that explained the truth conditions of a statement in terms of the extralinguistic reference of its component expressions—forged a link between the conceptual and doctrinal sides of 'foundations' studies (a link that is already implicit in the assumption that the obviousness, or certainty, of truth is a function of the clarity and distinctness of the ideas it contains). The analytic version of the semantic conception of truth is, indeed, the formal expression of the analytic conception of language with which we have been concerned since chapter 1. It embodies the principle that the meanings of words are logically prior to the truth of statements formed from them, so that philosophy (as the analysis of meaning) is in the same way prior to science (the discovery of truth). Just as analysis of 'number' in terms of sets was meant to provide 'foundations' for mathematics, and analysis of 'body' in terms of sense impressions 'foundations' for our knowledge of the physical world, so explication of truth in terms of semantic concepts of meaning or reference represents a parallel effort to provide the conceptual foundations of analytic philosophy itself.

4   The Positivists' Dilemma and the Relevance of Tarski's Work

What really caught the imagination of early positivists was the opportunity the new method of "logical analysis" seemed to present to overturn speculative metaphysics while simultaneously pursuing traditional Cartesian epistemology within the scientifically secure parameters of a study of language. They were captivated by the idea of a logically pure language in which all genuine knowledge and significant thought could be precisely and explicitly stated in such a way that the more complex and remote theoretical concepts and truths were derived by simple logical rules and definitions from the clearer, simpler, and more obvious ones. Positivists united around the conception of a favored subset of simple "basic," "atomic," or "protocol" sentences as the ultimate repository of all truth and of a favored subset of primitive undefined terms—out of which such sentences were to be exclusively composed—as the ultimate repository of all *meaning*. Where they finally parted company was over the crucial question as to an adequate account of the truth and significance of these favored expressions themselves—the limits of analysis and reduction—which would link the conceptual (philosophical) and doctrinal (scientific) studies in the desired fashion.

One group, led by Schlick, followed in what were essentially the tracks of Russell and Wittgenstein. They applied the semantic analysis of correspondence, or truth, within a framework of traditional empiricism and construed "basic propositions," or "protocols," as reports of direct observations whose truth conditions or meanings—the 'facts' or experiences that would verify them—depended solely upon the direct extralinguistic reference of their primitive constituents. This was also, of course, the orientation exemplified by the tentative constructions of Carnap's early *Aufbau*.

As in Russell's original account, the precise links between primitive components of basic propositions and determinate aspects of reality or immediate experience could only be learned through a process akin to that of "direct acquaintance," so that verification of such a proposition would consist in simply "confronting" or "comparing" it directly with given experience:

> . . . when do I understand a proposition? When I understand the meanings of the words which occur in it? These can be explained by definitions. But in the definitions new words appear whose meanings cannot again be described in propositions, they must be indicated directly: the meaning of a

word must in the end be *shown*, it must be *given*. This is done by an act of indication, of pointing; and what is pointed at must be given, otherwise I cannot be referred to it.

Accordingly, in order to find the meaning of a proposition, we must transform it by successive definitions until finally only such words occur in it as can no longer be defined, but whose meanings can only be directly pointed out. The criterion of the truth or falsity of the proposition then lies in the fact that under definite conditions (given in the definition) certain data are present, or not present. If this is determined then everything asserted by the proposition is determined and I know its meaning.[57]

Disputes quickly arose among positivists as to whether the observations reported by basic propositions were infallible, and whether they concerned private sensations or publicly observable events.[58] These arguments over the nature of the ultimate facts, or experiences described by basic propositions, or the kinds of things to which their primitive terms *really* refer, proved to be a source of considerable discomfort and embarrassment to early positivists. Such naked discussion of extralinguistic reality and of our direct, preanalytic perception or awareness of it seemed to fatally compromise their stringent antimetaphysical posture and threatened to undermine the validity of their conception of philosophy by suggesting that the whole program of analysis was itself based on a footing of speculative metaphysics.

Another group, led by Neurath, turned away entirely from talk of correspondence or any other supposed semantic relations between linguistic expressions and external reality. These philosophers, including Hempel and Popper in addition to Neurath and eventually Carnap, came to view semantics as a thoroughly suspect discipline and held that all that linguistic expressions could properly be related to or compared with—logically speaking—were other linguistic expressions. The result was a formal account of truth and meaning that paralleled in many ways the "coherence theories" of traditional idealism.

During his formalistic phase, Carnap followed Neurath in attempting to refrain from any explicit mention of the "primitive data" to which language might ultimately refer, and sought to explain the meaning, or truth conditions, of a statement solely as a function of its grammatical form and its logical interrelations with other statements. The meaning of a word was, then, to be determined by its pattern of occurrence within such a system of logically related statements:

> What now is *the meaning of a word*? What stipulations concerning a word must be made in order for it to be significant? . . . First the *syntax* of the word must be fixed, i.e. the mode of its occurrence in the simplest sentence form in which it is capable of occurring; we call this sentence form its *elementary sentence*. . . . Secondly, for an elementary sentence S containing the word an answer must be given to the following question, which can be formulated in various ways:
> (1.) What sentences is S *deducible* from, and what sentences are deducible from S?
> (2.) Under what conditions is S supposed to be true, and under what conditions false?
> (3.) How is S to be *verified*?
> (4.) What is the *meaning* of S?[59]

In his *Logical Syntax of Language*, Carnap introduces a host of purely formal, syntactical formulations for a whole range of both logical and semantic notions: deducibility, consequence, entailment, equivalence, meaning, content, designation, analyticity, synonymity, and so on. To explain the apparent preoccupation of philosophers with the seemingly semantic issues of meaning and reference, Carnap again turns to his doctrine of "quasi-syntactical" sentences:

> The disguise of the material mode of speech conceals the fact that the so-called problems of philosophical foundations are nothing more than questions of the logic of science concerning the sentences and sentential connections of the language of science, and also the further fact that the questions of the logic of science are formal—that is to say, syntactical—questions.[60]

Accordingly, Carnap shows how to translate all such statements that purport to treat of the relations between language and non-linguistic reality into purely syntactical statements concerning the forms and formal relationships of expressions themselves.[61]

Despite his increasing uneasiness over talk of any relationship

between protocol sentences and immediate experience as the ultimate source of linguistic meaning, Carnap, for a while, found it
difficult to reject altogether the notion of protocol sentences as still
somehow providing the privileged, observational base relative to
which the meaning, or empirical content, of all other expressions
in a language is fixed:

> . . . it is certain that a sequence of words has a meaning only
> if its relations of deducibility to the protocol sentences are
> fixed, whatever the characteristics of the protocol sentences
> may be; and similarly, that a word is significant only if the
> sentences in which it may occur are reducible to protocol
> sentences.[62]

According to this early doctrine of Carnap's, the scientist is free to
adopt any covering laws and higher-level hypotheses he wishes,
based only on such practical considerations as theoretical economy,
expediency, and fruitfulness, just as long as these do not themselves
entail any "protocols" that conflict with any of the multitude of
"ever-emerging" protocols already "stated" or "acknowledged" by
working scientists.[63]

However, while the privileged relation of protocols to direct observation remained implicit in Carnap's account, his stringent formalism prevented him from making any serious attempt to explore
the nature of the observational circumstances (notwithstanding his
early *Aufbau*) that might prompt and warrant a scientific observer
to "state" or "acknowledge" a protocol in the first place. The rather
unsatisfactory result was that even the question as to the nature
of protocols themselves was reduced—so far as logical analysis
was concerned—to questions concerning the conventionally determined syntactical forms of this class of sentences:

> The problem of empirical foundation (problem of verification)
> is an inquiry into the form of the protocol sentences and the
> consequence relations between the physical sentences—
> especially the laws—and the protocol sentences.[64]

This relatively early view of Carnap's presents a highly formalized
picture of language in which the empirical significance of all
expressions is precisely determined by their systematic logical relationships with a core of basic propositions or protocol sentences.

Yet Carnap could offer no intelligible account of how to tie this basic core of language to the world, or our experience of it, in a way that might conceivably justify our extraordinary confidence in it as the final tribunal for the acceptability and significance of all other theoretical claims. The favored protocols, as Schlick and Ayer so clearly recognized, were left "hanging in the air" with nothing to warrant them but their own internal consistency and conventional appeal.[65] Eventually, both Carnap and Neurath ceased to regard protocol sentences as differing in any philosophically significant way from the rest of the statements of science, and consequently less emphasis was put on their peculiar formal, or syntactical, character.

What is conspicuously lacking in such an account of language is a semantic theory, such as Russell originally proposed, sufficient to anchor protocol sentences, or language generally, to observation so as to account for the existence of objective truth and meaning in the first place. To find such a theory that would not violate the positivists' own prohibitions against metaphysics remained a challenge that had to be met before philosophers like Carnap could feel really secure in their new pursuit of logical analysis. Russell's correspondence theory purported to bind the basic statements of science directly to the 'facts' that ultimately made them true or false by means of their individual constituent terms. With the linguistic base thus firmly in place, one could feel free to proceed with a clear conscience to analyze the rest of theoretical science relative to it. Positivists eager to get on with the analytic task of a "rational reconstruction" of science faced a dilemma: either to risk metaphysics and nonsense by talking about the ineffable relations between language and reality, or to risk divorcing scientific truth from objective fact altogether. Neurath and the early Carnap held out for the formal rigor and logical precision so highly prized by analysis, whereas Schlick and Ayer placed a premium on common sense and the need for an intelligible account of objective truth.

The work of Alfred Tarski eventually resolved this dilemma. Tarski's celebrated semantic definition of truth[66] rescued the notion of truth from the resurgent tide of metaphysical debate that threatened to engulf it and vindicated the intuitions of early analysts by providing a formally correct and explicit semantic analysis of truth in terms ultimately so unobjectionable that even Carnap could readily accept them. Tarski furnished a procedure that, when applied to formalized language of a particular type, explained truth for each sentence of the language in terms of carefully specified semantic properties of its component expressions. Under Tarski's formulation (the details of which will be outlined shortly), the concept of satisfaction—a notion more or less equivalent to that of denotation—is first introduced as a relation between the open sentences (or predicates) of a language and various sequences of objects. Truth for all closed sentences of the language, then, emerges as a function of the satisfaction of open sentences from which they are formed.

Tarski took the technical resources of logic and set theory that had been employed so dramatically in the analysis of concepts of mathematics and physical science and brought them directly to bear on the philosophical concept of truth itself. His definition figured as a reduction in two important respects. First, it represented a reduction of the concept of truth, or correspondence, to more elementary semantic concepts. Until Tarski's work, formulations of the correspondence notion of truth had been figurative and suggestive at best, fraught with imprecision and ambiguity. Tarski gave the notion literal sense by capturing antecedently perceived relations between truth and meaning (reference) in a rigorous logical symbolism that linked the ancient and ill-disciplined concept of truth in precise and systematic fashion with a simple semantic notion whose own narrowly circumscribed significance was itself clearly established at the outset. Second, the definition represented a reduction of semantics itself to scientifically acceptable, non-semantic concepts. Under Tarski's procedure, introduction of the concept of satisfaction requires no prior introduction of any other undefined semantic concepts, or of any other concepts—aside from those of logic, grammar, and set theory—whose significance is any more questionable than those of the language for which truth and satisfaction are being defined. This means, for example, that for so-called physicalist language—which, because of its intersubjectivity, Carnap, following Neurath, had adopted as the observational base for all theoretical discourse[67]—truth and satisfaction could now be introduced in terms as innocent and meaningful (apart from those of set theory, of course) as those of ordinary physical concepts. So it was that Tarski presented his results not only as a formal analysis of truth, but also as providing the very foundations of theoretical semantics itself.[68]

Popper, describing how he proposed to avoid use of the concepts of truth and falsity in the 'logic of science' by employing purely "logical considerations of derivability relations" to take their place, goes on, in a footnote added later, to recount his own reaction upon learning of Tarski's work:

> Not long after this was written, I had the good fortune to meet Alfred Tarski who explained to me the fundamental ideas of his theory of truth. It is a great pity that this theory—one of the two great discoveries in the field of logic made since *Principia Mathematica*—is still often misunderstood and misrepresented. It cannot be too strongly emphasized that Tarski's idea of truth . . . is the same idea which Aristotle had in mind and indeed most people . . . : the idea that *truth is correspondence with the facts* (or with reality). But what can we possibly mean if we say of a *statement* that it corresponds with the *facts* (or with reality)? . . . Tarski solved this apparently hopeless problem . . . by . . . reducing the unmanageable idea of correspondence to a simpler idea (that of 'satisfaction' or 'fulfillment').
>
> As a result of Tarski's teaching, I no longer hesitate to speak of 'truth' and 'falsity.'[69]

Carnap's response was no less enthusiastic. He viewed Tarski as having suddenly brought the entire field of semantics under the umbrella of legitimate scientific inquiry:

> In this way it becomes possible to speak about the relations between language and facts. In our philosophical discussions [i.e., those of the Vienna Circle] we had, of course, always talked about these relations: but we had no exact systematized language for this purpose. In the new metalanguage of semantics it is possible to make statements about the relation of designation and about truth.[70]

Once fully acquainted with Tarski's work, Carnap readily acknowledged the inadequacy, or "incompleteness," of his former, purely syntactical approach and quickly developed an array of semantic concepts to replace and supplement the syntactical concepts defined in *Logical Syntax of Language*.[71] From the late 1930s on, beginning with books like *Foundations of Logic and Mathematics* and *Formalization of Logic*, he employed the new "semantical method"—by which he meant chiefly the strict adherence to the object language/metalanguage distinction and use of a logical hierarchy of semantic types—almost exclusively in the investigation of philosophical issues. He now embraced semantics as wholeheartedly and unequivocally as he originally had shunned it:

> To me the usefulness of semantics for philosophy was so obvious that I believed no further arguments were required and it was sufficient to list a great number of the customary concepts of a semantical nature.[72]

However, whereas Tarski's definitions of truth, satisfaction, and some other related semantic notions were purely extensional (that is, belonged not to the theory of meaning but to the theory of reference), Carnap sought to use these results as a basis from which to introduce purely intensional concepts as well. These efforts included a semantic definition of logical truth, the construction of modal logics, and the development of a theory of meaning aimed at demarcating analytic and synthetic statements from scientific (internal) and philosophical (external) existence questions. These later semantic doctrines of Carnap's have already been dealt with extensively here, and our main concern now is with Tarski's original extensional treatment of truth. It was this formal analysis of truth, in terms of the semantic concept of satisfaction, that first legitimatized semantic analysis as a whole in the eyes of early positivists and provided the springboard from which Carnap and so many others since have tried to attack virtually the whole range of outstanding philosophical issues.

5 Tarski's Method

In one of his rarer, more philosophical essays, "The Establishment of Scientific Semantics,"[73] Tarski presents a remarkably concise and lucid exposition of his views on the nature of semantics, the specific steps to be taken in constructing its "foundations," and the philosophical significance of his own technical results in this field. His characterization of the discipline of semantics is that of a purely extensional science, very much along the lines of Quine's own later account of the theory of reference:

> The word "semantics" is used here in a narrower sense than usual. We shall understand by semantics the totality of considerations concerning those concepts which, roughly speaking, express certain connections between the expressions of a language and the objects and states of affairs referred to by these expressions. As typical examples of semantical concepts we may mention the concepts of *denotation, satisfaction,* and *definition* . . . [74]

And there is one more concept to be added to this list, to which Tarski draws special attention:

> The concept of *truth* also—and this is not commonly recognized—is to be included here, at least in its classical interpretation, according to which 'true' signifies the same as 'corresponding with reality.'[75]

While truth, unlike other semantic concepts, seems to represent a *property* of expressions (sentences) rather than a *relation* between such expressions and objects referred to, it is still to be counted among the concepts of semantics, Tarski explains elsewhere, because

> it is easily seen that all the formulations which were given earlier and which aimed to explain the meaning of the word, referred not only to sentences themselves, but also to objects "talked about" by these sentences, or possibly to "states of affairs" described by them. And, moreover, it turns out that the simplest and the most natural way of obtaining an exact definition of truth is one which involves the use of other semantic notions, e.g., the notion of satisfaction.[76]

Though semantic notions are routinely employed in philosophy, logic, and philology, and though the sense of these notions as they occur in everyday discourse seems intuitively clear and unproblematic, all systematic efforts to clarify their meaning in a precise way—from Plato and Aristotle down through Moore, Russell, and Wittgenstein—have failed, Tarski observes, and the use of these concepts in connection with other rather elementary and seemingly obvious assumptions has continued to generate the troublesome

paradoxes mentioned above in section 1. While such historical difficulties have, by and large, warranted the skepticism with which
many have regarded semantic concepts, Tarski concedes, the source
of these difficulties can be traced to rather basic misunderstandings
and confusions about language. These errors, which according to
Tarski went largely unnoticed until Lesniewski, consist of the failure
to appreciate that all semantic concepts must be relativized to the
language to whose expressions they apply, the failure to carefully
distinguish between the language talked about (the "object language") and the language used to talk about it (the "metalanguage"),
and the failure to appreciate the fact that any language that contains
its own semantic vocabulary, and within which the usual laws of
logic hold, will be inconsistent. Tarski contends that once appropriate steps (as outlined above) are taken to avoid these mistakes,

> the task of laying the foundations of a scientific semantics,
> i.e., of characterizing precisely the semantical concepts and of
> setting up a logically unobjectionable and materially adequate
> way of using these concepts, presents no further insuperable
> difficulties.[77]

The task of "laying the foundations of scientific semantics" consists, then, of constructing what Tarski terms materially adequate
and formally correct definitions of all semantic concepts. A "materially adequate" definition is one that successfully captures or
expresses the ordinary or "intuitive" sense of the term defined.
This means, in the case of the semantic concept of truth, "grasping
the intensions which are contained in the so-called *classical* conception of truth ('true—corresponding with reality'). . . ."[78] A "formally correct" definition, on the other hand, fixes the extension of
the term defined precisely and unambiguously by employing in
the definition only terms that are explicitly specified and admit of
no vagueness or ambiguity on their own account. Given the questionable theoretical status of semantic notions generally, this means
that in proposing to define any one such concept Tarski is obliged
to adopt the following resolution: "I shall not make use of any
semantical concept if I am not able previously to reduce it to other
concepts."[79] The entire project is, of course, conceived from within
the framework of the positivist-analytic tradition: "Naturally . . . we
must proceed cautiously, making full use of the apparatus which

modern logic provides and carefully attending to the requirements of present-day methodology."[80]

Tarski sets forth the following "essential conditions" that must be satisfied if definitions of semantic concepts are to be realized: First, the object language, whose semantics is to be constructed, must possess a completely formalized logical and grammatical structure. That is to say, all of its primitive expressions must be listed and the rules of definition by means of which new expressions are introduced by means of primitive ones must be stated. Among the totality of all expressions, those that are sentences must then be specified, and from these the axioms must be separated out. Finally, the rules of inference by means of which the theorems are derived from the axioms must be given.[81]

On the other hand, the metalanguage, within which the semantic concepts applicable to expressions of the object language are to be constructed, must possess its own distinctive terminological resources if it is to be capable of describing the relations between expressions of the object language and the objects they refer to. This means that, in addition to a full stock of conventional logical and set-theoretic devices, it must contain expressions that refer to the expressions of the object language themselves as well as expressions that refer to the same objects as do those of the object language. Expressions of the former sort belong to what Tarski calls the morphology of language and describe structural characteristics and relationships of expressions of the object language. Expressions of the latter sort consist of the expressions of the object language themselves or of "translations" of such expressions. Beyond this, Tarski requires that the metalanguage possess variables of higher order than any of those of the object language.

The paradigm schemata Quine regards as so clearly revealing the sense of concepts of reference are in fact equivalent formulations of those originally devised by Tarski in order to establish conditions for the materially adequate use of the semantic terms he wished to define. According to Tarski, these schemata represent the forms of partial definitions that fix the use of the semantic term in question for appropriately selected individual expressions of the object language. Any "materially adequate" use or definition of a semantic concept is, then, required to entail all its corresponding partial definitions.

Desiring that the definition of truth, for example, "do justice to the intuitions which adhere to the *classical Aristotelian conception of truth*,"[82] Tarski requires that a definition of the term 'true'—in the sense of 'correspondence with reality'—must entail all such statements as " 'Snow is white' is true if and only if snow is white," which are obtained from his formulation of the truth schema,

(T)   X is true if and only if p,

by replacing "X" with the name of any sentence of the object language and "p" with the sentence itself (or a suitable "translation" of it within the metalanguage):

> Statements of this form can be regarded as partial definitions of the concept of truth. They explain in a precise way, and in conformity with common usage, the sense of all special expressions of the type: *the sentence x is true*.[83]

The requirement that a definition of truth entail all equivalences of form T is referred to as Convention T.[84]

An analogous approach is also taken with regard to the semantic concept of satisfaction, which plays an important role in Tarski's semantics. The form of its "partial definitions" (for sentential functions, or open sentences, with one free variable) is schematized as follows:

> For all a, a satisfies the sentential function x if and only if p.

From this schema we can obtain individual "paradigms" of the materially correct use of satisfaction, such as "For all a, a satisfies the sentential function 'x is white' if and only if a is white," by replacing "x" in the schema with the name of any individual sentential function (with one free variable) and "p" by the function itself (after replacing its free variable with "a"). Any materially adequate use or definition of the concept of satisfaction for such sentential functions would, then, be required to entail all partial definitions of this form.[85] (The form of "partial definitions" for the more general case of satisfaction of sentential functions with an arbitrary number of free variables will be discussed in the next section.)

Having thus clarified how we shall recognize the materially adequate use or definition of any semantic term, and being mindful of the formal and expressive requirements that object language and metalanguage respectively must each fulfill, we are now ready to consider the ways in which semantic concepts applicable to expression of a given object language might actually be introduced into a metalanguage. Tarski describes two fundamentally different approaches: axiomatic definition and full reduction to terms of the metalanguage.

Axiomatic definitions of semantic concepts would involve including undefined semantic terms among the primitive vocabulary of the metalanguage and then adding enough new axioms containing these semantic primitives to fix their use within the metalanguage (thus securing the entailment of all "partial definitions" of the term in question). "In this way," observes Tarski, "semantics becomes an independent deductive system based upon the morphology of language."[86]

Despite the apparent simplicity of this approach, however, it has some fairly serious drawbacks from the standpoint of a 'foundational' study of semantics. To begin with, any selection of axioms would be an unavoidably arbitrary and accidental matter based primarily upon practical considerations of convenience and deductive power and dependent upon our actual state of knowledge, or what does or does not happen to appear obvious or self-evident to us, at a given time. There would also be the problem of establishing the consistency of any such axiom system—a matter of particular concern in the present case because of the notoriously paradoxical history of the concepts involved. There is, furthermore, something "psychologically unsatisfactory," Tarski notes, in accepting as undefined primitives concepts that have fostered so much confusion and misunderstanding in the past. Perhaps the most significant objection, though, is to be raised from the point of view of "present-day methodology," to which Tarski has pledged to adhere:

> It seems to me that it would then be difficult to bring this method into harmony with the postulates of the unity of science and of physicalism (since the concepts of semantics would be neither logical nor physical concepts).[87]

Simply put, the axiomatic approach would assume as primitives the very notions positivists and other empirically minded philosophers were most anxious to have explicitly defined in empirically significant terms.

What was wanted, then, was not simply an independent deductive theory of semantics, but rather full explications of semantic notions in terms of scientifically acceptable concepts of logic and physical science. And this is precisely what would be accomplished by Tarski's second approach—the introduction of semantic terms via full reduction to the concepts of the metalanguage. For the metalanguage, as described above, contains only concepts of logic (including set theory) and the "morphology of language," in addition to those of the object language, which will itself contain—if it is a suitably formalized portion of empirically significant physicalist discourse, or reducible to such—only essentially logical or physical concepts. And it is precisely this kind of reduction of semantic concepts, Tarski claims, that can be carried out so long as the metalanguage remains "essentially stronger" or "richer" than the object language; this is to say that the metalanguage must contain expressions of higher order or logical type than any of those of the object language, so that although the object language may be contained in or translated into the metalanguage, the reverse will be impossible.

Tarski therefore proposes to achieve materially adequate reconstructions of traditional semantic concepts without introducing any new realm of empirically suspect or unverifiable discourse. He strictly limits himself to a conceptual base that is essentially no stronger than that employed by Carnap in his syntactical constructions of *Logical Syntax of Language*. While Carnap resorted only to a limited range of physical concepts (those pertaining to the forms and arrangements of linguistic expressions) in addition to the usual notions of logic and set theory, Tarski simply admits physical concepts generally by including expressions of the object language themselves (or their translations) among the conceptual resources of the metalanguage. His goal is not merely to provide syntactical facsimiles for untrustworthy semantic notions, but rather to provide intuitively satisfying reconstructions of the traditional semantic notions themselves.

This entire project revolves around the introduction of the semantic concept of *satisfaction*:

It can only be pointed out that it has been found useful, in defining the semantical concepts, to deal first with the concept of satisfaction; both because a definition of this concept presents relatively few difficulties, and because the remaining semantical concepts are easily reducible to it.[88]

This use of satisfaction is especially significant in the case of truth, in particular, since—as indicated by its partial definition—satisfaction purports to be a relation between an individual sentential function, or open sentence, and the particular objects to which its predicate(s) applies. Thus an account of truth in terms of satisfaction represents an analysis of the truth of a statement as a function of the references of its component terms and raises concerns about the relativity of ontology in a way which an unanalyzed notion of truth does not.

6 Tarski's Definition of Truth

Tarski, and Quine after him, viewed the truth schema as adequately capturing truth for each sentence of a language to which it is applied, but clearly recognized that the truth schema is not itself a general definition nor can it easily be turned into one in any straightforward and grammatically acceptable fashion.[89] What leads Tarski to employ the concept of satisfaction, then, and the particular procedure he proposes for defining truth, are largely technical considerations of what is required of a "formally correct" definition. Tarski discusses these considerations in great detail in his classic paper "The Concept of Truth in Formalized Languages," which appeared in German in 1935 under the title "Der Wahrheitsbegriff in den formalisierten Sprachen."[90] In what follows I will briefly sketch the procedure Tarski proposes, and his reasons for doing so.

The "universal" character of natural languages guarantees they will contain, or can be made to contain, their own semantic predicates, and thus that they will give rise to the infamous semantic antinomies mentioned earlier. In addition, the inherent grammatical ambiguity and "open" nature of natural languages rule out any possibility of formally specifying all their sentences, let alone all *true* ones. Thus, Tarski reasons, a "formally correct" definition of truth is possible only for so-called formalized languages (languages satisfying the requirements of an object language set down in the preceding section).[91]

The language Tarski selects as his object language is that of a fragment of set theory known as Boole's calculus, or algebra, of classes. This language possesses an extremely limited vocabulary and an exceedingly simplified grammatical structure. Its four constants consist of three standard logical particles—the negation sign, the disjunction sign, and the universal quantifier—in addition to the single, two-place predicate of class inclusion, "$\supset$" (to be read "is included in"). Its only other primitive expressions are an unlimited supply of variables, "x_1," "x_2," ..., "x_n," taking classes of individuals as values. From these basic elements all other expressions of the language can be formed.

The simplest grammatical construction in this language is the inclusion, formed by adjoining any two variables to the inclusion sign in the following fashion: "$x_2 \supset x_1$." All other constructions are then obtained from inclusions by the familiar logical operations of negation, disjunction, and universal quantification. The elementary formulas—inclusions—contain free variables and are therefore only sentential functions, or open sentences, neither true nor false in themselves but only satisfied or not satisfied by given classes. Since there are no names available in this language, actual closed sentences occur only when all variables in a sentential function are bound by universal quantifiers.[92]

In striking contrast to the meager vocabulary and streamlined grammatical structure of his object language, Tarski's metalanguage contains a rich supply of logical, set-theoretical, and other specialized devices designed to facilitate its use in studying the object language.[93] Among these terminological resources are translations of all object-language expressions[94] and expressions for referring to object-language expressions.[95] The metalanguage is thus understood to be "essentially stronger" than the object language in the manner required and satisfies the other conditions of a metalanguage set forth in the preceding section.

After stating in terms of his metalanguage exactly what constitutes an "expression" of the language of the class calculus,[96] Tarski proceeds to introduce a series of "metalogical" concepts—including those of *sentential function* and *sentence*, as well as *axiom, consequence, provable,* and others sufficient to establish the class calculus as a formalized deductive system.[97] Although such complete formalization goes far beyond what ultimately turns out to be required to define truth, it does enable Tarski to derive some important "metalogical" results once the notion of truth has been introduced. In addition, given a system whose sentences, axioms, and logical consequences have indeed been thus specified, one naturally asks whether we might not simply define "true sentence" as "provable sentence." The answer to this question is negative, for even in the case of the language of the class calculus Tarski demonstrates that the extension of "true" does not coincide with that of "provable."[98] Moreover, Gödel's results have shown that any deductive system capable of expressing the arithmetic of natural numbers will always contain more true than provable sentences.[99]

Another possibility Tarski considers is that of simply listing all "partial definitions" of truth obtained by applying the truth schema to each formally specified sentence of the object language. However, while a complete list of partial definitions would certainly satisfy the criterion of material adequacy (Convention T) and would fix truth precisely and unambiguously for the language concerned, since the language of the class calculus (like all but the most trivial languages) possesses an infinite number of sentences, a complete list of partial definitions is out of the question.[100]

Tarski therefore considers the alternative strategy of a recursive or inductive definition that would capture truth for each of the object language's infinitely many sentences by first defining truth for all simple, or elementary, sentences (by means of the corresponding "partial definitions" of form T) and then explaining truth for all compound sentences as a function of that for simple ones. However, the elementary formulas of the language of the class calculus, from which all other compounds are formed, are not, we may recall, sentences at all, but rather sentential functions containing free variables, which are not themselves either true or false but only satisfied or not satisfied by given classes. Actual closed sentences are formed by the binding of such variables in quantification, and thus comprise a special class of compound sentential functions.

A direct recursive definition of truth for a language like that of the class calculus would require not only that its expressions include names to replace free variables and form simple closed sentences out of simple sentential functions, but also that there be enough names to make quantification dispensable altogether as a sentence-forming operation; that is, the quantification of the language in question must be open to substitutional interpretation.[101] Such a requirement, however, would significantly restrict the strength of languages that could be considered and would raise additional complications for languages possessing infinitely many names, which could themselves only be specified in a recursive fashion. For these reasons, the approach Tarski finally settles on is that of first defining recursively the concept of *satisfaction* itself for all sentential functions of the language of the class calculus, and then explaining the notion of *truth* for sentences per se in terms of the satisfaction of sentential functions.

In the preceding section we considered Tarski's schema for satisfaction of a sentential function with one free variable. However, in order to explain the notion of satisfaction as applied to sentential functions with any arbitrary number of free variables, Tarski finds it necessary to first introduce into the metalanguage the mathematical notion of an *infinite sequence*, saying not that given classes but instead that given infinite sequences of classes satisfy the sentential functions of the language of the class calculus. The classes that constitute the individual terms, or elements, of each infinite sequence are ordered, or enumerated, in such a way that each variable in a sentential function is correlated with a distinct element (class) of every sequence. The infinite length of sequences ensures that there will always be enough classes to correlate with the variables in any sentential function, while all those extra classes in a sequence that correspond to no variables in a given sentential function are simply to be disregarded.[102] Tarski thus schematizes satisfaction for sentential functions generally as follows:

> For all infinite sequences of classes f, f satisfies the sentential function x, if and only if p,

where "x" is to be replaced by the name of any sentential function and "p" is replaced by the function itself (with its free variables "v_i," "v_j," ... replaced by "f_i," "f_j," ...). By application of this schema, satisfaction conditions for an elementary sentential function of the language of the class calculus, such as "$x_2 \supset x_1$," can be simply stated as follows:

For all infinite sequences of classes f, f satisfies the sentential function "$x_2 \supset x_1$" if and only if f_2 is included in f_1.

Tarski's recursive definition of satisfaction begins, then, with a statement of what it means for any elementary sentential function of the language of the class calculus—any simple inclusion—to be satisfied by a given sequence of classes. Now, it is easy to state satisfaction conditions for given individual inclusions, as was illustrated above, but to state satisfaction conditions generally for any inclusion that can be formed by adjoining the inclusion sign "$\supset$" to any two of the object language's infinitely many variables requires an essentially greater degree of abstraction and generality—to wit, the following:

(1) For all i and j, and sequences of classes f, f satisfies the sentential function formed by adjoining "$\supset$" to the variables, v_i and v_j, if and only if f_i is included in f_j.

Thus (1) states satisfaction conditions outright for all simple inclusions and constitutes the *direct* clause of Tarski's recursive definition of satisfaction. With satisfaction thus directly defined for all elementary sentential functions, the *inductive* clauses of the definition, which explain satisfaction for the three types of compound sentential functions—negation, disjunction, and universal quantification—can now be formulated.

The negation of any sentential function is easily explained as satisfied by any sequence that does not satisfy the sentential function itself, and the disjunction of any two sentential functions as satisfied by any sequence satisfying at least one of the sentential functions. Thus clauses (2) and (3) of Tarski's definition are stated as follows:

(2) For all sequences of classes f and sentential functions x, f satisfies the negation of x if and only if f does not satisfy x.

(3) For all sequences of classes f and sentential functions x and y, f satisfies the disjunction of x and y if and only if f satisfies x or f satisfies y.

Universal quantifications are a trickier, more subtle case; indeed, it is in order to define truth conditions for such constructions that recourse to the concept of satisfaction is required in the first place.

For a sequence to satisfy a universally quantified sentential function with respect to a certain variable, the sequence must satisfy the sentential function itself without regard to what the element of the sequence corresponding to the variable quantified over happens to be. Say, then, that x is a sentential function and that we already know what sequences satisfy it. We will say that a given sequence f satisfies the universal quantification of x with respect to its ith variable if and only if it continues to satisfy x for every choice of its ith element—in other words, if and only if every other sequence identical to f (except, perhaps, in its ith place) also satisfies x. This is formally stated as follows:

(4) For all i and j, sequences of classes f, and sentential functions x, f satisfies the universal quantification of x with respect to v_i if and only if, for all sequences g such that $g_j = f_j$ for all $j \neq i$, g also satisfies x.

Clauses (1)–(4) represent Tarski's full recursive definition of satisfaction for the language of the class calculus, and all that remains now is for truth to be introduced in terms of satisfaction.

We can easily appreciate that whether a given sequence of classes satisfies a given sentential function depends, generally, upon the nature of the particular classes in the sequence that correspond to the free variables in the sentential function. However, when such variables are bound by a universal quantifier, the sentential function will remain satisfied only if originally satisfied no matter what the corresponding classes in the sequence are. In the extreme case of sentences, then, when all variables are bound by universal quantifiers, a sequence must satisfy a sentential function without regard to what any of its elements are, or else not at all. Such a sentence will therefore be either satisfied by all sequences or by none. And from this, an explicit definition of truth—as satisfaction by all sequences—naturally arises:

(5) For every sentential function x, x is a true sentence if and only if x is a sentence and for every sequence of classes f, f satisfies x.[103]

Tarski thus succeeds in directly defining satisfaction for all elementary sentential functions, in inductively characterizing satisfaction for all compound sentential functions in terms of that for elementary ones, and in explicitly defining truth itself for all compound sentential functions with no free variables (sentences) in terms of satisfaction. This definition satisfies the criterion of material adequacy imposed by Convention T,[104] and in the case of the completely formalized system of the class calculus it also permits the derivation of the laws of contradiction and excluded middle,[105] "metalogical" versions of Gödel's consistency and incompleteness proofs,[106] and a number of other more specialized metamathematical results.[107]

It is interesting to note how closely Tarski's formal construction of truth in terms of satisfaction parallels a more traditional, less technical formulation such as that exemplified by Russell's version of the correspondence theory. In each case the central idea is to take a logically streamlined language, identify all its basic grammatical elements and constructions, and then to so plot relations between these grammatical elements and extralinguistic things as to form the basis from which the semantic properties, or relations, of all other grammatical forms—especially the truth of sentences—can be constructed.

For Russell, working with the "ideal" language of his *Principia Mathematica*, the basic linguistic elements are (proper) *names* and *predicates*, which are joined to form (atomic) *propositions*. According to Tarski's procedure, as applied to languages employing standard quantificational logic such as that of the class calculus, these elements are (free) *variables* and *predicates*, which are joined to form (elementary) *sentential functions* (or just inclusions, in the case of the language of the class calculus). The semantic relations Russell posits between (proper) names and the individual particulars to which predicates apply are reflected in Tarski's analysis by the relations of variables to the distinct elements of the sequences of things (classes) to which predicates, such as that of inclusion, apply. According to the Russellian scheme, the truth of a basic proposition is a function of its predicate actually applying to the thing named. According to Tarski's, satisfaction of a sentential function results from its predicate(s) (such as the inclusion predicate) actually applying to the individual things (such as classes) correlated with its free variables, pure truth, as it were, arising through the binding of such variables in quantification, which serves to activate the reference latent in free variables.

According to each scheme, the semantics of all complex constructions is, at least ideally, a function of the semantics of the most basic ones. Although Tarski was forced to reconstrue (somewhat artificially) basic formulas as sentential functions, which are satisfied or not satisfied, instead of propositions, which are either true or false in themselves, he thereby accomplished something that had stubbornly eluded Russell, Wittgenstein, and the early positivists: He managed to reduce the truth of all statements of standard quantificational form, including universal ones, to just the semantics of elementary forms. From this perspective, Tarski fulfilled the Russellian ideal of constructing all truth out of a primitive matrix of term-to-thing relations, designed to fasten the world and language together at their respective joints. That he did so in a vocabulary as chaste as even Carnap could ever have demanded is what sealed his accomplishment in the minds of philosophers like Carnap and Popper as "one of the two great discoveries in the field of logic since *Principia Mathematica*."

Though the full reductionist program was indeed doomed from the start, Tarski's account of truth (and other semantic terms) provided foundations for analytic philosophy in its broadest sense, the sense in which analysis proposes to investigate the *conditions of truth* generally, be it scientific or otherwise, by studying the nature of the *meanings* or *concepts* involved. Popper's allusion to the *Principia* is particularly apt here; just as the *Principia* reduced mathematics to logic and set theory, one might justly regard Tarski's semantic definition of *truth* (which is to philosophy what the concept of *number* is to mathematics) as a reduction of philosophy itself to semantics, reflecting the original positivist proposal to replace traditional metaphysics with linguistic analysis.

5 Truth, Semantics, and Philosophy

1 Applicability of Tarski's Procedure

Although Tarski's semantical methods made philosophers such as Carnap and Popper feel much more confident and secure in adopting an explicitly semantic approach to philosophical questions, the philosophical significance that can justly be accorded Tarski's formal analysis of truth depends heavily on the extent to which it provides a general track to truth for different languages—if not for all languages, then at least for all those we need care about. Tarski himself recognized two important restrictions on the use of his methods: First, he saw them as applicable only to "formalized" languages, as we have described, rather than to natural, or "colloquial," ones. Second, they were to apply only to languages of limited strength in relation to that of their metalanguages. As a result, much of the discussion regarding the philosophical significance of Tarski's work since it first became widely known has centered on the question whether these limitations reflect more the shortcomings of Tarski's methods than those of the particular languages to which these methods cannot be applied.

Tarski regards languages with the classical quantificational structure so admirably exhibited by his formulation of the language of the class calculus as capable, in principle, of expressing not only all formalized deductive knowledge but all empirical science as well.[1] Since it is to just such languages that his methods apply, their alleged sufficiency in this regard is central to his claim for the philosophical significance of his work. Notwithstanding such claims by Tarski, ordinary language philosophers have voiced great disdain for his formal account of truth because of its inability to cope with ordinary discourse. Since ordinary language is viewed as that mode of speech upon which all communication about and understanding of other languages ultimately depends, failure to explain truth for it is reckoned as failure to explain truth for the most philosophically interesting and pertinent case. Tarski's response has been to call attention once more to the source of the difficulties that preclude application of his procedure to colloquial language. These difficulties, he reminds us, reflect the inherent vagueness, ambiguity, and universal character of natural languages rather than any specific defect of his procedure:

> Whoever wishes, in spite of all difficulties, to pursue the semantics of colloquial language with the help of exact methods will be driven first to undertake the thankless task of a reform of this language. He will find it necessary to define the structure, to overcome the ambiguity of the terms which occur in it, and finally to split the language into a series of languages of greater and greater extent, each of which stands in the same relation to the next in [the way in] which a formalized language stands to its metalanguage.[2]

Another sort of response suggested by Tarski and strongly endorsed by latter-day philosophers like Quine and Donald Davidson is to view formalized languages themselves as partial extensions or fragments of the natural languages that contain them.[3] According to this view, a formalized language represents an alternative system of notation, if not an actual analysis of the underlying "deep structure," of a given fragment of a more encompassing natural language. With this in mind, Davidson has sponsored an entire philosophical program that enthusiastically accepts the "thankless task" of reforming those extensive remaining contexts of natural speech that have thus far resisted systematic explication within a system of quantificational logic.[4] From this point of view, then, formalized languages represent not merely portions of natural language but the most intelligible and well-behaved portions. The extent to which Tarski's methods are still inapplicable to remaining portions reflects the extent to which the task of reform has still to be completed.

Another important consideration is the relative strength of a language to which Tarski's procedure can be applied as compared with that of the metalanguage employed to construct its semantics. Tarski considers languages of primarily the Russell-Whitehead sort, which employ a syntactical hierarchy of logical types to differentiate variables that range over different classes of objects. He demonstrates how his procedure can be modified to fit various sorts of languages of "finite order,"[5] but he concludes, at least initially, that the same general procedure cannot be extended to deal with languages of "infinite order," such as that of the general theory of sets.[6]

Tarski's reasoning can be briefly summarized as follows: Assume that we are dealing with an object language that, like the language of the general theory of sets, can express elementary number theory, and that our metalanguage consists of the expressions of the object language plus the means of treating of their syntactical forms—what Quine would call its protosyntax.[7] There is a well-known set-theoretic technique, attributable to Frege, for converting an inductive or recursive definition, such as the one Tarski gives for satisfaction, into a direct, eliminative definition.[8] This gives rise to a problem: As Gödel has shown, any language capable of expressing arithmetic can also be made to treat of its own expressions, or protosyntax.[9] This means in the present case that, if the inductively defined semantics of the object language is indeed reduced to other terms within the metalanguage by Frege's method, then the entire metalanguage—including the semantic predicates applicable to object-language expressions—will be expressible in the object language itself, resulting in paradox within the object language. In such cases, then, truth would appear to be definable for such languages only if the language itself is inconsistent.

Thus, by at first requiring that the object language always be of finite order, Tarski sought to make sure that it would always be possible to so strengthen the metalanguage in relation to the object language as to enable introduction of "satisfies" and "true" as predicates applicable to values of variables of higher order than any contained in the object language, thereby precluding any possibility of introducing these semantic terms into the object language itself. Subsequent to the publication of the original Polish version of "Der Wahrheitsbegriff," Tarski devised a similar way of extending his method to languages of infinite order as well, by employing metalanguages equipped with variables of so-called transfinite order.[10] In either case, Tarski thus makes it a necessary condition of the applicability of his semantic methods that the metalanguage possess "essentially richer" syntactical resources—variables of higher order—than the object language, so that the sets introduced in the metalanguage in order to define semantic properties of object-language expressions will not themselves be definable within the object language.

This standard, however, is not applicable to languages that make no use of the theory of logical types and employ a single style of variable to range freely over all sorts of different objects, as in the Zermelo-Fraenkel and von Neumann versions of set theory. More-over, the requirement that any definition of truth always employ a metalanguage essentially stronger than the language for which truth is defined makes it appear that truth, and all other semantic concepts, will always remain undefined for some metalanguage on which we will have ultimately to depend for our semantic constructions.

Happily, there is, at least in some cases, a satisfactory resolution of these difficulties. The fact that one can inductively define sat-isfaction for a given language is by itself no guarantee that this inductive definition can then be turned into a direct one by means of the Frege technique. Quine has shown how to construct, within a metalanguage consisting of just the notation of his system of *Mathematical Logic* and the basic means of describing these expres-sions (its "protosyntax") an inductive definition of satisfaction for the language of *Mathematical Logic*, which in fact resists conversion into a definition of the direct sort.[11] While all the rest of the notation employed in the various clauses of the inductive definition goes over neatly into the logic and protosyntax of the object language, the predicate "satisfies," recursively defined for each formula of the object language, remains untranslatable within the metalan-guage. Construction of a direct definition of satisfaction in this case would be possible only if the system of *Mathematical Logic* were itself inconsistent.

So long as we are willing to eschew recourse to a direct definition of satisfaction, then, we may still be able to apply Tarski's pro-cedure—even to languages of full set-theoretic power, such as that of *Mathematical Logic*—without having to impose any limitations on the strength of the object language with respect to that of the metalanguage. Both may employ the same logic and appeal to the same ontology, the only palpable difference between them being the presence in the metalanguage of the inductively defined, unreduced predicate "satisfies," which applies to object-language expressions without in any way being interpretable by means of them. Still, if we wish to avail ourselves of the direct kind of definition in order to eliminate semantic terms in favor of the logical and (proto-) syntactical expressions of the metalanguage, the set theory of the metalanguage can always be strengthened relative to that of the object language to permit such a definition while still preventing introduction of the defined semantic terms into the object language. In this case the semantic vocabulary is resolved in favor of a more potent predicate of set membership than can ever be encompassed within the language for which truth is defined.[12]

We may conclude, then, that Tarski's procedure provides a general method of defining truth for any systematized language of standard quantificational structure. Let us agree, in addition, that such languages, whether or not they actually suffice for every conceivable intellectual pursuit, may represent, at least, a standard, or ideal, of logical rigor, precision, and clarity toward which all theoretical discourse strives.

2 Ontological Relativity and Tarski's Definition

Not only did Tarski succeed in formally explicating the semantic intuitions of early analysts, but he did so in a way that lent substance and credibility to the move away from an absolute metaphysics like Russell's to a more language- or theory-relative view of the sort I have described as "linguistic Kantianism."[13] Tarski's analysis presupposes no privileged access to reality apart from the way reality may be represented by a particular language. His procedure provides a technically precise and explicit analysis of the classical correspondence concept of truth in terms of the structural relations between language and fact without appealing to either absolute "facts" or an "ideal" language. It accomplishes this by employing a specified metalanguage to construct truth and its underlying semantics for each given object language on the basis of the relations plotted between the individual terms of the object language and the corresponding elements of its domain of discourse, as described in the terms of the object language itself, or their metalinguistic equivalents. Tarski's semantics thus seems to provide a way of tying a language firmly to its subject matter, sufficient to anchor objective truth and meaning, without any pretense of trying to escape the confines of some particular language in the process of doing so.

Quine, in strongly rejecting any appeal to an absolute conception of truth or reality apart from encompassing theoretical or linguistic considerations, discusses the sense in which truth as defined by Tarski's procedure is meaningfully ascribed to sentences of a given language:

> It is rather when we turn back into the midst of an actually present theory, at least hypothetically accepted, that we can and do speak sensibly of this and that sentence as true. Where it makes sense to apply 'true' is to a sentence couched in the terms of a given theory and seen from within the theory, complete with its posited reality.[14]

It is not hard to understand why Tarski's analysis of truth appealed so strongly to Carnap with his emerging doctrine of the relativity of all significant discourse to a given "linguistic framework."[15] Tarski's methods provide a way of constructing an account of truth as correspondence for any well-defined framework without presuming that any one framework more faithfully represents or corresponds to reality as such than any other. Tarski's semantics seems to provide a way of plausibly representing each framework as a self-contained conceptual system within which objective truth and significance are secure while leaving full scope for the philosopher to exercise his individual discretion to fashion and select such frameworks based only on practical considerations of convenience, utility, power, and the like.

Tarski's relativization of truth to individual languages does not, of itself, entail the Kantian-like, or Whorfian, doctrine that all meaningful perception and conception of reality is necessarily conditioned by language. His semantic method is indeed applicable within such a scheme, but does not presuppose it, for his procedure applies as readily to uniquely "right," "correct," or "ideal" languages as to arbitrarily chosen ones. Tarski's semantics is simply neutral with respect to the more global philosophical questions; explicating ordinary theoretical truth for given theories or languages, it attempts to provide no absolute basis or criterion for deciding between competing theoretical frameworks themselves.[16]

However, although Tarski's procedure makes no appeal to absolute facts nor implies that there is any single right way in which a language or theory ought to describe reality, by defining truth in terms of certain structural relationships between a language and its purported domain of discourse it does require some assumptions concerning the nature of the facts, or of reality, as described or represented by the theory or language in question. This, then, raises concern about the objective significance of the concept defined by Tarski's procedure after all, for we concluded in chapter 3 that, as a consequence of the relativity of ontology, it makes no more sense to talk of how a particular language describes or represents the world apart from some translation of it into a background language than to talk of the nature of the world itself apart from any applied theoretical framework.

In the passage from *Word and Object* quoted above, Quine spoke forcefully of the relativity of all meaningful attributions of truth to a given theory "complete with its posited reality." However, ontological relativity has taught us just how relative a matter even the question of the nature of this "posited reality" itself can be. If truth defined by Tarski's procedure is essentially a function of the features of a given theory's universe of discourse—the objects comprising its ontology—then how can our understanding of 'true' as applied to sentences of the theory be any less relative than our description of the theory's universe? Tarski's relativization of truth to individual languages nicely accommodated the growing recognition that significant talk of the world is relative to some specified framework for discourse, but it is now also clear that the concept defined by any particular application of his procedure can itself be accorded objective significance only to the extent to which we can objectively describe the relevant features of a theory's universe on which application of the procedure depends.

Unlike the analyses of Russell, Wittgenstein, and Schlick, Tarski's recourse to a more primitive semantic concept like satisfaction for the purposes of defining truth was motivated purely by the technical considerations described in the last section of the preceding chapter.

Conformity with our ordinary intuitions about truth was to be ensured wholly through the definition's compliance with Convention T, which itself requires no further analysis of truth in terms of other more primitive semantic concepts but calls only for the entailment of all "partial definitions" of form T. We have observed that both Tarski and Quine regard the ordinary use of 'true' as best exemplified in these paradigms, which raise no specific questions themselves about the objective reference of individual terms in a language and display an ontological neutrality that transcends the twofold relativity of reference proper. They explain truth for individual sentences of a language without requiring so much as a grammatical analysis of the sentence in question, let alone the identification of objects purportedly referred to by any component terms.

However, whereas such individual truth paradigms as " 'Snow is white' is true if and only if snow is white" mention only an individual sentence, truth itself, and the *objective circumstances* under which the sentence is deemed to hold, Tarski's inductive characterization of satisfaction makes essentially stronger demands upon our information about a language. First, in order to explain satisfaction conditions for all complex sentential functions in terms of those for simpler ones, it invokes a full logico-grammatical analysis of the language under consideration, a segmentation of its infinitely many sentences into a finite number of truth-relevant expressions and truth-affecting constructions. This involves the identification of quantifiers, variables, sentential connectives, and other auxiliary devices, as well as all primitive predicates of the language. Second, in order to state outright satisfaction conditions for each simple sentential function, Tarski's procedure invokes specific interpretations of each object-language predicate. This it does, ostensibly, by appealing within the terms of the metalanguage to an ontology of sequences and of the particular classes or kinds of objects ordered by those sequences, to which object-language predicates presumably apply.

Because of this seemingly outright appeal to the specific interpretations of predicates of the object language on the basis of some prior determination of that language's ontology, one might naturally expect that because of the relativity of ontology, Tarski's procedure would encounter the following sort of difficulty: Suppose that we are considering a language interpreted as expressing arithmetic and we proceed to introduce satisfaction for its simple sentential functions by quantifying over an ontology composed of all the natural numbers, explaining satisfaction for each sentential function as a relation between it and the appropriate sequences of natural numbers. But suppose we then change our minds and reconstrue the same language as treating instead of its own notation its protosyntax. We shall now find ourselves appealing to an ontology comprised entirely of the expressions of the object language itself, and satisfaction will accordingly be introduced as a relation holding between the sentential functions of the object language and selected sequences of these and other object-language expressions. Alternatively, we may choose an ontology of one or another subsets of natural numbers, or of sets, each time construing satisfaction correspondingly as a different relation holding between sentential functions of the object language and sequences of different sorts of things.

Does it not follow, then, that a definition of satisfaction (and, derivatively, of truth) according to Tarski's procedure is destined to be as relative to a background language and a chosen manual of translation as are our assignments of numbers, sets, or expressions to a theory's universe of discourse? In such a case it would seem that the truth ascribed to a given set of sentences of arithmetic must be construed as retaining a distinctly numerical character so long as those sentences are understood to deal with the natural numbers, but must be viewed as assuming a different, set-theoretical or even protosyntactical character when the same sentences are taken instead as describing certain sets or the expressions of the language itself. So viewed, what it would mean to call one and the same set of sentences *true* would vary systematically according to how one (arbitrarily) chose to construe and reconstrue the interpretations of their predicates or the values of their variables—thus making, it would seem, objective nonsense out of talk of truth.

As paradoxical as it may first appear, however, this radical relativization of the significance of the concepts of truth and satisfaction is not after all forced upon us by Tarski's procedure, for reasons owing to the very inscrutability of reference itself. Our inability to objectively signal our preference for one among several equally qualified candidates to serve as the ontology of a given theory itself precludes any chance that Tarski's procedure might formally capture such evanescent ontological distinctions in the first place. Once we have determined the basic logical structure of a theory and have identified its quantifiers and its variables, we will get the same truth definition regardless of what objects we choose as values of those variables. As above, we are free to imagine that we are constructing different truth definitions by assuming different classes of objects quantified over in defining the satisfaction relation, but such supposedly different definitions will produce no discernible difference with respect to the total class of sentences each determines as true. Each attempt at a different account of truth will yield the same infinity of T sentences and other metalogical consequences, no matter how ontologies are switched and predicates correspondingly reinterpreted.

Consider, for example, the sentential function "x is a prime number." Dropping talk of sequences for convenience, we can state satisfaction conditions for this function as follows:

> For all a, a satisfies "x is a prime number" if and only if a is a prime number.

This quantified biconditional holds regardless of whether we choose to construe the objects of arithmetical discourse (the values of its variables) as natural numbers or as sets or expressions, interpreting and reinterpreting predicates accordingly. The formula fixes the use of "satisfies" with respect to "x is a prime number" without making any theoretical capital whatever of the purported semantic distinction between reference to numbers, reference to sets, or reference to expressions, or of the corresponding question whether the sentential function expresses a genuine arithmetical condition as opposed to a corresponding set-theoretical or protosyntactical one.

It appears, then, that we may speak intelligibly of given objects satisfying a given condition without necessarily being able to individuate these objects or conditions to the precise extent that has proved so distressingly arbitrary and relative. Our account of satisfaction for "x is a prime number" establishes that "x satisfies 'x is a prime number'" and "x is a prime number" are each applicable to the same things, while leaving considerable latitude for us to choose just what kinds of things these are. But although we may not need to fix the objects of our discourse so narrowly as to always be able to separate numbers from sets or from expressions, in defining satisfaction by means of Tarski's procedure we still need to make distinctions between those alternative selections of objects with which a theory may and may not properly be said to deal.[17]

Of course, only the nonlogical expressions of a theory can be freely reinterpreted without affecting the form or the logical consequences of a truth definition, whereas the interpretations of the logical constants to which the recursive clauses of the definition apply must remain fixed. Indeed, the predicates of the theory are themselves recognizable and distinguishable from one another only by reference to the various ways they are linked together in the laws of the theory by means of the logical apparatus of quantifiers, variables, and truth-functional connectives. When defining satisfaction for the expressions of a theory, then, we are free to quantify over only those domains of objects whose general structural properties permit interpretations of all the theory's predicates in their preestablished logical relations, while making all sentences of the theory come out true. Thus the objects we may choose to see as satisfying the expressions of a theory are just those domains that may serve as a *model*, or *true interpretation*, of the theory in question.

The definition of satisfaction by means of Tarski's procedure does not hinge, therefore, on generic distinctions between the correlated objects of isomorphic domains, but only on the broader, structural features of a universe required for it to serve as the model of a given theory. Separate definitions may proceed by employing as many diverse, albeit isomorphic, alternatives as one pleases without thereby introducing any objective distinction between the versions of truth and satisfaction thereby defined. What matters is not what the objects of a theory are in themselves (this may be conceded as a relative matter or simply relegated to the domain of what Weyl has called "immediate intuitive perception"[18]); what matters is that we can determine such objects "up to an isomorphic mapping." Any consistent quantificational scheme will have several true interpretations. Given such a scheme, Tarski's procedure will deliver one and the same rendition of 'true' and 'satisfies' no matter what decisions are ultimately made in interpreting individual predicates at the atomic basis of the satisfaction recursion.

However, even the significant ontological latitude permitted under

Tarski's procedure is insufficient, in the end, to rescue it entirely from the consequences of ontological relativity and indeterminacy of translation. The problem is that quantification, upon which even the most general sort of objective reference depends, and which, along with the truth-functional connectives, is essential to the applicability of Tarski's procedure, is not, according to Quine, objectively determined in a language at the level of radical translation, as are the truth functions themselves. Quantifiers and variables ultimately boil down to devices like relative pronouns, which belong to what Quine has called the "English apparatus of individuation." Quine contends that these kinds of devices can be read into a language in several mutually incompatible ways, if in any at all.[19] Still, once quantification has been fixed in a language, no matter how arbitrary this may be in principle, a Tarski truth definition for the language clearly transcends all remaining relativity involved in specifying the ontology of the language. In this sense both truth and satisfaction as defined by Tarski's methods remain significantly more absolute than reference proper.

It must also be noted, though, that to whatever extent the considerable ontological latitude allowed for under Tarski's formal procedure enables it to skirt the difficulties ontological relativity poses for questions of reference, or ontology generally, it falls short to the same extent of successfully expressing the more intuitive accounts of reference which analysts have presumed to underlie truth. Tarski's formal semantics makes the weakest possible demands on our understanding of linguistic meaning: It appeals to the *meanings* of words neither in the narrow intensional sense nor in the conventional extensional sense of objects referred to, but only in the still broader sense of the formal or structural properties of objects referred to. In constructing semantic concepts for a theory like arithmetic while making no capital of the difference between talk of numbers and talk of sets or expressions, formal semantics simply makes no capital of much of what is commonly regarded as semantics, or the theory of reference, in the first place. However, failure to render these deeper intuitions explicit can hardly be reckoned a failure of Tarski's formal methods, for it simply reflects the objective inscrutability of these intuitions to start with.

3   The Semantic Conception of Truth and Tarski's Definition

The basis of the semantic conception of truth Tarski seemed to have captured so brilliantly in his formal analysis is the idea that the truth of a sentence is a function of the references of its component terms. This conception of truth has been recognized as an expression of the more general view characteristic of philosophical analysis that has been called the *analytic conception of language*—namely, the view that questions of meaning are, generally speaking, logically prior to questions of truth, so that philosophy, viewed as a discipline essentially concerned with the study of meaning, is therefore engaged in a study of the logical foundations of theoretical science itself. Thus we came to appreciate that Tarski's attempt to formally explicate the semantic conception of truth can also be viewed as an effort to lay the foundations of philosophical analysis itself.

We may agree, then, that Tarski's analysis succeeds in explicating, formally and precisely, the analytic version of the semantic conception of truth to the extent that it is explicable at all, but it can hardly be credited with having captured the full semantic intuitions of the early analysts in a way that would support the view that talk of the meanings (references) of words is somehow on a logically firmer footing than talk of the truth of sentences. Still, this is precisely the significance that is apt to be ascribed to Tarski's work by philosophers who share such analytic intuitions and motivations. Hartry Field, for example, while disputing Tarski's claim to have reduced truth and satisfaction to genuinely nonsemantic terms, still credits him with having accomplished the important task of having reduced truth to a more primitive form of reference, which Field calls "primitive denotation":[20]

> To explain truth in terms of primitive denotation is, I think, an important task. It certainly doesn't answer *every* question that anybody would ever want answered about truth, but for many purposes it is precisely what we need. For instance, in model theory we are interested in such questions as: given a set Γ of sentences, is there any way to choose denotations of the primitives of the language so that every sentence of Γ will come out true given the usual semantics for the logical con-

nectives? For questions such as this, what we need to know is how the truth value of a whole sentence depends on the denotations of its primitive nonlogical parts. . . .[21]

Field's comments here about what allegedly takes place during the interpretation and reinterpretation of a formal linguistic system reveal one source of the subtle confusion about the relationship between truth and reference which underlies the semantic conception of truth.

A formal linguistic system is understood to be one that possesses a completely defined logico-grammatical structure but whose nonlogical vocabulary is left without any specified or intended interpretation. When we interpret such a system, we ostensibly do so by specifying a domain of objects to serve as values of the system's variables of quantification and the extensions of its predicates. The heretofore meaningless but grammatical strings of the system are thus transformed into meaningful sentences that are either true or false. If all of the system's theorems are transformed into true sentences, the selection of objects in question is said to constitute a model or *true interpretation* of the theory. Switching interpretations—universes or extensions—can alter the truth values of sentences of the system, and thus it is natural to think of the truth or falsity of each interpreted sentence as totally determined by the particular extensions assigned its predicates and values assigned its variables. In this way the truth of sentences generally seems to hinge on the prior question of the references of the terms they contain.

However, we saw in chapter 2, in relation to the development of non-Euclidean geometries and the interpretation of formally constructed artificial languages, that full interpretation of a theory or a language takes place only relative to a more inclusive background theory in which we already recognize truth and speak of objects.[22] It was noted there that, just as specifying a theory's universe is not meaningfully different from just reducing that universe to (part of) that of a background theory, clarifying the nature or basis of a theory's truths is not meaningfully different from just reducing those truths to (some of) those of a background theory.

When we choose extensions for the predicates of a system so as to achieve a "true interpretation" of that system, all we actually do is to equate these predicates with those of a background theory in such a way as to identify each formal theorem of the system with an antecedently held truth in the background system. Under the given set of term-to-term equations invoked, the once formal strings become, in effect, "conventional transcriptions" of sentences in the background theory held true apart from the interpretation in question.[23] Thus the chosen method of interpretation, which we construe parochially from within some accepted background framework as endowing terms of the system under interpretation with objective reference of some kind, provides no independent basis whatever for understanding the nature of truth and reference in the system; at most it simply equates truth and reference for the interpreted system with truth and reference for corresponding expressions of the background theory, whatever that may be understood to be.

We have, of course, also observed that in interpreting such a system any method of correlating the nonlogical vocabulary of the system under interpretation with that of the background theory will do as well as any other, so long as logical structure remains intact and each theorem of the system goes over into a true sentence of the background theory. Attainment of truth and preservation of logical structure sets limits on our interpretational options, then, relative to which we have seen that it makes sense to talk of the structure required of a given domain of objects for it to serve as a model of a theory. However, within these limits differences in choices of domains not only do not matter, they do not make any objective sense at all. So, while truth for each interpreted string is fixed relative to any acceptable method of interpretation or translation, reference itself—even if supposed fixed within the background language—will still vary with each such truth-preserving interpretation. The point here is that, just as was noted in connection with radical translation, it is ultimately prior considerations of truth that guide, shape, and define adequate translation and true interpretation and thus determine reference (to whatever extent it is determinable at all), rather than the other way around.

It is not hard to understand, then, how simply misreading what occurs when one proceeds to systematically interpret the terms of a hitherto uninterpreted language can easily encourage the mistaken idea that the truth of a sentence is essentially dependent upon the references of its component expressions. However, after a closer look at what is actually involved in such interpretation, it should also be much easier to appreciate that the reduction of truth to more primitive forms of reference, for purposes of philosophical explication, is problematic in two important respects. First, truth is more absolute, or objective, than reference; second, our understanding of reference itself, however relative and arbitrary, is ultimately dependent upon prior questions of truth.

It was noted earlier that Field views Tarski as having successfully completed only the desired reduction of truth to more primitive forms of reference, and insists that the purported secondary reduction of all semantic terms to nonsemantic ones somehow failed to come off. This puzzling assessment leads Field to offer some revealing comments on the sort of explanation he feels is ultimately required as a philosophically acceptable account of our understanding of truth. What Field seems to have in mind is a more empirical account of primitive reference as opposed to the account rendered in Tarski's formal analysis. Field cites Russell's theory of "logically proper" names, whose connections with their designata are allegedly established by "direct acquaintance," as the "classic," if "wildly implausible," example of such an explanation.[24] As a more promising recent step toward the so-called physicalist reduction of truth and denotation he is seeking, Field points to Kripke's development of "causal theories" of denotation.[25]

Field concedes that individual paradigms of form T adequately "clarify the meaning" of the word 'true' for ordinary (nonphilosophical) purposes, but he rejects such paradigms as satisfactory philosophical explications of truth because they fail to explain truth in terms of more primitive (physical) "connections" between words and things. Field is quick to acknowledge the impossibility of climbing outside one's conceptual scheme in order to "glue it on to reality from the outside," citing the very passage quoted from *Word and Object* in the preceding section as well as Quine's theses of referential inscrutability and ontological relativity in support of this view. However, he goes on to explain that what he is seeking is an account of the connections between words and things from within an accepted physicalist framework, rather than from outside of it:

In looking for a theory of truth and a theory of primitive

reference we *are* trying to explain the connection between language and (extralinguistic) reality, but we are *not* trying to step outside of our theories of the world in order to do so. Our accounts of primitive reference and of truth are not to be thought of as something that could be given by philosophical reflection prior to scientific information—on the contrary, it seems likely that such things as psychological models of human beings and investigations of neurophysiology will be very relevant to discovering the mechanisms involved in reference. *The reasons why accounts of truth and primitive reference are needed is not to tack our conceptual scheme onto reality from the outside; the reason, rather, is that without such accounts our conceptual scheme breaks down from the inside.*[26]

It was pointed out in the preceding section that one of the more admirable attributes of Tarski's procedure for defining truth is precisely that it appears to capture traditional semantic intuitions about the relationship of language to the world as viewed from within a given theoretical framework. Field, now, in seeking a stronger semantic theory than is provided by Tarski, is in fact courting the most extreme consequences of ontological relativity, for it is the consideration of just such an empirical linguistic investigation as Field proposes, undertaken from within an already accepted physicalist framework, with which Quine is concerned in his examination of "radical translation" in *Word and Object*, "Ontological Relativity," and elsewhere, and upon which his dire assessment of the possibilities for meaningful talk about meaning and reference is based. Far from attempting to "step outside of our theories of the world" in order to connect words and things on the basis of "philosophical reflection prior to scientific information," radical translation is conceived as an enterprise proceeding entirely from within our total currently accepted theory of nature.

Working within an explicitly acknowledged physical theory that includes both relevant portions of neurophysiology and a behavioristic theory of learning and verbal behavior, Quine himself develops, in chapter 2 of *Word and Object*, his own very carefully considered "causal theory" of "stimulus meaning," in an all-out effort to make empirical sense of traditional philosophical concepts of meaning while providing a basis for the "radical" translation of one language into another. It was, indeed, the inherent obstacles he encountered in this effort that led to his initial formulation of the thesis of the indeterminacy of translation and the two collateral theses of the inscrutability of reference and the relativity of ontology. The "relativistic thesis" is not, as I have pointed out, simply a reiteration of the familiar point that we can never escape our linguistic or theoretical frameworks in order to view them in their 'true' or 'correct' relationships to extralinguistic reality, but rather that, even if we work unabashedly from within our most credible and creditable theory of the world, talk of what things the words of a language are connected with or refer to makes sense only relative to a largely arbitrary translation of the language in terms of some chosen background language.

Field is right to conclude that our inability to make objective sense of reference results in the breakdown of our "conceptual scheme"—at least to the extent that such conceptual schemes are viewed as frameworks of objective meaning or reference underlying, or implicit in, any particular body of theoretical truth.[27] However, he is wrong to conclude that this would require us to abandon the concepts of truth as well as those of reference,[28] for this conclusion follows only if one insists, with Field, on construing truth in terms of more primitive reference—an attitude we have come to recognize as being in need of drastic reappraisal. If there are, as I have urged, independent considerations governing attributions of truth that not only are prior to questions of reference but also hold constant while reference itself varies, then perhaps truth itself is as close to a 'physical' or empirical concept as we need worry about.

Tarski's procedure, in contrast with the sort of theory Field desires, does not attempt to find an empirical basis for relating words and things. Instead, Tarski simply takes our understanding of the various terms of the object language "at face value" and then proceeds by employing these same expressions, under their assumed interpretations, to formally introduce the notions of satisfaction and truth. It is this characteristic of Tarski's account of truth that renders it formally indifferent to the more extreme sort of relativity encountered when the interpretation of individual terms is explicitly called into question in the manner Field proposes. Still, to view Tarski's analysis as presenting a philosophically adequate analysis, reduction, or clarification of truth remains problematic, for in reducing truth to satisfaction Tarski's account still construes truth as a function of a more primitive form of reference (less relative though this form is than reference intuitively understood). And what has become increasingly clear upon consideration of the truth schema and the methodology of both radical translation and the more conventional interpretation of formally constructed systems as well is the primary character of the concept of truth as opposed to the more derivative nature of meaning and reference. This is what ultimately most seriously undermines the analytic conception of language, for it means that the preference of analytic philosophers for a study of meaning as the basis of theoretical truth is misguided from the start, even if we imagine them satisfied with so rarefied and disembodied a semantic theory as Tarski's formal account of satisfaction would provide.

4 The Primacy of Truth

If one wishes, then, to tie language firmly to its subject matter from within the accepted terms of an applied theory of the world, one can hardly expect to improve significantly upon Tarski's methods. Though use of Tarski's procedure presupposes the more general sort of objective reference associated with those logical and individuative devices whose interpretation at the level of radical translation is itself relative and arbitrary according to Quine, it still displays the considerable ontological latitude noted earlier, formally transcending all relativity arising out of the interpretation of the nonlogical expressions of a language. However, if we are simply viewing our theories parochially, from within, taking their terms "at face value"—as we do naturally enough whenever we put them to good practical use—then Tarski's procedure surely provides as clear and precise a formulation of the classical correspondence theory of truth as we could reasonably ever hope to express formally. Given a full interpretation of a theory, Tarski's procedure reconstructs truth from the inside out, presenting a view of truth for a language as seen through the scaffolding of the given interpretation. That this is ultimately a relative and parochial view is hardly a fault of Tarski's procedure, but simply reflects the nature of our understanding of the language itself, as any account of the 'facts' must necessarily do.

So far as the purposes of formal semantics go, the power and precision of Tarski's methods are unrivaled. But whatever the theoretical status of this discipline is finally determined to be, it can never provide philosophical foundations for theoretical truth. Tarski's defined concept of satisfaction demonstrates broad utility and applicability in charting the internal structures of given linguistic systems, but it hardly qualifies as a clearer or more empirically meaningful concept than truth itself. Tarski's procedure codifies systematic internal relations between the infinitely many sentences of a language and provides a finite, effective method for correlating each such sentence with a corresponding one from the metalanguage, antecedently perceived as stating its truth conditions. In this sense a Tarski truth definition identifies and illuminates structure relevant to adequate translation and true interpretation. However, rather than explaining the basis or ground of truth in a language, the significance of the structural-semantic features Tarski's methods bring to light itself derives from prior judgments and observations about truth in the language under study. Taken in abstraction from questions of truth entirely, formal semantics reduces to a comparative study of the logical structures of quantificational systems, helping to establish the potential expressive power of one system with respect to another and revealing the semantic hierarchy needed to avoid paradox upon interpretation.

The mistaken assumption that truth must necessarily be conceived in terms of more primitive forms of reference leads Hartry Field to conclude erroneously that we must abandon the concept of truth unless we can first make sense of reference. While Tarski's procedure nicely explicates the truth of a theory relative to any given interpretation, we have seen that in achieving such an interpretation or translation in the first place we seem already to be guided by antecedent considerations of truth. The priority of such considerations is already implicit, we have noted, in Quine's method of radical translation,[29] for there the field linguist was seen to proceed forthwith to establish, on the basis of available empirical evidence, what are in effect *truth conditions* of certain native sentences, without having any similar empirical basis for projecting our own object-positing pattern, or indeed any object-positing pattern, on native speakers. It was, indeed, the apparent indifference of such determinations of truth conditions for whole sentences to various possible alternative attributions of internal semantic content that first prompted the theses of the inscrutability of reference and the relativity of ontology.

This same priority of matters of truth with respect to the more subsidiary issues of meaning and reference has been dramatically and explicitly addressed by Donald Davidson in his recent proposal to apply Tarski's procedure for the purposes of constructing empirical theories of meaning, or interpretation, for natural languages.[30] Rather than view Tarski's procedure as a method for formally defining the truth predicate of a given language whose interpretation is assumed in advance, Davidson's idea is to apply the same procedure to a language whose interpretation is not assumed, but for which truth is understood already, and then reverse the direction of explication: "Our outlook inverts Tarski's: we want to achieve an understanding of meaning or translation by assuming a prior grasp of the concept of truth."[31]

Davidson's methodology is most clearly illustrated in his account of the extreme case of "radical interpretation," which is patterned closely after Quine's own description of radical translation in chapter 2 of *Word and Object*.[32] Here the task is understood to be one of constructing a theory of interpretation for a hitherto unknown language on the basis of empirical evidence concerning the truth and the truth conditions of whole sentences in the language. The theory is to analyze the language under study into a finite number of terms and grammatical constructions, which are then equated with those of the interpreter's own language so as to achieve for each sentence of the language in question an individual interpretation in the language of the interpreter. Whereas in Quine's approach the theory takes the form of a *manual of translation* (a dictionary and grammar for the alien tongue, yielding explicit correlations of sentences from one language to the other), Davidson chooses to construe the theory in the form of a Tarski truth definition, yielding, instead of explicit sentence-to-sentence correlations, biconditionals of form T that purport to state explicitly the truth conditions of each alien sentence in terms of a corresponding one from the interpreter's language. Davidson's proposal to make a theory of interpretation fit the form of a Tarski truth definition thus requires that the logical grammar of the language being investigated be resolved into the standard devices of quantificational logic upon which the application of Tarski's procedure depends.

The acceptability of a theory of interpretation when construed in the form of a truth definition is to be judged by its success in predicting truth conditions for individual sentences of the object language, just as when taken in the form of a manual of translation it is deemed acceptable to the extent that it yields satisfactory translations of individual sentences. The evidence upon which the truth of an individual T sentence or the adequacy of a corresponding sentence translation is to be determined is the observed attitudes, or dispositions, of native speakers toward individual sentences. For Davidson these are attitudes of holding a sentence true (or false) under certain circumstances; for Quine they are viewed more behaviorially as dispositions to assent to (or dissent from) a given sentence under certain stimulus conditions. However it is the basis of Quine's thesis of the indeterminacy of translation that such empirical considerations are so inherently limited that they will never provide a basis for choosing among various possible manuals of translation that would all fit (equally well) observed verbal dispositions yet deviate from one another in translations of sentences beyond the reach of independent verification.[33] Under Davidson's approach, the requirement that the language be fitted with standard quantificational logic considerably diminishes the possible scope of such indeterminacy.

The change in Davidson's orientation with respect to Tarski's is reflected by the role assumed by T sentences under Davidson's proposal. Instead of being viewed as formal consequences of a definition of truth, these biconditionals now become empirical consequences of a theory of interpretation. For Tarski the truth of individual biconditionals of form T as "paradigms" or "partial definitions" of the correct use of 'true' for individual sentences of a language was taken for granted on the basis of the assumed interpretation of the language in question, and thus he was interested only in securing their formal entailment as consequences of a "materially adequate" definition of truth for such a language. Once the interpretation of the language becomes the question to be resolved, however, the truth of such biconditionals as statements of the truth conditions of individual sentences of the language can no longer be simply assumed, but becomes instead subject to independent verification.

The change of methodology involved in Davidson's use of Tarski's procedure has significant philosophical implications. Whereas Tarski sought in more or less traditional philosophical fashion to lay foundations for semantics by formally reducing concepts like truth and satisfaction to others of presumably superior epistemological standing, under Davidson's proposal both truth and satisfaction are adopted outright as *undefined primitives* of an *empirical theory of meaning*, or *interpretation*. *Satisfaction*, rather than being formally introduced on the basis of a prior understanding of the expressions and constructions to which it applies, is now invoked as a *theoretical term* in order to help explain the meanings of these same expressions and constructions. *Truth*, on the other hand, assumes the role of an *observational term*, whose applicability to certain sentences under certain conditions is to be determined by considerations independent of the theory itself.

Once the effort to provide a *philosophical clarification, analysis,* or *reduction* of truth in terms of ontologically or epistemologically favored notions is abandoned, the issue of ontological relativity ceases to be so urgent. In Davidson's scheme, "satisfies" plays the role of an unreduced theoretical term invoked to help explain the more familiar phenomena of truth as in physics appeal is made to concepts like "atom" or "molecule" to explain the behavior of ordinary physical things. In neither case are the theoretical terms intended to replace or supplant the more familiar notions intuitively understood at the pretheoretical level of ordinary experience. From this perspective, truth is no longer essentially dependent upon such semantic notions as satisfaction, but only hypothetically linked to them via one or another theory of interpretation. Any difficulties posed for such theories as a result of ontological relativity would then militate only against acceptance of the theory rather than against the significance of talk of truth per se.

There are two fundamental principles that guide the approaches of both Quine and Davidson to radical translation or interpretation. The first and most widely recognized is that our ability to understand and construct the full potential infinity of sentences in a language depends on our prior understanding of the various basic component parts (words) from which all sentences are formed and the basic principles (rules of grammar) governing the ways these parts may legitimately be assembled into whole sentences. In the programs of radical translation and interpretation, this kind of understanding is represented by the translator's/interpreter's fully developed *theory of interpretation*, whether it is put in the form of a manual of translation or a Tarski truth definition. The fact that the full understanding of a language rests on a grasp of basic vocabulary and grammar has, of course, been widely recognized by philosophers from Plato down through Russell and his modern-day successors and has exercised a profound influence on the development of traditional theories of meaning and knowledge. The second principle has been much less widely appreciated. It is that individual words are first learned by abstraction from their roles in sentences, rather than (as classically supposed) in isolation, by associating them one by one with individual presented objects, ideas, or impressions. This crucial feature of early language learning is represented in the methodology of radical translation and interpretation by the translator's/interpreter's explicit concern for sentences held true (or false) or assented to (or dissented from) under various circumstances by native speakers as the entering wedge into a previously unknown language. This fact about the first learning of words seems to have been almost totally unrecognized until the work of the later Wittgenstein, and Quine's explicit recognition of it in his account of radical translation represents a fundamental departure from more traditional theories of language learning.[34]

Appreciation of how our understanding of whole sentences is generally a function of our understanding of the words out of which those sentences are constructed leads one to think that the way to start learning an unknown language is to start pinning down the 'meanings' (references) of individual words independent of their occurrences in such sentences, and this fosters the idea that questions about the meanings of words are somehow logically prior to questions about the truth of sentences—the view I have called the analytic conception of language. While much, if not most, learning of words occurs through defining or explicating them individually by means of other words of the same or another language, the first learning of words is commonly acknowledged as deriving from *observed instances* of their 'correct' *use* or *application*, with or without the additional benefit of direct ostension. This has traditionally been conceived as the setting up of some kind of cognitive or psychological connection between individual words and corresponding elements of the speaker's physical environment, mental life, or sense experience, which then become recognized as the 'meanings' or 'designata' of the words in question. This is the classical picture of language acquisition as a methodical, deliberate, and linear process, beginning with the direct apprehension of the 'meanings' of a few simple and discrete linguistic elements and rules of combination and proceeding step by step to a full mastery of the infinite variety and complexity of all linguistic forms in a language. This picture of language acquisition is also at the root of traditional epistemology, whereby it is imagined that we can methodically abstract from the fullness of our current understanding of nature to a few simple ideas, clearly and distinctly perceived, and then reconstruct all knowledge anew on the basis of only clearly enunciated principles of reason or understanding.

However, though most sentences are surely built up from words previously learned and most learning of new words typically occurs by associating them individually with other words, the initial learning of words does not involve establishing links between individual words and corresponding things named or referred to by those words, but involves, as Quine describes in sections 3 and 4 of *Word and Object*, the learning of words either as sentences or as fragments of sentences.[35] Ultimately all learning of words depends on learning them in full sentential contexts—specifically, *true* sentential contexts. To observe the correct "use" or "application" of a word is simply to observe it *truly* applied—that is, to observe its use or application in true sentential contexts, whether at the observational level in single sentences like "Red" or "This is red" or Quine's classic illustration "Gavagai," or far from direct observation in sentences with rich intratheoretical connections, such as those concerning sets or numbers.

Thus we arrive at a conclusion in direct opposition to the analytic conception of language and the classical analytic version of the semantic conception of truth: that ultimately understanding the meanings of words depends upon a prior understanding of the truth conditions of sentences containing them. This is the crucial principle that is incorporated in both Quine's account of radical translation and Davidson's parallel description of radical interpretation. According to Quine's view of radical translation there appears to be less direct access to truth conditions of individual sentences than under Davidson's analogous approach to radical interpretation, but the important thing is that in either case this access, limited or not, is prior to and independent of access to the meanings or references of individual words. Quine has recently summed up these matters as follows:

> What were observational were not terms but observation sentences. Sentences, in their truth or falsity, are what run deep; ontology is by the way. . . .
>
> Perhaps then our primary concern belongs with the truth of sentences and with their truth conditions, rather than with the reference of terms. If we adopt this attitude, questions of reference and ontology become quite incidental. Ontological stipulations can play a role in the truth conditions of theoretical sentences, but a role that could be played as well by any number of alternative ontological stipulations.[36]

A philosopher-linguist who, like Davidson, has sought to build a semantic theory based upon just such an explicit prior assumption of the concept of truth is Henry Hiz. Hiz describes the point of view of his "aletheic semantic theory" as follows:

> Truth being the basic primitive term of the semantic theory, the spirit with which the theory is built may be called aletheism from ἀλήθια, truth. Aletheism may be also a philosophical point of view, according to which we know first of all that some sentences are true or we know the content of some true sentences; the knowledge of objects, relations, properties is a secondary construction on the bases of known true sentences. And aletheic philosophy may be an epistemic hypothesis or may be a methodological device of organization of our knowledge.[37]

The details of Hiz's program differ somewhat from those of Davidson's. Hiz thinks aletheic semantics can get along with just three "linguistic universals": the concepts of *sentence*, *true sentence*, and the operation of *negation*. Davidson, as we have seen, assumes not only all truth functions, but referential quantification and the theoretical concept of *satisfaction* as well. Also, under Hiz's approach all constructed semantic concepts are treated as relations between linguistic entities only, while Davidson appeals to the notion of satisfaction as a genuine semantic relation between object language expressions and given values of the metalanguage's variables of quantification. The fundamental common denominator lies in the recognition that meaningful talk about the meanings of words pre-supposes meaningful talk of truth, or true sentences, rather than the other way around. And this priority of truth holds firm no matter how determinate meaning, or translation, may eventually be determined to be; demonstrations of either determinacy or in-determinacy of meaning presuppose, as it were, at least some de-terminacy of truth.

5   Indeterminacy and the Status of Semantic Inquiry

There is, then, no privileged access to the truth conditions of sentences in a language through the independently "grasped" meanings of individual words, either for the philosopher or for the field linguist. A theory of interpretation can be judged, it has been noted, only by its success in predicting truth conditions for individual sentences that seem consistent with the circumstances under which those sentences are observed by the interpreter to be held true, or assented to. Davidson explains what this involves:

> The general policy . . . is to choose truth conditions that do as well as possible in making speakers hold sentences true when (according to the theory and the theory builder's view of the facts) those sentences are true.[38]

This policy reflects the large-scale agreement about questions of truth that must be assumed to exist between speakers of a language and anyone undertaking to interpret that language before such interpretation can begin.[39] The circumspect linguist will, of course, further minimize any chance of error, confusion, or disagreement as best he can by concentrating heavily at first on the interpretation of those sentences that are keyed most directly to more mundane and obvious matters of fact until he has developed a comprehensive system of interpretational ("analytical") hypotheses upon which he feels sufficiently confident to rely as a basis for interpreting most other sentences of the language in question.[40] He will venture to construe as false sentences earnestly affirmed by native speakers (individually or collectively) only as a last resort, when it is necessary to salvage a natural and manageable system (theory) of interpretation.[41] However, all such decisions as to what individual sentences are finally to be regarded as truthfully or falsely asserting can only be made relative to the interpreter's own opinion of what the pertinent facts in any particular case happen to be, as viewed and judged from within his own particular theory of the physical world.

All interpretation, then, whether undertaken as a purely conventional enterprise or conducted solely on the basis of an empirical investigation of established speech usage, takes shape only against a fixed matrix of truth and falsity within the interpreter's own language. This fact is of considerable methodological importance for semantic inquiry, for it sets the interpreter—and the philosopher *qua* analyst—apart from the theoretical scientist, though not in a way that supports any claim to a special awareness or understanding of the nature of theoretical truth itself. The scientist may be viewed as working within the evolving fabric of science, helping to reshape and restructure that fabric to the extent that he initiates genuine theoretical innovations and modifications. The interpreter, however, works relative to the fabric of science, or a good-sized portion of it, as fixed and static; he operates outside the normal sphere of theoretical activity along a dimension defined by preestablished truth. This helps explain why Davidson views concepts of meaning and belief—which he regards as interrelated theoretical constructs—as not reducible to conventional scientific terms:

> Theories of belief and meaning may require no exotic objects but they do use concepts which set such theories apart from physical and other non-psychological sciences: concepts like those of meaning and belief are, in a very fundamental way, not reducible to physical, neurological, or even behavioristic concepts. . . . It is . . . the methods we must invoke in constructing theories of belief and meaning that insures the irreducibility of the concepts essential to those theories. Each interpretation and attribution of attitude is a move within a holistic theory, a theory necessarily governed by concern for consistency and general coherence with the truth, and it is this that sets these theories forever apart from those that describe mindless objects, or describe objects as mindless.[42]

Philosophical analysis conceived as a discipline exclusively concerned with an analysis of linguistic meaning occupies no superior vantage point to that of theoretical science, but just the reverse. As a form of semantic inquiry concerned with the interpretation of words, philosophical analysis is dependent upon the thorough-going theoretical presuppositions that guide all interpretation. If interpreting the meanings of another's words seems to occur independently of any conscious considerations of truth or falsity, this is probably just because such interpretation most typically takes place when it would never occur to anyone to challenge or doubt the unexceptional truths upon which it implicitly relies.

Perhaps it is now possible to shed some light on a long-standing controversy. Several of Quine's critics, beginning most notably with Chomsky, have argued that Quine's thesis of the indeterminacy of translation adds nothing of significance to the already widely acknowledged view that physical theory is itself underdetermined relative to all possible empirical evidence.[43] Quine, for his part, has continued to maintain since *Word and Object* that the indeterminacy of translation does in fact constitute a distinct, second dimension of underdetermination, over and above that of theory itself:[44]

> Though linguistics is of course a part of the theory of nature, the indeterminacy of translation is not just inherited as a special case of the underdetermination of our theory of nature. It is parallel but additional.[45]

The distinction which Quine has thus attempted to draw has proved to be elusive for philosophers—including many sympathetic with Quine's overall point of view—to grasp, but it should be easier to understand once one has come to appreciate fully the priority of truth over meaning, and the secondary, dependent character of semantic issues generally, relative to those of truth, or theory, proper.

The point is this: We know, or think we know, as part of our own theory of nature, that any such theory is underdetermined by available evidence. However, the translator or interpreter necessarily undertakes his investigation by first presupposing—no matter how implicitly or un-self-consciously—some such theory (presumably his own) and then proceeds to seek a satisfactory way of reading this theory, more or less intact, into the language he is investigating. That there will always be many alternative, equally valid, yet mutually incompatible ways of reading such a theory into another

language without significantly disturbing the totality of truth asserted by the theory—as underdetermined as this truth itself may
be—is, in essence, Quine's thesis of the indeterminacy of translation,
or meaning:

> . . . for now adopt my fully realistic attitude toward electrons
> and muons and curved space-time, thus falling in with the
> current theory of the world despite knowing that it is in prin-
> ciple methodologically underdetermined. Consider, from this
> realistic point of view, the totality of truths of nature, known
> and unknown, observable and unobservable, past and future.
> The point about indeterminacy of translation is that it with-
> stands even all this truth, the whole truth about nature. This
> is what I mean by saying that where indeterminacy of trans-
> lation applies, there is no real question of right choice; there
> is no fact of the matter even to *within* the acknowledged un-
> derdetermination of a theory of nature.[46]

Indeterminacy of translation enters when translational options
present themselves relative to the same matrix of truth and falsity
within the translator's own language, and only after all questions
of genuine theoretical significance have, at least for the time being,
been put aside. Our interpretations of, or attributions of meaning
to, the expressions of a language are thus essentially dependent
upon our prior perceptions of the truth about matters of fact generally, from within the parochial confines of our own (underdetermined) theory of the world, in a way that more genuine
theoretical hypotheses are not. The point here is not the familiar
one of the interdependence of hypotheses within a single system,
but rather the dependence of one system of hypotheses (the translator's) upon another (the theoretician's).

It is evidence, together with holistic considerations of convenience,
simplicity, and the like, that warrants our adoption of a system of
hypotheses or assertions as true. But such evidence does not in
any straightforward way equate with the truth conditions, or meanings of individual sentences, upon which the meanings and references of individual terms in a language ultimately turn. Where
interpretation begins is where theorizing proper leaves off. What
are firmest and most absolute for theory proper are observation
sentences.[47] What are firmest and most absolute for interpretation

are in effect sentences describing the truth conditions of observation sentences (namely, T sentences of observation sentences). If we think of our currently accepted system of beliefs about the world in terms of Quine's famous figure from "Two Dogmas" as a "field of force whose boundary conditions are experience,"[48] then perhaps it is not too farfetched to think of a theory of interpretation, analogously, as a field of force whose boundary conditions are just some such theoretical system. Thus, although theory remains underdetermined relative to evidence, Quine's contention is that meaning or translation is similarly underdetermined relative to theory itself.[49]

Once the secondary, dependent methodological character of semantic inquiry relative to that of theoretical science proper is recognized, issues such as those of the indeterminacy of translation, the inscrutability of reference, and the relativity of ontology likewise assume only a secondary importance. Once meaning and reference are seen as limited and conditioned by prior considerations of truth in very much the same fashion that classical philosophical analysis has supposed truth to be a function of meaning or reference, then any arbitrariness or relativity allegedly involved in determining meaning or reference ceases to have any direct implications whatever so far as objective truth or our understanding of it is concerned.

Disagreement is still possible, of course, with regard to Quine's thesis of the indeterminacy of translation, even when this thesis is clearly distinguished from that of the underdetermination of theory and one is fully prepared to acknowledge the priority of truth over meaning. For example, Davidson's a priori requirement that a theory of interpretation assume the form of a Tarski truth definition necessitates, as we have seen, "fitting" the language in question "to the procrustean bed of quantification theory," thereby ruling out in all likelihood the kind of radical indeterminacy arising out of Quine's more Humean attitude toward the form an acceptable manual of translation may take.[50] However, any differences here between Quine and Davidson with respect to the indeterminacy of translation are actually of only very limited philosophical interest, given their much more important common methodological orientation to translation and interpretation. For this reason it may be that the real value of Quine's critical examinations of traditional concepts of meaning lies ultimately in the positive light they have helped to shed on the true nature and method of semantic inquiry, and it is in this spirit that Davidson has called the "basic ideas" set forth in Quine's critical discussions of these matters, upon which his own program of radical interpretation is admittedly based, "one of the few real breakthroughs in the study of language."[51]

The theoretical scientist, then, is concerned with the construction and development of systems of truths about the world; the translator, or interpreter, is concerned only with the translation or interpretation of such truths. When evidence wanes, the theoretical scientist chooses among genuine *theoretical* alternatives; his interest is ultimately in reasons, pragmatic and otherwise, for adopting or rejecting given sentences as true or false. The interpreter, confronted with the choice among various possible alternative manuals of translation, is choosing among *notational* alternatives; his interest is in reasons, pragmatic and otherwise, for couching one and the same set of truths in one system of notation or another. The decisions of the theoretical scientist effect changes in theory; those of the interpreter effect only changes in the formal or notational properties that may be ascribed to a given set of truths.

If the task of grammar is to provide a finite specification of the sentences of a language in terms of a finite list of basic expressions and constructions,[52] then the task of semantics may be described as to map sentences from one language onto those of another, or from one part of a language onto those of another part of the same language, through a correlation of these basic expressions and constructions, but subject to the additional constraint that the mapping preserve both truth and truth conditions to the extent that these are theoretically determinable. Where theoretically equivalent sets of interpretational hypotheses determine different truth conditions, or even different truth values for the same sentences, these apparent material differences ultimately reflect only different choices of basic vocabulary and grammar and the method by which these are correlated with those of the background language.

It should be of little surprise, then, that semantic analysis can provide no original information about the world or our knowledge of it. We can expect only an indirect reconstruction or reflection of what our own empirical science and common understanding already tell us, together with information about how this might be expressed within different systems of notation. Semantic analysis discovers notational rather than theoretical options. Given the full corpus of antecedently established truth as parameter, it seeks formal principles for constructing that truth, or for correlating it (or parts of it) with other truth. It seeks truths only about the forms and formal relations of true sentences. It is constrained at its borders not by observation or experience but by antecedently perceived truth. Semantic interpretation is shaped by the truth as seen from the vantage point of some accepted theory of the natural world, rather than by the evidence that shapes such a theory. The interpretational hypotheses of the interpreter or analyst have extra-linguistic significance only relative to the already accepted doctrine of a background theory, but they provide no independent basis even for understanding that doctrine let alone believing it.

The characterization of semantics as primarily a formal or notational discipline brings to mind Carnap's original description of logical analysis as the "mathematics and physics of language" in *Logical Syntax of Language*. It was, as I have noted, Carnap's original view that all semantic statements are reducible to syntactical ones concerning the form and shape of symbols, and indeed his early syntactical doctrine bears a remarkable resemblance to something like Hiz's "aletheic semantics." Like Carnap, Hiz construes semantic relations as relations holding between linguistic entities and explains the meanings of expressions in terms of the class of their formal "consequences." The major and very crucial difference is that whereas Carnap also sought to define truth formally and viewed such syntactical investigations as clarifying the "foundations" of scientific knowledge, Hiz's program relies on a prior appeal to a primitive, undefined concept of truth in order to build a semantic theory that aims much more modestly to elucidate only translation and interpretation themselves:

> The theory is rather simple, maybe even simple-minded. It minimizes philosophical involvement; its content is more neutral philosophically than is the case in other semantic theories. By this and, perhaps, by some other properties the presented theory should be more useful in establishing a scientific study of semantics and in discovering some non-trivial facts about the semantics of languages.[53]

Such an outlook is a far cry from that of classical analysis, which wanted to reduce all philosophy to something like syntax, semantics, or both.

It may seem, however, that a problem still remains in explaining how we come to learn and understand a language if Quine is right about indeterminacy of translation and there is no single right way to construe the grammar and meanings of words in a language, even from within a clearly defined theoretical perspective. The answer is, of course, that understanding a language no more requires grasping individual 'meanings,' 'ideas,' or 'concepts' than scientific knowledge requires prior perception of "essences" or "basic categories of existence." The idea of a fixed conceptual scheme mediating between us and our theories of the world is as useless and as meaningless as the idea of a fully determinate extralinguistic reality lying beyond all theoretical construction.

Just as the search for absolute metaphysical truth represents a failure to perceive the indeterminacy, as it were, of extralinguistic reality—the underdetermination of our theories of the world by brute experience—so semantic or linguistic analysis undertaken with high philosophical purpose represents a comparable failure to perceive the indeterminacy of meaning—the underdetermination of our theories of interpretation or translation by theory in general. As Quine expresses it in *Word and Object*,

> The indefinability of synonymy by reference to the methodology of analytical hypotheses is formally the same as the indefinability of truth by reference to scientific method. . . . Also the consequences are parallel. Just as we may meaningfully speak of the truth of a sentence only within the terms of some theory . . . so on the whole we may meaningfully speak of interlinguistic synonymy only within the terms of some particular system of analytical hypotheses.[54]

Both our understanding of the world and our understanding of that understanding are equally underdetermined. The indeterminacy of meaning need represent no insuperable difficulty to a semantic theorist, though, just as long as he, like Hiz, clearly recognizes semantics' lack of direct philosophical import as well as the considerable debt it owes to our prior grasp of truth within our working theory of nature. Semantic inquiry reveals neither metaphysical truth about the nature of the world nor epistemological data about our conception of it. It is concerned not with ideas, meanings, and concepts, but with largely relative matters concerning the structural properties of symbol systems.

The implications of this picture of semantic inquiry are perhaps most damaging for philosophical analysis in the form of classic logical positivism, as well as for those more modern versions of analysis that reject traditional metaphysics out of hand yet continue to advocate a special sort of philosophical inquiry directed solely at the study and understanding of human linguistic activity. This substitute form of first philosophy may seek new ways of answering the old philosophical questions, may interpret such questions as only disguised linguistic or conceptual questions, or may simply declare them to be pseudo-questions altogether. Whether the language of philosophical explication is conceived as ideal or ordinary matters little. Whether the stated objective is descriptive metaphysics or conceptual anthropology, the consequences are the same. The nature of the meaning or conceptual content imagined inherent in language remains essentially beyond the scope of objective determination and systematic expression. It can be described meaningfully only relative to some background theory and a particular manner selected for translating into it.

For those philosophers who would pursue linguistic analysis only as an adjunct to more traditional metaphysical inquiry, the implications of our assessment of semantics is perhaps less serious. Philosophical analysis is no worse off than metaphysics, but it is no better off either. Perhaps Cornman's meanderings through language and back again to metaphysics in order to help answer questions about linguistic reference itself best illustrate the thoroughgoing interdependence of absolute metaphysical questions and absolute questions concerning the meaning or reference of words.

6   Philosophy

Perhaps our concern here with what appear to be the primarily negative metaphilosophical implications of Quine's writings on meaning and translation has tended to raise questions concerning what the proper role of philosophy could conceivably be, or whether there is indeed any legitimate function to be served by philosophy at all. With regard to the idea of a special philosophical realm of inquiry completely distinct from that of theoretical science, where philosophers roam free to exercise their extraordinary powers of insight, intuition, and imagination unhampered by the mundane constraints of the ordinary empirical scientist, the implication of Quine's work is clearly that such a realm is a dream world pure and simple. There remain, however, at least three distinguishable kinds of philosophical activity that may be legitimately pursued within the overall Quinean perspective sketched here, and in a manner and spirit continuous with that of theoretical science generally. In addition, each of these three modes of philosophizing displays a characteristic concern with linguistic issues of one form or another, though none of them can be equated with first philosophy or analysis in any standard metaphilosophical sense.

Science has been called "self-conscious common sense." This self-consciousness manifests itself in language, in the systematic articulation of sentences—one hopes, true sentences—about the world. Science thus tries to make explicit in theory that which is implicit in practice, and by means of this explicit systematization to provide additional guidance for practice. There is, then, a rather clear sense in which philosophy may be said, somewhat analogously, to represent science itself gone self-conscious. From this point of view, philosophy tries to make explicit in theory (philosophy) that which is implicit in scientific practice. The characteristic scientific concern with the systematic construction of sentences about the world is reflected by the philosophical concern with the formulation of sentences about such sentences. As the product of scientific activity is theory of nature, so that of philosophy, construed as self-conscious science, is theory of theory. And as the most prized feature of the product of scientific activity is the truth of its sentences or theories, so, too, the most prized feature of the product of this kind of philosophical activity is truth about such truth—its origin and extent, its ground and nature. Philosophy as the theory of theory, or the science of science, is simply philosophy as the theory of truth.

The philosopher as theorizer about theorizing is the epistemologist. He is preoccupied with the theory of knowledge—of scientific or theoretical truth. He seeks theoretical truths about truth, not just the structural properties of systems of notation. Truth is not simply to be defined away in some other terms, nor treated as an inessential concomitant of a notational investigation. It takes its place as the principal theoretical concept of a portion of empirical science whose scope is the entire domain of scientific activity. "True" is for the science of science what $\in$ is for set theory: an undefined primitive, our understanding of which depends pretty much upon the degree to which we succeed in systematically articulating its various theoretical interconnections. Likewise, its initial intuitive intelligibility is just as invaluable an aid in helping us to originate explicit theoretical postulates in the first place. Such a theory is, in outline, like the "axiomatic definition" of truth suggested by Tarski,[55] except that what Tarski has in mind is a set of axioms whose other nonlogical primitive terms are entirely semantic, whereas the scope of the postulates envisioned here would encompass the entire range of human theoretical activity.

Philosophy as the theory of truth includes portions of psychology, sociology, anthropology, and biology, in addition to physics and the science of science proper. The demarcations cannot be drawn sharply but simply grade off, the theory of truth being after all continuous with the rest of theoretical science and thus enjoying the same observational base. One excellent example of philosophy as the theory of truth is the doctrine of the underdetermination of theory itself. Quine describes this as follows:

> . . . theory in physics is an ultimate parameter. There is no legitimate first philosophy, higher or firmer than physics, to which to appeal over physicists' heads. Even our appreciation of the partial arbitrariness or underdetermination of our overall theory of nature is not a higher-level intuition; it is integral to our underdetermined theory of nature itself, and of ourselves as natural objects.[56]

The great bulk of the research central to this theory of truth is, then, simply most of what has historically been carried on as the philosophy of science and the theory of knowledge. Other interesting and significant examples are such investigations as Quine's extensive scrutiny of the tasks of the grammarian and the translator, which involve a (theoretical) assessment of the methods and theoretical status of these disciplines, from which Quine's doctrine of the indeterminacy of translation was, of course, derived. The philosopher, as theoretician of truth, makes decisions that make a difference to theory. Like the theoretician generally, his determinations relate directly to the total amount of truth purported to hold at any given time. They are genuinely theoretical, therefore, and quite unlike the notational decisions made by the translator or the interpreter.

Of course, philosophy as the science of science includes metaphilosophy (the theory of philosophy) as well, and any further such meta-investigations that could conceivably be launched. Thus even the extensive writings of Carnap and other positivist or linguistic philosophers concerning the proper method of philosophizing can easily be granted full theoretical and "philosophical" status, even though their claims are rejected as false and erroneous. The same is the case with Tarski's endorsement and defense of his semantic definition of truth (as distinct from the definition itself). This is not a view of philosophy, after all, that precludes the possibility of meaningful philosophical dialogue.

Now there also remains a good deal that may still be said for philosophy in a residual sense of conceptual, linguistic, or semantic *analysis*. This is philosophy viewed as a notational enterprise in which broad considerations of theoretical truth are only indirectly involved. Its business is the creative mathematical exploration of the formal properties of linguistic or theoretical systems. Though its direct theoretical import is minimal, a true picture of its importance for science can be reached only by appreciating the role it plays in the context of actual theory construction. The results of analysis do not constitute theoretical discoveries, but they can strongly suggest theoretical innovation in the form of the adoption of new theories or the simplification and refinement of existing ones.

Analysis thus seeks to delineate the formal properties of linguistic or theoretical "coordinate systems" and bring to light structural analogies and relationships between different systems or different portions of the same system. In so doing, it reveals possible channels of intertranslation or the chance for more localized definition and paraphrase. Theoretical innovation of a genuine sort, then, may come as a response to the possibility for increased theoretical power and simplicity revealed by the analyst's "analytical hypotheses." Truth or falsity in the systems explored is not the direct concern of the analyst qua analyst. He is obliged only to pursue the truth concerning the mathematical relations he plots from system to system. The net product of such analysis is the discovery of notational options and the possibilities of theoretical reduction and consolidation.

The most illustrious successes of analysis as described here are still those that have been achieved in work on the "foundations" of mathematics. This includes Descartes' invention of analytic geometry, the formal construction of non-Euclidean geometries and their various interpretations, and the various set-theoretic reductions of mathematics. Similarly, "phenomenalist" constructions of the sort attempted by Carnap in the *Aufbau* or by Goodman in *Structure of Appearance*, representing similar thoroughgoing and systematic efforts aimed at physical language, are also included in this view of analysis. The theoretical reduction of thermodynamics to mechanics, on the other hand, represents striking analytical success within a more limited systematic sphere. Indeed, the plethora of attempts in twentieth-century philosophical literature to reduce the mental to the physical, or to analyze the language of ethics, and so on, are all representative of analysis in the current sense, fragmentary and piecemeal as these efforts are. The point is, however, that the establishment of such analytical hypotheses of itself is entirely neutral as to whether entities such as sets or numbers really exist; nor do they lend the slightest support to the epistemological thesis that our knowledge of physical objects derives from our knowledge or acquaintance with sense data. These constructions, no matter how simple and straightforward, will never prove by themselves that mentalistic theories of human behavior and action are false. These are the decisions of the scientist or philosopher qua theoretician, not of the "analyst."

Thus there is truth in the view that analysis is independent of empirical science in general—not, as positivists and many linguistic analysts have thought, because it asks questions that are somehow logically prior to those of science itself concerning the actual meaning or the conceptual content of the language of science, but only because they do not as a rule touch directly on issues of truth and falsity to begin with. The fact that numerous false claims have been and will no doubt continue to be made concerning the significance of analysis militates not at all against its indubitable merits properly characterized. The true value and utility of the analyst's work is hardly to be measured in relation to what he may have erroneously supposed himself to be doing, nor according to what others may just as mistakenly have supposed him to have done. Analysis need make no inflated claim to ontological or epistemological insight in order to merit the kind of attention it has received from philosophers.

The third sort of philosophical enterprise is most familiar from Quine's writings. This is philosophy that, like the theory of truth, is fully continuous with theoretical science proper; however, rather than dealing with the epistemological sort of question about theory and truth, it treats the questions that are more apt to be termed "metaphysical" and that more directly concern the world and existence. These are questions concerning the existence of minds, intentions, and ideas in psychology; sets and numbers in mathematics; molecules, atoms, waves, and particles in physics; and so on. These are questions of linguistic reference according to some philosophers and linguistic proposals according to others. The position here is that they may be considered linguistic proposals just as long as all scientific questions are taken so—that is, as questions about whether to adopt some particular sentence or theory as true. The point, of course, is that there is no sharp demarcation to be made between purely "factual" and purely "linguistic" questions in the sense intended by proponents of the proposal theory (such as Carnap, according to his doctrine of "linguistic frameworks").

Quine has repeatedly addressed the task of characterizing this kind of philosophical activity,[57] and I will not dwell on it here except to underscore that the more "philosophical" kinds of existence questions are regarded simply as those farthest from the observational level at which, or nearer to which, scientific agreement is more readily achieved. These are issues with the broadest systematic implications, and disagreement over them is indicative of deep differences in overall theoretical perspective. It is for this reason, Quine has explained, that discussion in these areas so often "ascends" to explicit treatment of the theories themselves.[58] This move to talk of language which Carnap saw as signifying the pseudo-scientific nature of these questions really serves, according to Quine, only to sidestep time-wasting confusion and needless question begging by making theoretical commitments clear and explicit. As Quine has pointed out, all questions of existence, about anything from wombats to classes, involve making practical theoretical choices; it is just that those about wombats or unicorns will be resolved with minimal disturbance to the encompassing theoretical network, while those about numbers or classes, for example, may require wholesale theoretical shifts and realignments on the broadest scale when minds are changed.

The assimilation of philosophy to general theoretical science is frequently thought to deprive philosophy of its normative or critical role in telling us how we *ought* to think as opposed simply to how we *do* think as a matter of fact. Such views, which accentuate sharply the normative/descriptive distinction, usually tend to exaggerate the purely factual nature of science; those who hold them fail to see that science is also a discipline of enormous normative scope. Legislative postulation, the general mode of scientific hypothesis, is essentially a matter of human proposal and decision. Theory is not simply and unequivocally "determined by the facts," but instead involves theory-wide "practical" considerations of simplicity, convenience, utility, and efficacy, which have become increasingly recognized for their important role in theory construction. Thus the problem of deciding what is the best or most desirable of alternative views of the same set of "facts," so to speak—deciding what we ought to think—is a regular feature of standard scientific operating procedure.[59]

The idea that construing philosophy as an integral part of theoretical science strips it of its normative, critical, or regulative role is itself a by-product of the outworn view that there is, after all, a hard and fast distinction to be made in such matters between questions of value and questions of fact. Rejection of the fact/value (or pragmatic/theoretical) distinction in this context no more entails that all questions of value are *really* questions of fact than that all questions of fact are *really* questions of value. It represents, rather, an appreciation of the subtle reciprocity of factual and normative considerations, in varying degrees, throughout the entire realm of scientific inquiry. That a theoretical account of truth and theory construction should tell us how we should think is no more anomalous than that physics should tell us how we should look at the world in general. It is no more surprising that philosophy in this fashion should provide rules for the scientist or the theoretician to follow than that the physicist should similarly provide rules for the engineer. The move that treats philosophy as a fully scientific discipline involves no abdication of critical-normative responsibility so long as one is not committed to an impoverished and outmoded view of theoretical science.

The "naturalist" view outlined here thus makes room for distinctive characterizations of philosophy in three of its primary modes: epistemological, metaphysical, and analytical. In so doing, it has been argued, it neither precludes the possibility of significant philosophical and metaphilosophical disagreement nor arbitrarily excludes from the realm of philosophical issues questions traditionally deemed meaningful. Yet this view also makes clear a sense in which it is still legitimate to continue to characterize philosophy as a peculiarly "linguistic" endeavor.

The linguistic character of philosophy as the theory of truth is seen in the explicitly linguistic character of its subject matter, namely theories and their component sentences. Indeed, truth remains essentially a property of linguistic expressions—sentences and theories. Similarly, the "semantic ascent" routinely employed by philosophers when treating of the most general sorts of theoretical issues has also been accounted for in a way that makes these linguistic concerns seem natural enough but hardly indicative of a serious breach with conventional scientific methodology. And, of course, analysis itself has not been rejected outright as a philosophically relevant activity, but merely restricted drastically with respect to the nature of its purported theoretical import. As a matter of fact, our characterization of analysis was such as to portray it as so purely a linguistic activity as to have virtually no direct bearing at all on genuine theoretical issues. Analysis, when separated from erroneous metaphilosophical doctrines, is actually more linguistic than originally supposed, while the admittedly linguistic character of the epistemological and metaphysical tasks detracts in no way from their scientific status but serves only to clarify it.

This characterization of philosophy as a linguistic enterprise is therefore thoroughly consistent with the rejection of philosophy as essentially logical, semantic, or conceptual analysis. According to the classical view, best exemplified by early positivism, analysis is a source of ontological and/or epistemological insight and goes the furthest toward answering traditional philosophical questions about the world and our knowledge of it—questions of truth and existence—whereas according to the view offered here it contributes by far the least in these same respects. Traditional metaphysical questions about what exists or is real can ultimately be accommodated quite comfortably within the legitimate bounds of theoretical science, as can the investigations of the epistemologist into the source and extent of truth and human knowledge. However, when understood as a separate form of philosophical inquiry, analysis must be relegated to a purely secondary and ancillary theoretical status, only indirectly related to the others.

It is ironic, then, in light of the "linguistic turn," that, rather than provide the underpinnings for theoretical science, analysis comes up short, methodologically, relative to the rest of science. Indeed, to the extent that it is prior considerations of truth upon which interpretation and translation both depend, rather than the other way around, it is more correct to view theoretical science as providing the underpinnings of analysis. Thus, Rorty, noting Quine's rejection of a "first philosophy" to which to appeal "over physicists' heads," objects that Quine, in holding the indeterminacy of translation to be other than just a special case of the underdetermination of physics, is himself suggesting that there *is* such a "first philosophy" to which to appeal over linguists' (interpreters', translators', analysts') heads.[60] And, interestingly enough, there is now a very clear sense in which Rorty can be said to be right in this assessment, just so long as the "first philosophy" in question is understood to be none other than the whole of theoretical science itself, including philosophy as metaphysics and epistemology.

Notes

Chapter 1

1 Wittgenstein (2), 4.46—4.4661, 5.142.

2 Ayer (3), p. 29.

3 Schlick (2), p. 48; (5), pp. 55–57.

4 Carnap characterized philosophy as the "mathematics and physics of language" in (9), pp. 282–284; but later came to see investigations of meaning as reducing ultimately to a task like that of the field linguist. See, e.g., his (11).

5 Carnap (7), p. 250.

6 See, e.g., the preface to Wittgenstein (2), as well as Bradley, pp. 1–6.

7 Thompson, p. 138.

8 Schlick (2), p. 44.

9 Ayer (3), p. 33.

10 See, e.g., Sagal.

11 Schlick (2), p. 48.

12 Ayer (3), p. 52.

13 Ibid.

14 Ibid., pp. 52–53.

15 Thompson, pp. 142–149.

16 Russell (5), pp. 135–158.

17 Russell (4).

18 Wittgenstein (2, 4.003) thus saw Russell's chief philosophical contribution as his recognition of the fact "that the apparent form of the proposition need not be its real form." Ibid., 4.0031.

19 See, e.g., Carnap (1), p. 75.

20 Ibid., pp. 60–61.

21 Carnap (8), pp. 88–92, 270–272, and especially 284–287. See also his comments in (6), p. 18.

22 Ayer (3), pp. 57, 59.

23 Carnap, as noted earlier, later rejected this purely "syntactical" approach in favor

of one that gave "semantical" considerations far more prominence. This discrepancy is, however, irrelevant to the present point at issue, which concerns only the broader question of the reinterpretation of traditional philosophical issues as essentially linguistic. Even Ayer, who stresses his own indebtedness to Carnap's general approach as set forth in Carnap's (9), rejects Carnap's contention that it is only the formal or "syntactical" features of language that count for philosophical purposes. See, e.g., Ayer (2), pp. 84–92.

24 Carnap (9), p. 285.

25 Kraft, p. 69.

26 Carnap (9), p. 300.

27 Ibid., p. 299.

28 Prior to his determinedly syntactical bent in (9), Carnap, in an identical context, had expressed this same relation as "is of equal content with" (13), p. 59. His use of the purportedly syntactical expression "is equipollent to" here does not represent his rejection of the notion of *content* or *meaning*, but, again, only his conviction at the time that such notions were fully definable in syntactical terms.

29 Carnap (9), p. 301.

30 That this is, after all, only a suggestion is indicated by Carnap's remarks to this effect in (9), p. 302.

31 Ibid., pp. 51–52.

32 Ibid., pp. 299–300.

33 Carnap (2), p. 73.

34 Carnap's conversion to semantics having occurred long before the appearance of (2), what he means here by the "thing-language" is roughly equivalent to "the language whose expressions refer to, or designate,—according to its semantical rules—physical objects." A corresponding formulation from Carnap's syntactical period would have characterized the "thing-language" as composed of certain forms of expressions designated by the language's syntactical rules as "thing-expressions."

35 Carnap (2), p. 78.

36 Compare here the earlier discussions of Carnap's views as set forth in (9) concerning assertions made about physical objects or numbers, as made *from within* a specifically phenomenalist, or logicist, language, respectively.

37 Carnap (2), pp. 73–74.

38 Bergmann (3), p. 40.

39 Ibid., p. 43.

40 Ibid., p. 41.

41 Bergmann (2), p. 93.

42 Bergmann (3), p. 41.

43 Schlick (2), p. 48.

44 Ibid., p. 49.

45 Ibid.

46 Wittgenstein (2), 4.113–114.

47 Schlick (5), p. 56.

48 That is, the stock criticism of the verifiability criterion, to the effect that it is itself unverifiable, and thus meaningless, unless we postulate some further standard of significance after all. See Hempel (1), pp. 101–120.

49 Wittgenstein (2), 4.1121.
50 Ayer (3), p. 34.
51 Russell (1), p. 34.
52 See, e.g., Carnap (1), pp. 61–65.
53 As, e.g., in Schlick (2), pp. 55–57.
54 See Goodman (1), pp. 6–19 and (4).
55 Goodman (4), pp. 29–31.
56 Ibid., p. 29.
57 Goodman (1), p. 8.
58 Ibid., pp. 7–8.
59 Wittgenstein (2), 4.003–4.0031.
60 Ryle (3), p. 100.
61 Ayer (3), p. 57.
62 What I mean by "absolute linguistic questions" should not be confused with what Carnap calls "external questions," which are not theoretically significant but are simply questions as to the practical utility of a framework as a whole. Absolute linguistic questions, on the other hand, are those which concern the structure, or content, of any particular framework, and thus do not concern how we ought to speak, but seek only to clarify the conceptual import of the various alternative frameworks among which we may choose.
63 Wittgenstein (2), 2.1.
64 Ibid., 2.12.
65 Ibid., 4.022.
66 Goodman (4), pp. 31–32.

Chapter 2

1 Quine (22), ch. 2; (11), ch. 1.
2 Quine (11), p. 32.
3 Ibid.
4 Ibid., p. 33.
5 Ibid., p. 34.
6 Ibid., p.38.
7 Ibid., pp. 43–44.
8 Ibid., p. 47.
9 Ibid., p. 48.
10 Ibid., p. 49.
11 Ibid.
12 Ibid., p. 50.
13 Ibid., p. 51.
14 Ibid., p. 54.
15 Ibid., pp. 54–55.
16 Quine (4), pp. 1–19.
17 Quine (11), p. 64.
18 Ibid., p. 67.
19 Carnap (2), p. 76.

20 Ibid., p. 73.
21 Ibid., p. 74.
22 Ibid., p. 73.
23 Ibid., p. 78.
24 Ibid.
25 Ibid., p. 75.
26 Ibid., p. 77.
27 Ibid.
28 Martin, p. 73.
29 Martin, p. 177.
30 Ibid.
31 Ibid.
32 Ibid.
33 Ibid.
34 Ibid.
35 Carnap (2), p. 76.
36 Quine (11), p. 43.
37 Ibid., pp. 43–44.
38 Ibid., p. 50.
39 See Quine's discussion in his (22), pp. 14–16.
40 Ibid., p. 16.
41 Quine (1), p. 109.
42 Ibid.
43 Ibid.
44 Ibid.
45 Ibid., p. 111.
46 Ibid., p. 120.
47 Carnap (15).
48 Ibid., p. 916.
49 Quine (1), p. 110.
50 Ibid.
51 Ibid., p. 113.
52 Ibid., p. 114.
53 Ibid.
54 Quine (11), p. 44.

Chapter 3

1 Carnap (11).
2 Bergmann (3), pp. 17–29.
3 Strawson (2), pp. 513–514.
4 Wittgenstein (1), p. 120.
5 Austin, p. 47.
6 Hare.
7 Royaumont Colloquium, p. 305.
8 Thus, e.g., Austin speaks as follows: "When we examine what we should say

when, what words we should use in what situations, we are looking again not merely at words (or "meanings", whatever they may be) but also at the realities we use the words to talk about: we are using a sharpened awareness of words to sharpen our perception of . . . the phenomena" (p. 47).

9 Wittgenstein (1), p. 197.
10 Ibid., p. 340.
11 Strawson (2), p. 517.
12 Wittgenstein (1), 30.
13 E.g., Toulmin.
14 Strawson (1), p. 320.
15 Ibid., p. 327.
16 Quine (11), p. 32.
17 See, e.g., Wittgenstein (1), 27–30.
18 Strawson (1), p. 318.
19 Quine (11), p. 34.
20 Ibid., p. 47.
21 Ibid., p. 49.
22 Ibid., p. 50.
23 Cornman (3), p. xvi.
24 Ibid., pp. xvii–xviii.
25 Ibid., pp. 90–91.
26 Ibid., pp. 134–136.
27 Ibid., p. 174.
28 Ibid., pp. 137–138.
29 Ibid., p. 138.
30 Quine (4).
31 Ibid., p. 14.
32 Cornman (3), p. 150.
33 Ibid., p. xviii.
34 See Malcolm.
35 Husserl.
36 Weyl, pp. 25–26.
37 Black, p. 15.
38 Tarski (1).

Chapter 4

1 Quine (7), p. 130.
2 Harman (1), p. 125.
3 Quine (19).
4 Ibid., p. 22.
5 Ibid., p. 23.
6 Ibid., p. 24.
7 Ibid., p. 27.
8 Ibid., pp. 29–30.
9 Ibid., p. 32.

10 Ibid., pp. 32–36.

11 Ibid., p. 36.

12 See especially Quine (13) and (22), pp. 26–79.

13 Quine (7).

14 Ibid., p. 134.

15 Ibid., pp. 134–135.

16 Ibid., p. 136.

17 Ibid.

18 Ibid., p. 138.

19 Ibid., pp. 137–138.

20 Witness the sorts of appeals to meaning in the narrow, intensional sense noted above.

21 Quine (11), p. 35.

22 See, e.g., Davidson (6), and Hintikka.

23 Quine (11), p. 20.

24 Plato (1), 240D and 260C–263D.

25 Aristotle (l), 4a–22b19 and 14b2–23; and (2), 1011b26 ff.

26 Empiricus, VIII.100. See also commentaries by Mates, p. 36, and Long, p. 140.

27 Hintikka, p. 182.

28 Field, pp. 359–360.

29 Though the "connection" Field has in mind here is indeed the semantic one between individual words and things, the actual point of the passage here excerpted has to do chiefly with the reluctance of some philosophers during the early 1930s to employ such semantic concepts to begin with. (See discussion, below, section 4.)

30 Quine (7), p. 138.

31 Obviously, by "acceptable" translations I do not have in mind only those translations that purport to preserve 'meaning' in either the usual intensional or extensional sense, but simply those translations achieved by any acceptable "manual of translation" in accordance with empirical considerations as outlined in ch. 2 of Quine (22).

32 Ibid.

33 This special status of the concept of truth will be explored and discussed more extensively in chapter 5, particularly section 4.

34 Carnap (10). It is interesting to note that Mates has discovered parallels between Carnap's "method of intension and extension" employed in this book and aspects of early Stoic logical doctrine. See Mates, pp. 11–26.

35 Carnap (10), p. 5.

36 Ibid.

37 Carnap (5), p. 6.

38 Ibid., pp. 10–11.

39 Quine (11), p. 68.

40 Plato (2), 188E–189A.

41 See, e.g., Moore (2), pp. 301–302.

42 Plato (1), 240D and 260C–263D.

43 Russell had initially treated truth and falsity as properties of the *act* of believing

itself. According to his original "multiple relation" theory, believing is a many-termed relation holding between a person and the various objects and relations actually comprising a 'fact.' Such a belief was to be counted as true when it "knit together" its various objects in an order corresponding to the way these same objects were actually ordered by a relation in reality. See Russell (4) and (7), pp. 119–130. Spurred by Wittgenstein's criticism, Russell later dropped the "multiple relation" theory and adopted propositions ("complex symbols") as the objects of beliefs, and as the proper vehicles of truth and falsity. See Russell (2), pp. 178–189. Russell still avoided the consequences of construing belief as a simple two-term relation (i.e., between a person and a proposition), however, since propositions themselves—as well as the 'facts' they expressed—were still regarded as essentially "complex" in nature, and therefore incapable of standing in a simple relation to a believing person, Russell had to accommodate *beliefs* themselves as unique sorts of facts, possessing their own peculiar logical form— "a new beast for our zoo." Russell (2), p. 226.

44 Russell (2), pp. 179–281.
45 Ibid., p. 179.
46 See, e.g., ibid., pp. 194, 201.
47 Ibid., pp. 197–198.
48 Wittgenstein (2), 4.024.
49 Ibid., 4.01–02.
50 Ibid., 2.1–3.
51 Ibid., 5–5.641.
52 Russell discusses the difficulties with Wittgenstein's treatment of quantification in his introduction to the first edition of Wittgenstein's (2), pp. xiv–xix. Insofar as Wittgenstein's reduction of quantificational to propositional logic would have worked for a world with a finite number of individuals, however, his logical atomism presumably bears some relation to the finitistic nominalism once espoused by Quine in collaboration with Goodman. See Quine and Goodman's "Steps toward a Constructive Nominalism."
53 These are the "positive" and "negative" results of which Carnap later spoke in his (1), pp. 60–61.
54 Russell (2), p. 181.
55 Quine (11), pp. 69–70.
56 For a more detailed yet still concise summary and evaluation of these points, see Quine's (11), pp. 69 ff.
57 Schlick (4), p. 87.
58 See, e.g., Neurath (1) and (2); Schlick (1); Ayer (5); and Hempel (2) and (4).
59 Carnap (1), p. 62.
60 Carnap (9), p. 288.
61 Ibid., pp. 288–292.
62 Carnap (1), p. 63.
63 Carnap (9), pp. 317 ff.
64 Ibid., p. 323.
65 See Schlick (1), pp. 214–218; and Ayer (5), pp. 228 ff; for criticisms of the "coherence" doctrine as set forth in Carnap (3) and (1), Neurath (1) and (2), and Hempel (2), (3), and (4).

66 Tarski (1).

67 See Carnap (14).

68 Though it runs directly counter to the assessment offered here, it is perhaps interesting to note that Church views Tarski as having actually succeeded in reducing semantics to syntax itself, in the very fashion that Carnap originally undertook to do in his (9). See Church, pp. 64–68, and Kleene.

69 Popper (2), p. 274 n.

70 Carnap (6), p. 60.

71 Carnap outlines the modifications and supplementation of his syntactical doctrine, which he now feels is required in light of the "new semantical method" provided by Tarski, in Carnap (7), pp. 246–252.

72 Carnap (6), p. 62.

73 Tarski (2).

74 Ibid., p. 401.

75 Ibid.

76 Tarski (4), p. 345.

77 Tarski (2), p. 402.

78 Tarski (1), p. 153.

79 Ibid., pp. 152–153.

80 Tarski (2), p. 402.

81 Strictly speaking, we do not need to know what the axioms or rules of deduction are for a language in order to define its truth predicate.

82 Tarski (4), p. 342.

83 Tarski (2), p. 404.

84 Tarski (1), pp. 187–188. (Convention T also has a clause requiring that 'true' apply only to expressions that are actually *sentences*.)

85 Tarski actually cites only an example of one partial definition in his (2), p. 405. The schema for satisfaction of a sentential function with one free variable is given in (1) on p. 190.

86 Ibid., p. 405.

87 Ibid., p. 406.

88 Ibid., pp. 406–407.

89 See Tarski's discussion in (1), pp. 155–163.

90 Tarski (6).

91 Tarski (1), pp. 163–167.

92 Tarski's description of his object language is found ibid., pp. 168–169.

93 Tarski's full description of these resources is found ibid., pp. 171–172.

94 The metalanguage, if one prefers, can simply be made to contain all the expressions of the object language themselves rather than their translations, in accordance with Quine's and Tarski's own later suggestion. This reduces the number of different kinds of expressions which must be dealt with and helps avoid certain methodological misgivings arising out of the unnecessary appeal to the notion of 'translation' in describing the metalanguage.

95 Whereas Tarski's metalanguage here relies exclusively on so-called structural-descriptive designations—see ibid., p. 172—I shall employ quotation marks to simplify my exposition.

96 These are specified in axioms of Tarski's metatheory which are listed individually and discussed ibid., pp. 173–174.

97 The definitions in question are found ibid., pp. 175–185.

98 Ibid., p. 186. Also see Tarski's Lemma E, ibid., p. 199, along with his accompanying footnote.

99 Tarski also discusses another reason why definition of "true" as "provable" would be philosophically unacceptable, ibid., p. 186 n.1.

100 Ibid., pp. 185–188.

101 For an account of truth for such languages, see Quine (18), pp. 318–321. This is also the general subject of discussion by Tharp and by Wallace (1), (2), and (3).

102 One alternative to assuming the notion of an infinite sequence is to adopt the convention of simply lengthening any sequence that is too short by successive repetitions of its last element until all variables in the sentential function are reached. See Quine (12), p. 38.

103 Tarski's original formulation of the actual definition sketched here is found in his (1), pp. 189–197. My formulation is essentially the same apart from some notational differences. Quine provides a lucid account of Tarski's procedure as applied to a language more representative of a formalized portion of empirical discourse than is Tarski's mathematical example. Quine's object language contains conjunction and existential quantification, though, instead of disjunction and universal quantification, as the basic logico-grammatical constructions, in addition to that of negation; and instead of Tarski's single predicate of class inclusion, there are supposed any arbitrary number of finitely listed one-place, two-place, . . . n-place predicates. Accordingly, a separate clause corresponding to (1) of my formulation is required in Quine's formulation for each such predicate in order to give satisfaction conditions for predications *generally*. Quine also employs the notion of a *sentence* to play the role of Tarski's notion of a sentential function, distinguishing between *open sentences*, which contain free variables, and *closed sentences*, which contain none. A further difference worth noting is that Quine does not restrict the application of "true" to closed sentences, so that open sentences, such as, e.g., "$x = x$," which are also satisfied by every sequence, are also regarded as true. See Quine (12), pp. 35–42.

104 Tarski demonstrates the procedure by which, for any arbitrary sentence of the object language, the corresponding equivalence of form T can be proved in the metatheory in his (1), pp. 195–196.

105 Ibid., p. 197.

106 Ibid., pp. 198–199.

107 Ibid., pp. 199–209.

Chapter 5

1 Tarski (1), p. 209, and (5), p. 68.

2 Tarski (1), p. 267.

3 See, e.g., ibid., p. 165 n.2; Quine (22), pp. 157–161; and Davidson (2), p. 82.

4 These contexts are primarily of three types: those involving *indexicals*; those

involving attribution of *propositional attitudes;* and those involving the use of *modal operators.* See Davidson (4), pp. 318–320, and (6), pp. 10–18.

5 Tarski (1), pp. 209–241.

6 Ibid., pp. 241–255.

7 See Quine (5), ch. 7.

8 See Quine (8), p. 144; and (12), pp. 42–43.

9 See Quine (5), pp. 313 ff.

10 Tarski (1), pp. 268–278.

11 Quine (8), pp. 141–145.

12 Quine (12), pp. 45–46.

13 See above, Ch. 1, sec. 4.

14 Quine (22), p. 24.

15 See above, Ch. 1, sec. 4.

16 Popper nonetheless seems to have discovered just such an absolute standard— a "regulative ideal" (*verisimilitude*)—in Tarski's account of truth. Popper (1), pp. 223–238. Also, for Tarski's replies to criticisms that his definition implies a "naive realism," or involves other 'metaphysical' elements, see his "polemical remarks" in (4), pp. 361–364.

17 This remains the case at least as long as we remain concerned essentially with abstract objects where ostension is unavailable.

18 See the passage quoted above from Weyl, p. 104.

19 See above, Ch. 2, sec. 1 and Ch. 3, sec. 3 for discussion of this "individuative apparatus."

20 Field finds Tarski's formulation of his definition misleading, and he provides his own suggested reformulation in order to bring out certain features which he feels are implicit in Tarski's. Field, p. 350.

21 Ibid., p. 351.

22 See above, Ch. 2, sec. 3.

23 Ibid.

24 Field, pp. 365–366.

25 Kripke.

26 Field, p. 373.

27 See the discussion of "conceptual schemes" above, Ch. 3, sec. 3.

28 Field, p. 373.

29 Compare discussion of the methodology of radical translation above, Ch. 4, sec. 2.

30 Davidson (2) and (6).

31 Davidson (1), p. 318.

32 Davidson (1) and (4).

33 See Quine (22), pp. 27, 71–72.

34 Compare Carnap's account of the learning of a language in his (5), discussed above, Ch. 4, sec. 2, as well as his later treatment in his (11).

35 Quine (22), p. 13.

36 Quine (3), p. 190–191.

37 Hiz, p. 443.

38 Davidson (1), p. 320.

39 See Davidson's discussion of this point in (1), pp. 320–321, as well as his interesting elaboration upon this theme in (3).

40 Thus Quine speaks of "banal messages" as the "breath of life" for translation, Quine (22), p. 69. See also in this connection his discussion of observation sentences, ibid., pp. 40–46.

41 Ibid., p. 69.

42 Davidson (1), p. 322.

43 Chomsky; See also Putnam (3); Rorty (1); Friedman; and Soames.

44 Quine (22), pp. 73–79, and (17).

45 Quine (17), p. 303.

46 Ibid.

47 The notion of "observation sentence" I have in mind here is that described by Quine in (22), pp. 40–46, and (11), pp. 85–89.

48 Quine (19), p. 42.

49 For an excellent discussion of these points relative to the basic Quine-Davidson approach to translation and interpretation, see Føllesdal.

50 See Davidson's comments in his (1), pp. 319–320; and (4), p. 328 n.14.

51 Davidson (1), p. 317.

52 Compare Quine's characterization in (12), ch. 2.

53 Hiz, p. 438.

54 Quine (22), p. 75.

55 See Ch. 4, sec. 5.

56 Quine (17), p. 303.

57 Most notably, perhaps, in his (4), pp. 42–47, and (22), pp. 270–276.

58 Quine (22), pp. 270–276.

59 See the earlier discussion of legislative postulation above, Ch. 2, sec. 4.

60 Rorty (1), p. 451.

Bibliography

Achinstein, Peter, and Stephen F. Barker, eds., *The Legacy of Logical Positivism*. Baltimore: Johns Hopkins University Press, 1969.

Aristotle (1), *Categories and De Interpretatione*. Oxford: Clarendon, 1963.

Aristotle (2), *Metaphysics*. Ann Arbor: University of Michigan Press, 1960.

Austin, John L., "A Plea for Excuses," in Chappell, ed., *Ordinary Language*.

Ayer, Alfred J. (1), "Editor's Introduction," in Ayer, *Logical Positivism*.

Ayer, Alfred J. (2), *Foundations of Empirical Knowledge*. New York: St. Martin's, 1969.

Ayer, Alfred J. (3), *Language, Truth, and Logic*. New York: Dover, 1950.

Ayer, Alfred J. (4), ed., *Logical Positivism*. Glencoe, Ill.: Free Press, 1959.

Ayer, Alfred J. (5), "Verification and Experience," in Ayer, *Logical Positivism*.

Bergmann, Gustav (1), *Logic and Reality*. Madison: University of Wisconsin Press, 1964.

Bergmann, Gustav (2), *Meaning and Existence*. Madison: University of Wisconsin Press, 1959.

Bergmann, Gustav (3), *The Metaphysics of Logical Positivism*. Madison: University of Wisconsin Press, 1967.

Bergson, Henri, *Introduction to Metaphysics*. New York: Bobbs-Merrill, 1955.

Black, Max (1), "Carnap on Semantics and Logic," in Black, ed., *Problems of Analysis*.

Black, Max (2), "Language and Reality," in Black, ed., *Models and Metaphors*.

Black, Max (3), *Models and Metaphors*. Ithaca, N.Y.: Cornell University Press, 1962.

Black, Max (4), *Problems of Analysis*. Ithaca, N.Y.: Cornell University Press, 1954.

Black, Max (5), "Russell's Philosophy of Language," in Rorty, *The Linguistic Turn*. Reprinted from *The Philosophy of Bertrand Russell*, Vol. 5, Library of Living Philosophers, ed. Paul A. Schilpp. Evanston and Chicago: Northwestern University Press, 1944.

Black, Max (6), "The Semantic Definition of Truth," in Black, *Language and Philosophy*. Ithaca, N.Y.: Cornell University Press, 1949.

Bradley, F. H., *Appearance and Reality*. London: Oxford University Press, 1969.

Carnap, Rudolf (1), "The Elimination of Metaphysics through the Logical Analysis of Language," in Ayer, ed., *Logical Positivism*.

Carnap, Rudolf (2), "Empiricism, Semantics, and Ontology," in Rorty, ed., *The Linguistic Turn*. 1967. Reprinted from *Revue Internationale de Philosophie* 4 (1950), 20–40.

Carnap, Rudolf (3), "Erwiderung auf die vorstehenden Aufsätze von E. Zilsel und K. Duncker," *Erkenntnis* 3 (1932–33), 177–188.

Carnap, Rudolf (4), *Formalization of Logic*. Studies in Semantics, Vol. 2, (1943). Cambridge, Mass.: Harvard University Press.

Carnap, Rudolf (5), *Foundations of Logic and Mathematics*. University of Chicago Press, 1939.

Carnap, Rudolf (6), "Intellectual Autobiography," in Schilpp, *The Philosophy of Rudolf Carnap*.

Carnap, Rudolf (7), *Introduction to Semantics*. Cambridge, Mass.: Harvard University Press, 1948.

Carnap, Rudolf (8), *The Logical Structure of the World and Pseudoproblems in Philosophy*, tr. Rolf A. George. Berkeley: University of California Press, 1967.

Carnap, Rudolf (9), *Logical Syntax of Language*, tr. Amethe Smeaton. London: Routledge and Kegan Paul, 1937.

Carnap, Rudolf (10), *Meaning and Necessity*. University of Chicago Press, 1956.

Carnap, Rudolf (11), "Meaning and Synonymy in Natural Language," in Carnap, *Meaning and Necessity*.

Carnap, Rudolf (12), "Meaning Postulates," in Feigl, Sellars, and Lehrer, eds., *New Readings in Philosophical Analysis*.

Carnap, Rudolf (13), "On the Character of Philosophical Problems," in Rorty, *The Linguistic Turn*.

Carnap, Rudolf (14), "Psychology and Physical Language," in Ayer, ed., *Logical Positivism*.

Carnap, Rudolf (15), "Quine on Logical Truth," in Schilpp, *The Philosophy of Rudolf Carnap*.

Carnap, Rudolf (16), "Remarks on Induction and Truth," *Philosophy and Phenomenological Research* 6 (1946), 590–602.

Carnap, Rudolf (17), "Testability and Meaning," in Herbert Feigl and May Brodbeck, eds., *Readings in the Philosophy of Science*. New York: Appleton-Century-Crofts, 1953.

Carnap, Rudolf (18), "Über Protokollsätze," *Erkenntnis* 3 (1932–33), 215–228.

Caton, Charles E., ed., *Philosophy and Ordinary Language*. Urbana: University of Illinois Press, 1963.

Cavell, Stanley, "Austin on Criticism," in Rorty, *The Linguistic Turn*. Reprinted from *Philosophical Review* 74 (1965), 204–219.

Chappell, Vere, ed., *Ordinary Language*. Englewood Cliffs, N.J.: Prentice-Hall, 1964.

Chisholm, Roderick, et al., *Philosophy*. Englewood Cliffs, N.J.: Prentice-Hall, 1964.

Chomsky, Noam, "Quine's Empirical Assumptions," in Davidson and Hintikka, eds., *Words and Objections*.

Church, Alonzo, *Introduction to Mathematical Logic*, Vol. 1. Princeton, N.J.: Princeton University Press, 1956.

Cornman, James (1), "Language and Ontology," *Australian Journal of Psychology and Philosophy* 12 (1963), 291–305.

Cornman, James (2), "Linguistic Frameworks and Metaphysical Questions," *Inquiry* 7 (1964), 129–142.

Cornman, James (3), *Metaphysics, Reference, and Language*. New Haven, Conn.: Yale University Press, 1966.

Davidson, Donald (1), "Belief and the Basis of Meaning," *Synthese* 27, nos. 3/4 (1974), 309–323.

Davidson, Donald (2), "In Defense of Convention T," in Leblanc, ed., *Truth, Syntax, and Modality*.

Davidson, Donald (3), "On the Very Idea of a Conceptual Scheme," *Proceedings of the American Philosophical Society* 47 (1974), 5–20.

Davidson, Donald (4), "Radical Interpretation," *Dialectica* 27 (1973), 314–328.

Davidson, Donald (5), "True to the Facts," *Journal of Philosophy* 66 (1969), 748–764.

Davidson, Donald (6), "Truth and Meaning," in Davis et al., eds., *Philosophical Logic*.

Davidson, Donald, and Gilbert Harman, eds., *Semantics of Natural Language*. Dordrecht: Reidel, 1972.

Davidson, Donald, and Hintikka, Jaakko, eds., *Words and Objections: Essays on the Work of W. V. Quine*. Dordrecht: Reidel, 1969.

Davis, J. W., Hocking, D. J., and Wilson, W. K., eds., *Philosophical Logic*. Dordrecht: Reidel, 1969.

Evans, Gareth, and McDowell, John, eds., *Truth and Meaning: Essays in Semantics*. Oxford: Clarendon, 1976.

Feigl, Herbert, and Sellars, Wilfrid, eds., *Readings in Philosophical Analysis*. New York: Appleton-Century-Crofts, 1949.

Feigl, Herbert, Sellars, Wilfrid, and Lehrer, Keith, eds., *New Readings in Philosophical Analysis*. New York: Appleton-Century-Crofts, 1972.

Field, Hartry, "Tarski's Theory of Truth," *Journal of Philosophy* 69, no. 13 (1972), 347–375.

Føllesdal, Dagfin, "Meaning and Experience," in Guttenplan, ed., *Mind and Language*.

Frege, Gottlob, "On Sense and Nominatum," in Feigl and Sellars, eds., *Readings in Philosophical Analysis*.

Friedman, Michael, "Physicalism and the Indeterminacy of Translation," *Nous* 9 (1975), 353-374.

Goodman, Nelson (1), *Languages of Art*. New York: Bobbs-Merrill, 1968.

Goodman, Nelson (2), *Problems and Projects*. New York: Bobbs-Merrill, 1972.

Goodman, Nelson (3), *The Structure of Appearance*. New York: Bobbs-Merrill, 1966.

Goodman, Nelson (4), "The Way the World Is," in Goodman, *Problems and Projects*.

Goodman, Nelson, and Quine, W. V., "Steps toward a Constructive Nominalism," *Journal of Symbolic Logic* 12 (1947), 105–122.

Guttenplan, Samuel, ed., *Mind and Language*. New York: Oxford University Press, 1974.

Hacking, Ian, *Why Does Language Matter to Philosophy?* Cambridge University Press, 1975.

Hampshire, Stuart, "The Interpretation of Language: Words and Concepts," in Rorty, *The Linguistic Turn*. Reprinted from *British Philosophy in the Mid-Century*, ed. C. A. Mace. London: Allen and Unwin, 1957.

Hare, Richard M., "Philosophical Discoveries," in Rorty, *The Linguistic Turn*. Reprinted from *Mind* 69 (1960), 145–162.

Harman, Gilbert (1), "Quine on Meaning and Existence (Part l)," in *Review of Metaphysics* 21, no. 1 (1967), 124–151.

Harman, Gilbert (2), "Sellars' Semantics," *Philosophical Review* 79 (1970), 404–419.

Harman, Gilbert, and Davidson, Donald, eds., *Semantics of Natural Language*. Dordrecht: Reidel, 1972.

Hempel, Carl (1), *Aspects of Scientific Explanation*. New York: Free Press, 1965.

Hempel, Carl (2), "On the Logical Positivists' Theory of Truth," *Analysis* 2, no. 4 (1935), 49–59.

Hempel, Carl (3), "Some Remarks on Empiricism," *Analysis* 3, no. 3 (1936), 33–40.

Hempel, Carl (4), "Some Remarks on 'Facts' and Propositions," *Analysis* 2, no. 6 (1935), 93–96.

Hintikka, Jaakko, "Semantics for the Propositional Attitudes," in Linsky, ed., *Reference and Modality*.

Hintikka, Jaakko, and Davidson, Donald, eds., *Words and Objections: Essays on the Work of W. V. Quine*. Dordrecht: Reidel, 1969.

Hiz, Henry, "Aletheic Semantic Theory," *Philosophical Forum* 1, no. 4 (1969), 438–451.

Husserl, Edmund, *Logical Investigations*. London: Routledge and Kegan Paul; New York: Humanities Press, 1970.

Jorgensen, Jorgen, *The Development of Logical Empiricism*. University of Chicago Press, 1951.

Kant, Immanuel, *Critique of Pure Reason*. New York: Anchor, 1966.

Kleene, Stephen C., "Review of Carnap's *Logical Syntax of Language*," *Journal of Symbolic Logic* 4, no. 2 (1939), 82–87.

Kraft, Viktor, *Vienna Circle*, tr. Arthur Pap. New York: Philosophical Library, 1958.

Kripke, Saul, "Naming and Necessity," in Davidson and Harman, *Semantics of Natural Language*.

Kuhn, Thomas S., *The Structure of Scientific Revolutions*. University of Chicago Press, 1970.

Leblanc, Hughes, ed., *Truth, Syntax, and Modality*. Amsterdam: North-Holland, 1973.

Lewis, C. I., "Experience and Meaning," in Feigl and Sellars, eds., *Readings in Philosophical Analysis*.

Linsky, Leonard (1), ed., *Reference and Modality*. London: Oxford University Press, 1971.

Linsky, Leonard (2), ed., *Semantics and the Philosophy of Language*. Urbana: University of Illinois Press, 1952.

Long, A. A., *Hellenistic Philosophy: Stoics, Epicureans, and Skeptics*. London: Duckworth, 1974.

Lyas, Colin, ed., *Philosophy and Linguistics*. New York: St. Martin's, 1971.

Malcolm, Norman, "Moore and Ordinary Language," in Rorty, *The Linguistic Turn*. Reprinted from *The Philosophy of G. E. Moore*, Vol. 4, The Library of Living Philosophers, ed. Paul A. Schilpp. Evanston and Chicago: Northwestern University Press, 1942.

Martin, Richard M., "Category-Words and Linguistic Frameworks," *Kant-Studien* 54 (1953), 176–180.

Mates, Benson, *Stoic Logic*. Berkeley and Los Angeles: University of California Press, 1953.

Moore, G. E. (1), "Proof of an External World," in G. E. Moore, *Philosophical Papers*. New York: Collier, 1962.

Moore, G. E. (2), *Some Main Problems of Philosophy*. New York: Collier, 1962.

Neurath, Otto (1), "Protocol Sentences," in Ayer, ed., *Logical Positivism*.

Neurath, Otto (2), "Radikaler Physikalismus und 'Wirkliche Welt,' " *Erkenntnis* 4 (1934), 346–362.

Passmore, John, *A Hundred Years of Philosophy*. Baltimore: Penguin, 1966.

Plato (1), *Sophistes and Politicus of Plato*. New York: Arno, 1973.

Plato (2), *Theaetetus*. Oxford: Clarendon, 1973.

Popper, Karl (1), *Conjectures and Refutations*. New York: Harper and Row, 1963.

Popper, Karl (2), *The Logic of Scientific Discovery*. London: Hutchinson, 1948.

Prior, A. N., "The Correspondence Theory of Truth," in *Encyclopedia of Philosophy*. New York: Macmillan, 1967.

Putnam, Hilary (1) *Meaning and the Moral Sciences*. London: Routledge and Kegan Paul, 1978.

Putnam, Hilary (2), *Mind, Language and Reality*. Cambridge University Press, 1975.

Putnam, Hilary (3), "The Refutation of Conventionalism," *Nous* 8 (1974), 25–40.

Quine, Willard Van Orman (1), "Carnap and Logical Truth," in Quine, *Ways of Paradox*.

Quine, Willard Van Orman (2), "Comment on Donald Davidson," *Synthese* 27, no. 3/4 (1974), 325–329.

Quine, Willard Van Orman (3), "Facts of the Matter," in Shahan and Merrill, eds., *American Philosophy*.

Quine, Willard Van Orman (4), *From a Logical Point of View*. Cambridge, Mass.: Harvard University Press, 1953.

Quine, Willard Van Orman (5), *Mathematical Logic*. New York: Holt, Rinehart, and Winston, 1972.

Quine, Willard Van Orman (6), *Methods of Logic*. New York: Holt, Rinehart, and Winston, 1972.

Quine, Willard Van Orman (7), "Notes on the Theory of Reference," in Quine, *From a Logical Point of View*.

Quine, Willard Van Orman (8), "On an Application of Tarski's Theory of Truth," in Quine, *Selected Logic Papers.*.

Quine, Willard Van Orman (9), "On Empirically Equivalent Systems of the World," *Erkenntnis* 9 (1975), 313–328.

Quine, Willard Van Orman (10), "Ontological Relativity," in Quine, *Ontological Relativity and Other Essays*.

Quine, Willard Van Orman (11), *Ontological Relativity and Other Essays*. New York: Columbia University Press, 1969.

Quine, Willard Van Orman (12), *Philosophy of Logic*. Englewood Cliffs, N.J.: Prentice-Hall, 1970.

Quine, Willard Van Orman (13), "The Problem of Meaning in Linguistics," in Quine, *From a Logical Point of View*.

Quine, Willard Van Orman (14), "Review of Evans and McDowell's *Truth and Meaning: Essays in Semantics*," *Journal of Philosophy* 14, no. 4 (1977), 225–242.

Quine, Willard Van Orman (15), *Roots of Reference.* La Salle, Ill.: Open Court, 1973.

Quine, Willard Van Orman (16), *Selected Logic Papers.* New York: Random House, 1966.

Quine, Willard Van Orman (17), "To Chomsky," in Hintikka and Davidson, eds., *Words and Objections.*

Quine, Willard Van Orman (18), "Truth and Disquotation," in Quine, *Ways of Paradox and Other Essays,* revised ed. Cambridge, Mass.: Harvard University Press, 1976.

Quine, Willard Van Orman (19), "Two Dogmas of Empiricism," in Quine, *From a Logical Point of View.*

Quine, Willard Van Orman (20), *Ways of Paradox and Other Essays.* New York: Random House, 1966. Revised ed., Cambridge, Mass.: Harvard University Press, 1976.

Quine, Willard Van Orman (22), *Word and Object.* Cambridge, Mass.: MIT Press, 1960.

Rorty, Richard (1), "Indeterminacy of Translation and of Truth," *Synthese* 23 (1972), 443–462.

Rorty, Richard (2), ed., *The Linguistic Turn.* University of Chicago Press, 1967.

Rorty, Richard (3), *Philosophy and the Mirror of Nature.* Princeton, N.J.: Princeton University Press, 1979.

Rorty, Richard (4), "Realism and Reference," *Monist* 59 (1976), 321–340.

Rorty, Richard (5), "Review of Hacking," *Journal of Philosophy,* 74 (1977), 416–432.

Royaumont Colloquium, "Discussion of Urmson's 'The History of Analysis,' " in Rorty, ed., *The Linguistic Turn.*

Russell, Bertrand (1), "Logical Atomism," in Ayer, ed., *Logical Positivism.*

Russell, Bertrand (2), *Logic and Knowledge: Essays 1901–1950,* ed. R. C. Marsh. London: Allen and Unwin, 1956.

Russell, Bertrand (3), "On Denoting," in Feigl and Sellars, eds., *Readings in Philosophical Analysis.*

Russell, Bertrand (4), "On the Nature of Truth," in *Proceedings of the Aristotelian Society* (1906–1907), pp. 28–49.

Russell, Bertrand (5), *Our Knowledge of the External World.* London: Allen and Unwin, 1922.

Russell, Bertrand (6), *The Principles of Mathematics.* New York: Norton, 1938.

Russell, Bertrand (7), *Problems of Philosophy.* London: Home University Library, 1912.

Russell, Bertrand, and Whitehead, Alfred North, *Principia Mathematica,* 3 vols. Cambridge University Press, 1910–13; second edition, 1925–27.

Ryle, Gilbert (1), *Concept of Mind.* Harmondsworth, England: Penguin, 1949.

Ryle, Gilbert (2), "*Meaning and Necessity* by Rudolph Carnap," *Philosophy* 24 (1949), 69–76.

Ryle, Gilbert (3), "Systematically Misleading Expressions," in Rorty, ed., *The Linguistic Turn.* Reprinted from *Proceedings of the Aristotelian Society* 32 (1931–32), 139–170.

Ryle, Gilbert (4), "Use, Usage, and Meaning." *Proceedings of the Aristotelian Society, Supplementary Volume,* 35 (1961), 223–230.

Sagal, Paul T., "Implicit Definition," *Monist* 57, no. 3 (1973), 443–450.

Schilpp, Paul A., *The Philosophy of Rudolf Carnap,* Vol. XI, Library of Living Philosophers. La Salle, Ill.: Open Court, 1963.

Schlick, Moritz (1), "The Foundations of Knowledge," in Ayer, ed., *Logical Positivism*.

Schlick, Moritz (2), "The Future of Philosophy," in Rorty, ed., *The Linguistic Turn*. Reprinted from *College of the Pacific Publications in Philosophy* 1 (1932), 45–62.

Schlick, Moritz (3), "Meaning and Verification," in Feigl and Sellars, eds., *Readings in Philosophical Analysis*.

Schlick, Moritz (4), "Positivism and Realism," in Ayer, *Logical Positivism*.

Schlick, Moritz (5), "The Turning Point in Philosophy," in Ayer, ed., *Logical Positivism*.

Shahan, R. W., and Merrill, K. R., eds., *American Philosophy*. Norman: University of Oklahoma Press, 1977.

Shapere, Dudley, "Philosophy and the Analysis of Language," in Rorty, ed., *The Linguistic Turn*. Reprinted from *Inquiry* 3 (1960), 29–48.

Soames, Scott, "Review of Davis, Leiber, and Stalker," in *Metaphilosophy* 11, no. 2 (1980), 155–164.

Strawson, Peter F. (1), "Analysis, Science, and Metaphysics," in Rorty, ed., *The Linguistic Turn*. A translation of a paper, and the ensuing discussion, presented at the Royaumont Colloquium of 1961, printed in the proceedings of the colloquium (*La philosophie analytique*). Paris: Editions de Minuit, 1962.

Strawson, Peter F. (2), "Carnap's Views on Constructed Systems versus Natural Languages in Analytical Philosophy," in Schilpp, *The Philosophy of Rudolph Carnap*.

Strawson, Peter F. (3), *Individuals*. London: Methuen, 1959.

Strawson, Peter F. (4), "Truth," *Analysis* 9, no. 6 (1949), 83–97.

Tarski, Alfred (1), "The Concept of Truth in Formalized Languages," in Tarski, *Logic, Semantics, Metamathematics*.

Tarski, Alfred (2), "The Establishment of Scientific Semantics," in Tarski, *Logic, Semantics, Metamathematics*.

Tarski, Alfred (3), *Logic, Sematics, Metamathematics*, tr. J. H. Woodger. London: Oxford University Press, 1956.

Tarski, Alfred (4), "The Semantic Conception of Truth and the Foundations of Theoretical Semantics," *Philosophy and Phenomenological Research* 4 (1944), 341–376.

Tarski, Alfred (5), "Truth and Proof," *Scientific American* 220, no. 6 (1969), 63–77.

Tarski, Alfred (6), "Der Wahrheitsbegriff in den Formalisierten Sprachen," *Studia Philosophica* 1 (1935 for 1936), 261–405, tr. J. H. Woodger. London: Oxford University Press, 1956.

Tharp, Leslie, "Truth, Quantification, and Abstract Objects," *Nous* 5, no. 4 (1971), 363–372.

Thompson, Manley, "Metaphysics," in Roderick Chisholm et al., *Philosophy*. Englewood Cliffs, N.J.: Prentice-Hall, 1964.

Thomson, J. F., "A Note on Truth," *Analysis* 9, no. 5 (1949), 67–72.

Toulmin, Stephen, "From Logical Analysis to Conceptual History," in Achinstein and Barker, eds., *The Legacy of Logical Positivism*.

Urmson, J. O., *Philosophical Analysis*. London: Oxford University Press, 1965.

Wallace, John (1), "Belief and Satisfaction," *Nous* 4, no. 2 (1972), 85–95.

Wallace, John (2), "Convention T and Substitutional Quantification," *Nous* 5, no. 2 (1971), 199–211.

Wallace, John (3), "Response to Camp," *Nous* 9, no. 2 (1975), 187–192.

Warnock, G. J., *English Philosophy since 1900*. London: Oxford University Press, 1958.

Weyl, Hermann, *Philosophy of Mathematics and Natural Science*. Princeton, N.J.: Princeton University Press, 1949.

Whitehead, Alfred North and Bertrand Russell, *Principia Mathematica*. See Russell.

Whorf, Benjamin Lee, *Language, Thought and Reality*. Cambridge, Mass.: Technology Press of Massachusetts Institute of Technology, 1956.

Wittgenstein, Ludwig (1), *Philosophical Investigations*, tr. G. E. M. Anscombe. New York: Macmillan, 1968.

Wittgenstein, Ludwig (2), *Tractatus Logico-Philosophicus*, tr. D. F. Pears and B. F. McGuinness. London: Routledge and Kegan Paul, 1961.

Index